Epic of the Dispossessed
Derek Walcott's *Omeros*

Epic of the Dispossessed

Derek Walcott's *Omeros*

Robert D. Hamner

University of Missouri Press

Columbia and London

Library of Congress Cataloging-in-Publication Data

Hamner, Robert D.

Epic of the dispossessed : Derek Walcott's Omeros / Robert D. Hamner.

   p.   cm.

  Includes bibliographical references and index.

  ISBN 0-8262-1124-0 (alk. paper)

  ISBN 0-8262-1152-6 (pbk.)

  1. Walcott, Derek. Omeros.   2. West Indian poetry, English—Greek
influences.   3. Epic poetry, English—History and criticism.
4. West Indies—In literature.   5. Saint Lucia—In literature.
6. Castaways in literature.   7. Exiles in literature.   8. Homer—
Influence.   I. Title.

PR9272.9.W04434   1997

811—dc21   97-13099

                                                    CIP

Designer: Stephanie Foley

Typesetter: BOOKCOMP

Printer and binder: Thomson-Shore, Inc.

Typeface: Minion

To
the legacy of
Warwick Walcott
and the memory of
Robert F. Hamner

Contents

Acknowledgments

Several people have given invaluable support in bringing this work to completion. I am grateful to Derek Walcott for patiently bearing my inquiries; to my wife, Carol, for her unstinting patience and encouragement; to Alice Specht, Corrine Shields, and Belinda Norvell of the Hardin-Simmons University library for research assistance; to Elaine Ferguson, Bruce King, Paul Breslin, and the staff of the University of Missouri Press for editorial and critical insights that eliminate many of my vagaries and make this a far more readable and accurate book than it might otherwise have been. The Academic Foundation of Hardin-Simmons University generously assisted in the payment of permissions fees.

I am especially grateful to Derek Walcott and Farrar, Straus and Giroux for allowing me to quote from the works of Derek Walcott. Reprinted with the permission of Farrar, Straus and Giroux, Inc., under the copyright of Derek Walcott are excerpts from *Another Life,* Copyright © 1964; from *The Arkansas Testament,* Copyright © 1987; from *Dream on Monkey Mountain and Other Plays,* Copyright © 1970; from *Omeros,* Copyright © 1990; and from *The Star-Apple Kingdom,* Copyright © 1979; from *The Odyssey,* Copyright © 1993; from the unpublished play "Ghost Dance." Excerpts from Derek Walcott's Nobel Prize acceptance speech, "The Antilles: Fragments of Epic Memory," are reprinted with the permission of the Nobel Foundation, © The Nobel Foundation 1992. Derek Walcott and Faber and Faber have also graciously granted nonexclusive English rights to reprint excerpts from the following works throughout the British Commonwealth excluding Canada: *The Arkansas Testament,* Copyright © 1987; *The Odyssey,* Copyright © 1993; *Omeros,* Copyright © 1990; *The Star-Apple Kingdom,* Copyright © 1979.

Permission to quote excerpts from J. P. White's "An Interview with Derek Walcott" is granted by J. P. White and *Green Mountains Review.*

Five of the illustrations for this book, including the cover portrait, are original works by Derek Walcott. The cover reproduction of Walcott's *Helen* was provided by Ken Roberts of Roberts Studio. Facsimile reproductions of Walcott's other paintings and *In God We Troust* by Jared Hamner were made by Larry Fink. The photograph of Walcott's birthplace was provided by Mary Love and augmented for publication by Larry Fink and Ken Roberts. The facsimile of Winslow Homer's *The Gulf Stream* is reproduced with permission, © The Metropolitan Museum of Art, all rights reserved, The Metropolitan Museum of Art.

Epic of the Dispossessed
Derek Walcott's *Omeros*

Introduction

Nobel prize–winning poet Derek Walcott was fully conscious of the classical influences that nurtured his epic poem *Omeros* in 1990. In telling D. J. R. Bruckner that he was not writing "a conundrum for scholars," he was anticipating the inevitable critical approaches that would seize upon the traditional aspects of *Omeros*. What he has in mind is a poem that expresses his West Indian vision of New World experience. Despite the obviously conventional epic paraphernalia, the poem is based on Walcott's creolized version of a wanderer called Homer (for whom *Omeros* is named) rather than a sanctified literary progenitor.

> Part of what I'm saying in the book is that the Greeks were the niggers of the Mediterranean. If we looked at them now, we would say that the Greeks had Puerto Rican tastes. Right? Because the stones were painted brightly. . . . The same thing is true of looking at art as exotica, barbarous exotica. All the purple and gold—that's what I'm saying is very Caribbean, that same vigor and elation of an earlier Greece, not a later Greece, not the sort of Romanesque Greece. . . . Everything is reduced, as soon as a comparison begins.[1]

Because he has reservations about reductive comparisons to classical models, and because he knows how tempting it is to seize upon obvious parallels, Walcott goes to some lengths to point out differences between his project and traditional heroic poetry. By marginalizing the accomplishments of his people, history has consistently denied his archipelago the trappings of military and political recognition. Rectifying that selective amnesia for

---

1. D. J. R. Bruckner, "A Poem in Homage to an Unwanted Man," 17; Robert Brown and Cheryl Johnson, "An Interview with Derek Walcott," 216–17.

indigenous West Indians, Walcott provides a unique literary experience, a highly allusive New World assimilation of disparate influences.

In this era of intertextual self-consciousness, only the naive critic assumes that the act of reading is simply a matter of comprehending the latent meaning in a finite document. Since the 1970s, Harold Bloom has been accounting for the history of poetic invention in terms of "misprision": successive generations of poets misreading their predecessors as a process of creating imaginative room for their own expression. If misunderstanding is one way to explain the development of poetry, it is even less remarkable that the literary critic's role has come to be considered equally subversive of the time-honored objective of disclosing the obscure "truth" of a text. Roland Barthes is prominent among theorists who go so far as to challenge the parasitic critic-artist hierarchy. According to Barthes, the subjective reader does not so much rediscover as compose the work at hand. By his definition, the science of literary criticism does not attempt to establish an infallible meaning. Barthes argues, "[I]t will neither *give* nor even *rediscover* any meaning, but it will describe according to which logic it is that meanings are engendered in a manner which is capable of being *accepted* by the symbolic logic of humankind." Despite the liberating effect of this pronouncement, Barthes denies that the reader therefore is granted license to exploit meaninglessness. The parameters he recognizes guarantee a modicum of productive dialogue between artifact and interpreter. He has sufficient appreciation of established structural patterns and genres to contend that the critical reader may choose from among available linguistic codes or methods of explanation. "All the objectivity of the critic," he suggests, "will depend then, not on the choice of code, but on the rigour with which he applies the model he has chosen to the work in question."[2]

As subjective as the process of reading, or perhaps more accurately the act of rewriting, is admitted to be, intersecting languages continue to convey understandings that may be derived from the interpretive encounter. I remind readers of these current trends in critical thought neither to proclaim their peculiar relevance nor to deviate from them into any innovative approach of my own. Reader-response criticism, deconstruction, feminist credos, serve to remind us of the tenuousness of all schools of

2. Harold Bloom, *The Anxiety of Influence: A Theory of Poetry,* 5; Roland Barthes, *Criticism and Truth,* edited by Katherine Pilcher Keuneman, 72, 79, 39.

interpretation. The analysis of Derek Walcott's *Omeros* that follows is essentially a modest attempt to explain my understanding of a richly diverse poem.

It is against the conventions of an entrenched classical tradition that Walcott protests when he contends that his *Omeros* is not truly a heroic poem. Since it lacks the superhuman characters and monumental battle scenes, he will concede only that, "I suppose in terms of the scale of it—as an undertaking—it's large and does cover a lot of geographic elements, historical ground. I think that's the word. I think the reason why I hesitate about calling it that is I think any work in which the narrator is almost central is not really an epic. It's not like a heroic epic." Never one to deny the fruitful influence of several writers who have established the milestones of Western tradition, Walcott still maintains that inventive imitation is creative and that as a scion of both white and black grandparents he fulfills his rightful heritage by gleaning influences from all branches of his family tree. As early as 1974, Walcott argues that "mimicry is an act of imagination"; he goes on to assert, therefore, that culture originates "by the force of natural surroundings. You build according to the topography of where you live."[3]

Omeros builds on Walcott's innate love for St. Lucia. It does not spring suddenly from his pen but is ultimately a culmination of the various influences that have permeated his career from the beginning. With the gift of hindsight, it is possible to detect vestigial epic elements among individual works since he began writing in the late 1940s. I have chosen to call *Omeros* an "epic of the dispossessed" because each of its protagonists is a castaway in one sense or another. Regardless of whether their ancestry is traced to the classical Mediterranean, Europe, or Africa, or is confined to the Americas, they are transplanted individuals whose separate quests all center on the fundamental need to strike roots in a place where they belong. Unlike Homer's Odysseus, who must return to an established kingdom, and Virgil's Aeneas, who has been promised a new empire, Walcott's humble colonists must create a home in the aftermath of Europe's failed dream of a New World Eden, using only their bare hands, faith, and imagination.

In this respect *Omeros* qualifies as a "foundation" epic, one that inscribes a people's rightful name and place within their own narrative. The

---

3. Rebekah Presson, "The Man Who Keeps the English Language Alive: An Interview with Derek Walcott," 9; Derek Walcott, "The Caribbean: Culture or Mimicry?" 10, 12.

immigrant population of the West Indies is the inauspicious legacy of imperialism, colonialism, and slavery. It is appropriate if not inevitable that Walcott's story line should reflect European affinities in order to dramatize the evolution of a creolized Caribbean identity. Peasant protagonists Achille and Hector are pitted against each other over the love of their black Helen just as their Greek namesakes fought three thousand years ago (17).[4] Achille is but one of the characters involved in a quest for his long-lost father that echoes Telemachus's search for Odysseus (136–39). Since the Greek siege of Troy is futile until the wounded bowman Philoctētēs is healed and restored among his people, Walcott's villagers of Gros Îlet suffer collectively until the obeah woman Ma Kilman cures Philoctete of his racial wound (246–48). A grizzled old Charon transports the poet/narrator to his Dantesque inferno (285). There the shade of Hector awaits just as Elpenor and Palinurus preceded Odysseus and Aeneas in their respective underworlds (292). Walcott's deceased father, Warwick, serves as another Anchises to admonish him to fulfill the destiny of his people (75–76). The historic Battle of the Saints may be seen as heroic conflict (84–86); there are numerous epic catalogs and the muse is eventually invoked (298). In the end, as the image of Virgil appears to lead Dante in the *Divine Comedy,* the ghost of Homer materializes to assure Walcott that if the world no longer goes to war over beauty or a woman he has a greater cause in "the love of your own people" (284). It is this love that inspires Walcott and his expatriate character Major Dennis Plunkett to undertake written tribute to St. Lucia, their "Helen of the West Indies."

Structurally, *Omeros* is a unified whole, comprised of sixty-four three-part chapters in seven books. Those seven books further subdivide quite naturally into three interrelated segments. The two opening and two closing books are set in St. Lucia. Books three through five reach out to encompass the major African, North American, and European influences that merge in the Caribbean. In keeping with Walcott's expressed desire to emulate the breathing rhythm of a person working in the hills of St. Lucia, the prosody of *Omeros* is measured but subtly flexible. He readily agrees with Robert Frost's dictum that there are ultimately only two meters—"strict iambic and loose iambic"—nevertheless, he describes the pattern in *Omeros* to be "roughly hexametrical with a terza rima form. It's like a

---

4. Quotations and references to Derek Walcott's *Omeros* are cited within the text.

combination of a Homeric line and a Dantesque design."[5] The "roughly" might be emphasized, since variations of the basic foot are frequent enough throughout the poem that the meter approximates free verse. While the poem is composed in terza rima stanzas, Walcott's overall pattern never really approaches Dante's intricately wrought hierarchical framework. From the outset, a Germanic language such as English does not lend itself as easily to rhyming as Dante's gender-inflected Italian. Challenged by the sheer scale of epic verse, of necessity, Walcott has to exercise considerable ingenuity in varying the rhyme scheme so that it never becomes monotonously predictable. Short passages occasionally adhere to variations on the standard interlocking terza rima, "a-b-a / b-c-b;" there is one grouping of seventeen pairs of couplets (173); and on two occasions he indulges in approximately rhyming triplets: eleven stanzas (169–70), four stanzas (193–94). The bulk of the verse, however, flows over and through unobtrusively pliable rhymed and unrhymed tercets. At the conclusion of Brad Leithauser's succinct enumeration of Walcott's exact and off-rhyme variations—anagrammatic, apocopated, macaronic, pararhyme, rime riche, double, triple, and visual rhymes—he concludes that "a teacher of versification might well employ *Omeros* as a rhyme casebook."[6]

Walcott is so attuned to the sensual texture of poetry that at the time of writing *Omeros* he confesses exasperation with the contemporary verse libre movement.

> I have come to the point now, not so much where I want to proselytize the idea of structure, but I'm exhausted by the quiet hostility one encounters in regards to saying simple things well. Poetry is communication and communication is memory. . . . memory can decay. If you encounter persistently the kind of convinced hostility that everything in rhyme is old-fashioned and free verse is the only way to write, then this position carries its own penalty.

This penchant for fluid structure may account for his lyrical expressiveness, but for the narrative impetus necessary to sustain *Omeros,* he discovered prose writers Conrad, Hemingway, and Kipling to be especially significant.

---

5. Brown and Johnson, "An Interview with Derek Walcott," 221; Robert Hamner, "Conversation with Derek Walcott," 418–19; J. P. White, "An Interview with Derek Walcott," 36.
6. Brad Leithauser, "Ancestral Rhyme," 93.

He tells D. J. R. Bruckner, "you find in them the wit of the paragraph; mentally, it keeps the rhythm up."[7]

There is a reciprocal overlapping of characters throughout *Omeros* that multiplies until it generates a doppelgänger effect. The technique manifests itself in at least three variations. In returning to Africa, Achille not only meets his ancestor and learns his name was originally Afolabe but also his alienated self stares back at him when he gazes into the village pool (141). Achille is doubled again when a scene is repeated on both sides of the Atlantic. On the first occasion, Achille surveys an African settlement devastated by slave traders, and Omeros is the blind griot reciting a litany of sorrow (145–46). The mirror image of the moment is repeated later when Catherine Weldon is the forlorn observer of an abandoned Sioux village in the Dakotas, with Omeros as the shaman (215–16). In another variation, the shade of Omeros states explicitly Walcott's own dual perspective. On one hand the poet is the island boy who has never left his native shore; on the other hand, he is the seafaring artist only now circling back home (291).

Undergirding the prosody and the narrative form of *Omeros* is always the controlling factor of Walcott's voice. In fact, he cites his unheroic participation in the action as reason enough to deny that the poem can be an epic. Based on his study of the subjective disclosure of an author's self-projection, Paul Eakin concludes that "autobiographical truth is not a fixed but an evolving process of self-discovery and self-creation, and, further, that the self that is the center of all autobiographical narrative is necessarily a fictive structure." In explaining the postmodern shift in emphasis away from the artist's traditional role of revealer to the reader's increasing burden of creative rewriting, Linda Hutcheon cautions in her *Narcissistic Narrative* that "metafiction, . . . fiction about fiction," is necessarily "self-conscious narrative by definition [which] includes within itself its own first contextual reading." The reader, therefore, "is no longer asked merely to recognize that fictional objects are 'like life'; he is asked to participate in the creation of worlds and of meaning, through language."[8]

Despite its fundamental unity, *Omeros* challenges the terms of its own existence. This phenomenon begins initially when Walcott qualifies the

---

7. White, "An Interview with Derek Walcott," 25; Bruckner, "Poem in Homage," 17.
8. Presson, "Man," 9; Paul John Eakin, *Fictions in Autobiography: Studies in the Art of Self-Invention,* 3; Linda Hutcheon, *Narcissistic Narrative: The Metafictional Paradox,* 1, 6, 30.

heroic dimensions of the poem. Soon after the story begins he is insisting "every 'I' is a fiction finally" (28). Next, authorial intrusions incorporate the poet and his personal life into the poem. The intertextuality increases with allusions to the lines, pages, images, and the very subject of the poem itself. Then two-thirds of the way through their concerted efforts to immortalize Helen, both Walcott and Plunkett discover a fatal error in their project. Heretofore, their veneration of Helen has borne the seed of self-aggrandizement. The essence of the woman diminishes as she is transformed into the object of their hegemonic designs. Each of them achieves the revelation that Helen, as the embodiment of their island, needs no monolithic inscription. Nothing they can offer Helen or St. Lucia's peasantry can match the beneficence of their very lives.

Ironically, as far as the unassuming fishermen and villagers of Gros Îlet are concerned, *Omeros* with its powerful lyricism and sincere intentions need not have been written. The screed of classical coincidences ultimately becomes a foil for the authentication of a national identity. As *Omeros* begins examining the terms of its own existence, Walcott takes the process of art to be one of his basic subjects. He brings into question not only the venerable epic genre but also the rights of the historian and artist to confiscate and colonize reality. The mirror art holds up to nature is fraught with distortions. Nevertheless it illuminates, focuses, heightens, and intensifies aspects of reality that might otherwise be marginalized in our personal quests for meaning. Having reached the conclusion that it is not necessary to mold Helen to fit his image, Walcott leaves *Omeros* appropriately open-ended. The final word is that when Achille turns homeward from the beach, "the sea was still going on" (325).

1 Walcott's Odyssey

The contemporary poet who undertakes to write an extended narrative poem invites comparisons with an august tradition that extends from Nikos Kazantzakis all the way back to Homer and the very roots of Western literature. Epic comparisons are practically inevitable regardless of the fact that for one reason or another more than one prominent voice has declared heroic poetry, the epic, to be outmoded or defunct. An early prominent critic, Edgar Allan Poe, goes so far as to deny the possibility of the genre's existence: "I hold that a long poem does not exist. I maintain that the phrase, 'a long poem,' is simply a flat contradiction in terms." Given Poe's devotion to symbolic and lyrical compression, he is naturally averse to the emotional diffusiveness of longer forms. As recently as 1969, William Anderson opens his *The Art of the Aeneid* declaring:

> Today, when we read an epic, we are dealing with a "dead" form. The word "epic" still possesses some power, especially for the advertisers of historical novels and the historical extravaganzas of Hollywood, but epic poetry no longer attracts poets, no longer is written. To read an epic like the *Aeneid*, then, is to grapple with unfamiliar poetic conventions, a strange culture, and a complicated historical background.[1]

At least two objectives are served in Anderson's remarks. Irony is implicit in the fact that popular usage of the term "epic" has degenerated to egregious

---

1. Edgar Allan Poe, "The Poetic Principle," 266; William Scovil Anderson, *The Art of the Aeneid*, 1–2.

hyperbole. Second, since the genre is alien to modern society, he prepares readers to appreciate the "otherness" of Virgil's age.

I raise the issue of epic viability not to rehearse the standard arguments regarding paradigms but to indicate merely that with *Omeros* in 1990, Derek Walcott has joined the extensive list of Western writers who have adapted the venerable genre to fit their own purposes. The classic prescription calls for an objective, extended, elevated, narrative poem commemorating a superhuman leader whose exploits are of interest to the gods and a race or a nation. In addition, structure and content are supposed to accommodate an objective point of view, ringing oratory, glorious battles, divine intervention, arduous journeys, epithets, lofty similes, etc. As a matter of fact, ancient practice in the *Iliad,* the *Odyssey,* and the *Aeneid* adhere to such guidelines. Nevertheless, even Virgil takes the liberty of manipulating the form in order to epitomize the Roman ideal of dutiful patriotism. Dante, in his turn, casts himself as protagonist in his vernacular Italian epic, juxtaposing low humor with high seriousness. Milton expanded beyond national boundaries to encompass the entire universe for Christianity. Long before James Joyce composed *Ulysses* (1922) in prose or Ezra Pound cobbled together *The Cantos* (between 1925 and 1948), deviations began to be introduced that have now proliferated to the extent that prescribed rules seem to exist more as points of departure rather than as definitive characteristics.

The number of works for which one scholar or another has claimed epic status is so great that it would be futile to attempt to account for any significant portion of them. From oral to written expression, from Babylonian *Gilgamesh* and Indian *Mahābhārata* to Joyce's *Ulysses,* epics transcend geographic, chronological, cultural, linguistic, and structural boundaries. Nevertheless, they hold recognizable shapes and continue to attract authors in every age. Whatever the motivation, even in our decidedly iconoclastic century, writers persist in undertaking works with epic aspirations.

Critical approaches to these attempts are equally eclectic. Nabaneeta Dev Sen suggests that comparative studies between Eastern and Western epics would disclose no more exotic differences than those that exist among the *Iliad, La Chanson de Roland, Nibelungenlied, Kalevala,* and *Beowulf.* Jan De Vries's *Heroic Song and Heroic Legend* looks not only at the usual Western epics but also at heroic works from Africa, India, Persia, and Samoa. Inspired by advances of Milam Parry and Albert Lord in understanding oral heroic tradition through the study of Serbo-Croatian singers, Isidore Okpewho published *The Epic in Africa: Toward a Poetics of the Oral Performance.* Karl Kroeber explores epic qualities of personalized narrative in *Romantic Narrative Art.* J. Schellenberger's 1983 entry in *Notes and Queries* simply lists more than thirty previously unrecognized epics published in the early nineteenth century.[2]

When it comes to the diversity of twentieth-century poets, James E. Miller settles on a subgenre he designates variously as "personal," "lyric-epic," or "anti-epic," which he traces back to Walt Whitman's *Leaves of Grass.* In a second article, Miller argues that the lyric-epic encompasses long poems or thematically integrated collections of poems—"a tradition resonant with interrelated images and allusions and rich in intertextual assumptions and implications: Ezra Pounds's *Cantos,* T. S. Eliot's *The Waste Land,* William Carlos William's *Paterson,* Hart Crane's *The Bridge,* Charles Olson's *Maximus Poems,* John Berryman's *Dream Songs,* and Allen Ginsberg's *The Fall of America.*" Miller's list in itself suggests that despite the reservations of a number of critics since Poe, the epic proliferates and criticism must still devise means for dealing with its Protean mutations. At the end of his 1971 book *The Epic,* Paul Merchant is forced to conclude, "The word 'epic' will perhaps never quite be defined; we began with formal hexameter poems and end with collage."[3]

Rather than attempt to settle the matter of definition or arbitrate among conflicting rules where so many others have ventured already, I need only point out that none of the principle elements of epic have remained intact from generation to generation. The type of hero; the nature of his exploits; national, racial, and religious significance; the putative objectivity of the author; and finally even the basic structure have been altered by one poet after another. Near the conclusion of his *Structuralist Poetics,* Jonathan Culler imagines a structuralist argument that resists an arbitrary textual interpretation: reading "competencies" that "give a privileged status to a particular set of rules . . . granting pre-eminence to certain arbitrary

    2. Nabaneeta Dev Sen, "Thematic Structure of Epic Poems in the East and West: A Comparative Study," 607; J. Schellenberger, "More Early Nineteenth-Century Epics," 213–14.
    3. James E. Miller Jr., "She's Here, Install'd Amid the Kitchen Ware: Walt Whitman's Epic Creation," 36; Miller, "Whitman's 'Leaves of Grass' and the American Lyric Epic," 297; Paul Merchant, *The Epic,* 93.

conventions and excluding from the realm of language all the truly creative and productive violations of these rules."[4] A genre as encrusted with tradition as the classical epic becomes moribund under its own weight or grows according to the inventive capacities of its audience.

For Derek Walcott, art begins in creative imitation or assimilation of alien influences. As early as a minor *Trinidad Guardian* review in 1966, Walcott advised "Young Trinidad Poets" that in order to establish their own voices it is first necessary to evolve through the acquisition of "other voices." He elaborates on this and makes it the central theme of his later essays "The Caribbean: Culture or Mimicry?" and "The Muse of History" (1974). Never having been intimidated by charges of "imitation," he finally dismisses Harold Bloom's phrase "anxiety of influence" as academic jargon.[5] The most thorough coverage of Walcott's mimetic artistry is Rei Terada's *Derek Walcott's Poetry: American Mimicry* (1992). Terada begins with the understanding that Walcott's New World depends not on originality but on permutations of the Old Worlds of Europe, Africa, and Asia.

As I shall indicate in successive chapters, Walcott exploits a variety of social, religious, historical, and literary resources for the style and content of his creolized, West Indian epic. Of all his epic references—Homer, Virgil, Dante, Milton, Hart Crane, and James Joyce—most are fairly traditional allusions that do not require extensive analysis. The title *Omeros* is itself homage to the Greek poet. The other authors, with the possible exception of Hart Crane, might reasonably be expected to have been prominent in his colonial educational regimen. Two of the writers just mentioned, Joyce and Crane, deserve a few preliminary remarks because Walcott has been inclined to comment on them discursively on several occasions.

In the autobiographical essay "Leaving School," Walcott recognizes the sacrilegious Stephen Dedalus as his idealistic hero. Later, in casting about for an archetype for a contemporary, earthy hero, he seizes upon Leopold Bloom. Significantly, Walcott stresses the paramount role of Bloom in giving *Ulysses* its most fundamental epic qualities. He maintains in his 1990 interview with J. P. White that

4. Jonathan Culler, *Structuralist Poetics: Structuralism, Linguistics and the Study of Literature*, 241.

5. Derek Walcott, "Young Trinidad Poets," 5; Brown and Johnson, "An Interview with Derek Walcott," 220.

> *Ulysses* is an epic because it breathes. It's an urban epic, which is
> remarkable in a small city. . . . The subject is a matter of a reflective
> man, not a man of action, but a sort of wandering Jew. That's the width
> of that epic, that Bloom is the wandering Jew. . . . I think a great poet
> has a deeper sense of evil, a wickedness of malice and malignity. You
> say, where is it in *Ulysses,* and it's there in *Ulysses* because Bloom is
> tormented.

On the surface Leopold Bloom may seem a poor descendant of Ulyssean
glory, yet W. B. Stanford argues that no author's characterization has done
justice to Homer's Odysseus until Joyce and Kazantzakis.[6] Had Stanford
been privy to Walcott's version of St. Lucian fishermen, he would have
encountered a third example of earthbound heroism.

Walcott shares even more intimately and consciously in Hart Crane's
epic undertaking. There is an affinity between these two poets because
Crane's *The Bridge* is an epic of the American psyche, and it too addresses
connections—Old and New Worlds, past and present, and disparate seg-
ments of an emerging nation. As writer and commentator for the *Hart
Crane* videotape in the *Voices and Visions* series, Walcott is interested both
in Crane's technique and in the fact that he draws rhythms and images
from the Caribbean Sea. Although the two poets pursue different ends,
certain aspects of Crane's approach to the epic are strikingly compatible
with Walcott's later practice.

As early as 1923, Crane writes to Gorham Munson regarding the dimen-
sions of his emerging work: "The more I think about my *Bridge* poem the
more thrilling its symbolical possibilities become, and . . . I begin to feel
myself directly connected with Whitman. I feel myself in currents that are
positively awesome in their extent and possibilities."[7] Four years later he
mentions to Otto Kahn that the "Cape Hatteras" section of *The Bridge* is a
"kind of ode to Whitman." Thus he proclaims his lineage in the poem itself:

> The stars have grooved our eyes with old persuasions
> Of love and hatred, birth,—surcease of nations . . .

6. Walcott, "Leaving School," 13; White, "An Interview with Derek Walcott," 23–24;
W. B. Stanford, *The Ulysses Theme: A Study in the Adaptability of a Traditional Hero,* 211.
7. The first quotation in this paragraph is from *The Letters of Hart Crane, 1916–1932,*
edited by Brom Weber, 128; five following quotations are taken from *The Complete Poems
and Selected Letters and Prose of Hart Crane,* edited by Brom Weber, 252, 93, 218, 254.

But who has held the heights more sure than thou,
O Walt!—Ascensions of thee hover in me now
As thou at junctions elegiac, there, of speed
With vast eternity, dost wield the rebound seed!

Whitman is merely one of the prominent figures Crane solicits to represent his heritage. He begins in "Ave Maria" with Columbus, later refers to Pocahontas, frontiersmen, seafarers, and writers Poe, Melville, and Dickinson. In his article "General Aims and Purposes," Crane takes a position regarding influences that anticipates Walcott's mimetic openness: "The poet has a right to draw on whatever practical resources he finds in books or otherwise about him. He must tax his sensibility and his touchstone of experience for the proper selections of these themes and details, however,— and that is where he either stands, or falls into useless archaeology." Thus he can compare the "historic and cultural scope of *The Bridge*" to the *Aeneid,* and he can range from the past of sailing ships to the world of suspension bridges, skyscrapers, trains, the airplane, and machinery in general. From his visit to Cuba in 1926, Crane claims that "The 'foreignness' of my surroundings stimulated me to the realization of natively American materials and viewpoints in myself not hitherto suspected." The problem facing Crane, or any expansive New World poet such as Whitman, Pound, or Walcott, is finding means to contain this amorphous body of American self-perceptions.

Several influential critics feel that Crane does not succeed in synthesizing his aims and the basic material. According to Brom Weber, the difficulty may be traced to Crane's failure to master American history sufficiently to achieve the poetic "task of organic assimilation." Yvor Winters cites incomprehensibly loose theme and structure, along with a pretentiousness of style. R. P. Blackmur argues, "The confusion of tool and purpose not only led him astray in conceiving his themes; it obscured at crucial moments the exact character of the work he was actually doing." Roy Harvey Pearce discerns no qualitative difference within the plethora of names and details, so that Crane "cannot conceive of history as something that really—and therefore uniquely—happened."[8] Actually, that supposed homogeneity may

---

8. Brom Weber, *Hart Crane,* 323; Yvor Winters, "The Significance of *The Bridge,* by Hart Crane," 139; R. P. Blackmur, "New Thresholds, New Anatomies," 274; Roy Harvey Pearce, *The Continuity of American Poetry,* 110.

play to Crane's advantage if we take into account the idea that in and of itself what "uniquely happened" is neutral. I am not suggesting that Crane had no organizing principle, but to present the characters and events of his poem so that their relative merits reflect an egalitarian, democratic picture would be in keeping with his explicit desire to follow Whitman's model.

Although there is no consensus on Crane's success as an epic writer, it is evident that he and Whitman both push lyric expression to unusual lengths. Thomas Vogler is of the opinion that Crane's search for a vision in *The Bridge* expands the lyric mode toward epic proportions. While Vincent Quinn comments on Crane's vatic power, he finds instead of an epic "a series of lyrics intended to quicken an affirmative, idealistic viewpoint."[9] Without concerning himself directly with the question of genre, Derek Walcott reads *The Bridge* sympathetically in the *Visions and Voices* series. Given Walcott's Caribbean background, it is not surprising that he should open his narrative by quoting Crane's lyric "O Carib Isle." He emphasizes the heat, the glaring sun, shadows against white sand, and the impact of the sea. In this environment, on his grandmother's Cuban estate in 1926, Crane wrote much of *The Bridge*.

To explain the unifying force that propels Crane's verse, Walcott looks to the example of surging waves. As he sees it, *The Bridge* is not held together simply by imagination, nor is it symphonic or montage; the only necessary source of propulsion is Crane's chosen meter. Citing lines from "The River" section, Walcott illustrates by the quickening flicker of signboards read from a speeding train. The verse gathers momentum, abridging advertisements ("Thomas / a Ediford") until the flow modulates into a rhythm suitable to the length of the poem. Walcott also singles out Crane's humor and his ability to dramatize encounters among characters, sketching a scene in the same way novelists encapsulate telling moments. Equally impressive to Walcott are the portraits of maladjusted individuals, "dangerous models . . . damned people . . . whose sense of doom could almost be a heroic concept on his part . . . the drunkenness and general chaos of his own life." Perhaps because Crane chooses to induct outsiders into his pantheon with Columbus, the Wright brothers, and famous authors, his work would be particularly interesting to a black artist from that neglected backwater of the

---

9. Thomas A. Vogler, *Preludes to Vision: The Epic Venture in Blake, Wordsworth, Keats, and Hart Crane,* 14; Vincent Quinn, *Hart Crane,* 79.

Americas, the islands of the West Indies. Walcott voices these impressions of Crane in 1988, a scant two years before publishing his own epic-length poem *Omeros*. The proximity in time adds poignancy to his estimate of the power and ambition he attributes to Whitman and Crane. If, as he claims, each sets out in turn to become "the poet of America,"[10] he is no less ambitious in undertaking an epic of the New World centered in his native St. Lucia.

To this point, I have been concerned with the indomitable urge that surfaces in poet after poet to give expression to the spirit of their cultures. Hart Crane and his mentor Whitman represent a facet of epic poetry that is rarely emphasized in its modern descendant. They celebrate a quality of faith that underlies even the most negative assessment of the human condition. While experimentation in structure and content requires considerable latitude in defining parameters, the question is not whether a contemporary epic exists or why writers keep manipulating the genre. What remains to be seen are the dimensions of the next permutation.

This cursory overview of the genre is simply a reminder of the shade under which Derek Walcott plants the seed of *Omeros*. In the tradition of most of his predecessors, Walcott also finds it necessary to declare a certain degree of independence from tradition. Although many of the features of previous epics insinuate themselves into *Omeros,* the poem is marked primarily by its deviations from the norm. By centering the work on his native island of St. Lucia and focusing on the local peasantry he reifies the virtues of common people. Certainly, marginal individuals have received notice in other epics from Homer to Kazantzakis—laborers, prostitutes, sailors, servants, tribal Indians—but in *Omeros* they emerge from the background to become protagonists. The progeny of aboriginals, slaves, indentured servants, explorers, colonists who have traditionally been Eurocentric society's "other," now find their narrative voice. In effect, Walcott writes the epic of the dispossessed.

Having as his point of departure the neglected colony of a fading empire, a people descended from slaves and provincial clerks, his subject matter might at first appear unpromising. In what may be one of the most frequently quoted passages from his first major publication, *In a Green Night* (1962), Walcott raises the existential question of his divided heritage: "how

10. Walcott, *Hart Crane,* videocassette.

choose, / Between this Africa and the English tongue I love?" His decision
was to deny neither, but to forge a New World identity out of the social
nexus of the West Indies. As early as 1964, in a column for the *Trinidad
Guardian* entitled "A Dilemma Faces W. I. Artists," Walcott castigates local
intellectuals who are more interested in the fate of a decadent, declining
England than in the prospects of their own islands. He notes that since
germinal cultures such as theirs have served to invigorate older societies in
the past, rare opportunities abound for colonial artists and intellectuals.
The "dilemma" of his title refers to the fact that West Indian artists who
are technically immersed in European expressionism must contend with a
representational urge to "re-create the visible world, which is, in terms of art
history, undocumented." Walcott's enthusiasm for his Caribbean material
is unmistakable in "Meanings": "I think that an archipelago, whether Greek
or West Indian, is bound to be a fertile area, particularly if it is a bridge
between continents, and a variety of people settle there." If this allusion
to Greece seems ostentatious, his estimation of the New World poet's
responsibilities is equally bold in "Poetry—Enormously Complicated Art."
In this 1962 address (the same year in which his first major collection of
poems appeared), Walcott claims "that the good poet is the proprietor of
the experience of the race, that he is and has always been the vessel, vates,
rainmaker, the conscience of the king and the embodiment of society, even
when society is unable to contain him." At the same time that he touts the
superhuman attributes of the poet, he acknowledges his expression may
sound "precocious and artificial for . . . a society which has not settled and
whose languages have a Protean vitality that has not yet formalised its own
syntax and accent." He suggests, to ensure a desired anchor in reality, that
his imitative expression must derive from personal feelings with "roots in
his own earth."[11]

From these few examples, it is evident that Walcott has great expectations
for his archipelago, his people, and the function of poetry. In order to
assess his consistency in fulfilling some of his own requirements, and to
see how elements of epic promise begin to appear in his earliest writing, it
is necessary to turn to the primary works themselves. With the advantage
of hindsight it is now possible to see an immature skeleton of *Omeros*

---

11. Walcott, *In a Green Night*, 18; Walcott, "A Dilemma Faces W. I. Artists," 3;
Walcott, "Meanings," 49; Walcott, "Poetry—Enormously Complicated Art," 3.

in Walcott's first long autobiographical poem, "Epitaph for the Young: A Poem in XII Cantos" (1949). At the time of composition, Walcott was nineteen years old and fancied himself to be in the shoes of James Joyce's "blasphemous, arrogant Stephen Daedalus." "Like Stephen," he writes for *London Magazine* years later, "I had my nights of two shilling whores, of 'tackling in the Alley', and silently howling remorse. Like him, I was a knot of paradoxes: hating the Church and loving her rituals, learning to hate England as I worshipped her language."[12] Although Joyce and other influences mark the lyrical verse of *25 Poems* (privately printed in 1948), a year later under the influence of Dedalus, he initiates his first extended narrative poem.

"Epitaph for the Young" has in common with *Omeros* the same interest in history and memory. Both works are circular in structure and rife with parallel allusions. Significantly, however, the earlier poem is more concerned with individual rather than communal identity, and raw nerves are closer to the surface. Perhaps the narrative voice is the most crucial measure of the voyage from "Epitaph" to *Omeros*. As he explains in a 1975 interview with Robert Hamner, Walcott not only sees "Epitaph" as an Urtext for his lengthy autobiographical *Another Life*, but also it provides extensive cohesion for the author's persona and affords points of reference for the reader's perspective. In 1949, assuming a burden heavy for his nineteen years, Walcott cries, "A heart cracked early / Never heals." Sounding world-weary, he complains,

> While like an arrowing pylon my hardening talent
> Shot to the clouds, the boy I was is weakening.
> I hear the power I possess knock at my roots,
> And see the tower of myself whose height attracts
> Destruction, begin a crazy crack and waltz of ruin.[13]

From the height of indulgent despair, the young poet solicits at one time or another the names of Telemachus, Hamlet, Stephen Dedalus, and Icarus—whose fates are all entangled with paternal legacies.

Beyond the explicit allusiveness, from the beginning, Walcott revels in the tone and style of the masters he has been reading. He admits in introducing

---

12. Walcott, "Leaving School," 13.
13. Hamner, "Conversation with Derek Walcott," 411; Walcott, "Epitaph for the Young: A Poem in XII Cantos," 4, 5.

his collection *Dream on Monkey Mountain and Other Plays* that he aspired to prolong the line of Marlowe and Milton.[14] Even a short list of authors from whom he borrows themes and ideas comprises a formidable pantheon. "Epitaph for the Young" (1949) is spoken through the voices of not only Joyce but also Dylan Thomas and T. S. Eliot. The early play *The Sea at Dauphin* (1954) was directly inspired by W. B. Yeats's *Riders to the Sea*. *In a Green Night* draws its title from Andrew Marvell's poem "Bermudas." *The Joker of Seville* (1978) is an adaptation of Tirso de Molina's Spanish classic *El Burlador de Sevilla*. *A Branch of the Blue Nile* (1983) centers around a West Indian production of Shakespeare's *Antony and Cleopatra*. After borrowing from Homer and Dante for *Omeros*, Walcott has gone on to recast Odysseus in his own Caribbean play *The Odyssey* (1992). Revealing as this partial catalog may be in and of itself, it is more important to observe that in each case Walcott is rewriting what he has read, through personal West Indian experience.

Just as he "rewrites" other influences, it is essential to observe, as well, that he continually recycles elements of his own fertile mind. Tempting as it may be to elaborate on Walcott's incremental assimilative technique, it is beyond the scope of this chapter. Nevertheless, to illustrate the fact that Walcott may have always harbored latent epic tendencies, it would be worth citing a few gestures that anticipate *Omeros*.

As a precocious colonial artist suspended between metropolitan influences and the unformed material of his own life, Walcott had to launch a quest for a viable alternative to the subject matter. From the plethora of "facts" already known and interpreted, pertinent details had to be reassembled and a fresh narrative thread had to join them along a newly created seam. The first option that occurs to Walcott is pursued in one of his earliest unpublished plays, *Henri Christophe* (1950). By turning to the period of Haiti's successful slave rebellion in the last decade of the 1700s, Walcott inadvertently comes close to fulfilling James Anthony Froude's suggestion that no hero is available in the Caribbean "unless philonegro enthusiasm can make one out of Toussaint." Toussaint L'Ouverture stands out because of his remarkable successes against some of the most formidable troops Napoleon could muster.[15] There is also the pathos of his dying alone in a

14. Walcott, "What the Twilight Says: An Overture," introduction to *Dream on Monkey Mountain and Other Plays*, 31.

15. James Anthony Froude, *The English in the West Indies: or the Bow of Ulysses*, 306.

French prison after having been betrayed by his own people. Despite these potent facets of Toussaint's life, however, when Walcott elected to dramatize this bloody revolutionary period he turned instead to Henri Christophe. Unlike the victimized Toussaint, Christophe exhibits the *hamartia* requisite in classical forms of tragedy. Here is a slave during the height of imperial rule not only defying his white masters but also envisioning a black nation to rival the greatest powers of Europe.

Walcott's fascination with these defiant rebels is spelled out in his introduction to *Dream on Monkey Mountain and Other Plays:*

> At nineteen, an elate, exuberant poet madly in love with English . . . Full of precocious rage, I was drawn, like a child's mind to fire, to the Manichean conflicts of Haiti's history. The parallels were there in my own island, but not the heroes: a black French island somnolent in its Catholicism and black magic . . . The fire's shadows, magnified into myth, were those of the black Jacobins of Haiti. . . .
> . . . Dessalines and Christophe, men who had structured their own despair. . . . They were our only noble ruins.

At the time of writing, being "white in mind and black in body," he understands their downfall strictly in terms of Christian tragedy. Their overweening pride led them to contest the will of God, the order of the universe. As he looks around on other islands, he begins to envy Frantz Fanon and Aimé Césaire, their greater anguish, poverty, and blackness. At his brother Roderick's urging, as he explains in "Meanings," he decided to give voice to these nobly tragic predecessors.[16]

Unfortunately, at this stage of his career, the amateur playwright cannot mold his raw material into his ersatz Jacobean verse. Throughout the play, this discrepancy between content and form is a telling weakness. In fact, Walcott's assessment of his own youthful enthusiasm twenty years later confronts the problem in two ways. First, he reevaluates the qualities that made these men fascinating: "Now, one may see such heroes as squalid fascists who chained their own people, but they had size, mania, the fire of great heretics." There was at least something magnificent in their having striven heroically. Second, he accounts for the seductive European style into which he had attempted to force his expression: "It is easy, twenty years

16. Walcott, "What the Twilight Says," 11–12; Walcott, "Meanings," 45.

later, to mock such ambition, to concede . . . its 'fustian,' yet the Jacobean style, its cynical, aristocratic flourish came naturally to this first play—the corruption of slaves into tyrants."[17] Uneven as the literary quality of *Henri Christophe* may be, it is nevertheless a significant indication of Walcott's desire to give artistic life to actual figures in West Indian history.

Added to his already considerable interest in the historical background of the Caribbean, he was commissioned in 1957 by the University of the West Indies to write a play appropriate for the opening of the first Federal Parliament of the West Indies. As part of the celebrations of that occasion in April 1958, he presented *Drums and Colours: An Epic Drama*. It is not only the subtitle and broad scope of this play that mark its significance in Walcott's preparation as an epic poet. Between the writing of *Henri Christophe* and *Drums and Colours,* Walcott has been learning to reconcile the contrary impulses generated by his indigenous environment and his Western classical education. In the latter play, an uneasy compromise is struck, giving each its due. The result is a loosely structured saga dramatizing four chronological periods: discovery, exploitation, rebellion, and independence (represented in order by Columbus, Raleigh, Toussaint, and George William Gordon). These sequential episodes share minor characters who bear the same names in each time period; there are common images, motifs, symbols; and most important of all, a band of contemporary carnival dancers introduces the action in a prologue, entertains during one interval, becomes involved in several scenes, and finally closes the play in an epilogue.

Significantly, even though *Drums and Colours* pays homage to major historical figures, lowly members of the population are prominently represented. In fact, fascination with the inevitable luminaries of art, history, and literature is equaled only by his obsession with commemorating the unsung heroism of outcasts whose greatest achievement may be their very survival. The type of protagonist Walcott is seeking to establish is found in Makak, the main character in *Dream on Monkey Mountain*. Makak is indigenous, coming directly out of his St. Lucian experience, yet Walcott sees him as having much broader archetypal lineaments. In "Meanings" he describes parallels for island societies, whether in Japan or the Caribbean, where peasants gather around communal fires to hear stories of questing warriors.

17. Walcott, "What the Twilight Says," 13.

> In the West Indies, from a slave tradition adapted to the environ-
> ment, the slaves kept the strength of the stories about devils and gods
> and the cunning of certain figures, but what was missing in the folklore
> was a single heroic warrior figure. . . .
> My Makak comes from my own childhood. But there was no
> king, no tribal chief, no warrior for a model in those stories. So the
> person I saw was this degraded, humble, lonely, isolated figure of the
> woodcutter. I can see him for what he is now, a brawling, ruddy drunk
> who would come down the street on a Saturday when he got paid and
> let out an immense roar that would terrify all the children in the
> street. . . . This was a degraded man, but he had some elemental force
> in him that is still terrifying; in another society he would have been
> a warrior.[18]

Makak's quest in *Dream on Monkey Mountain* is not to reclaim an anachro-
nistic African warrior's identity but to reify himself as a present-day West
Indian.

Makak's heroic struggle is with history's legacy of slavery and colonial
neglect, which has reduced him to an old charcoal burner living alone in the
mountains. A white goddess appears in a vision to inform him of his royal
African heritage. Acting on that vision, he heals people, encourages them
to believe in themselves, and promises to lead them triumphantly back to
Africa. By the end of the play, however, he discovers that home is neither
across the sea nor in the past. The schizophrenic muse that inspires *Henri
Christophe, Drums and Colours,* and *Dream on Monkey Mountain* wears
both a private and a public mask. While historical and fictional characters
speak and act with the authenticity of biography, other more lyrical poems,
such as "Epitaph for the Young," evolve into his autobiographical paean to
St. Lucia, *Another Life.* This book-length work is less esoterically derivative,
more fully developed and mature than its predecessor. When asked how a
reader might be expected to respond to obscure personal references within
Another Life, Walcott suggested two levels of interpretation:

> Well, it would be hard for one to leave out the details of a person's life
> in a book of that kind. It is a particular experience. But in a sense it
> is a biography of an "intelligence," a West Indian intelligence, using it
> in the Latin sense of spirit. . . .

18. Walcott, "Meanings," 50.

> You know I once wrote another thing called "Epitaph for the
> Young." Well, all the influences are there: I mean they are visible,
> deliberately quoted influences. There's Joyce, and "The Wasteland,"
> and Pound and it's all in there, I mean in terms of what one was
> learning. . . . So this is sort of like an Urtext of *Another Life*. It was
> not a conscious thing. I realize that what I've done, in a sense, is not
> brought that life up to its own date, but sort of re-essentialized it,
> given it more of an essence in fact, made it more focal.[19]

The book may also be seen as an effective amalgamation of Walcott's dual
quest for a communal and personal history. Fusion of the two spheres grows
out of the imaginative depiction of his own experience as an aspiring artist
within the St. Lucian context.

In addition to portraying the evolution of a keen intelligence, *Another
Life* urges the latent significance and beauty of Walcott's birthplace. While
it lacks the restraint, sweep, and depth of a classical epic, it is a crucial
milestone on the journey toward *Omeros*. As "Epitaph for the Young" had
done before it, *Another Life* is a preliminary exploration of traditionally
marginalized characters, settings, and themes that Walcott considers too
valuable to be discounted in the annals of New World literature. The third
chapter of the first book is a virtual catalog of his peasant heroes. With
self-deprecating humor he candidly admits a few pages later:

> Provincialism loves the pseudo-epic,
> so if these heroes have been given a stature
> disproportionate to their cramped lives,
> remember I beheld them at knee-height,
> and that their thunderous exchanges
> rumbled like gods about another life.[20]

Within these lines two separate evaluative measures are introduced. Youth-
ful enthusiasm may distort estimations of worth, but Walcott is equally
aware that the "cramped lives" of his people have also been systematically
discounted through the prejudice of colonial neglect.

This desire to reclaim the marginal pervades all of Walcott's work, and
is nowhere more explicit than in the early "Origins," from *Selected Poems*.

19. Hamner, "Conversation with Derek Walcott," 411.
20. Walcott, *Another Life*, 41.

Evoking a kind of racial memory, the persona recalls that from the log of
Christopher Columbus,

> I learnt your annals of ocean
> Of Hector, bridler of horses,
> Achilles, Aeneas, Ulysses,
> But "Of that fine race of people which came off the mainland
> To greet Christobal as he rounded Icacos,"
> Blank pages turn in the wind.[21]

In the absence of historic West Indian precedent, he may occasionally doubt
the efficacy of his own writing, yet he never has to feel that he is writing
within a void. Never subject to the illusion that originality is an end in
itself, Walcott consistently emphasizes the subtle linkages between the Old
World and the new one he is in the process of inscribing.

Rather than inhibit his freedom to create, ancient models provide
catalysts for Walcott's innovative treatment of indigenous material, for the
renovation of staid tradition. His version of the active relationship between
past and present becomes the subject of "A Latin Primer."

> I had nothing against which
> to notch the growth of my work
> but the horizon, no language
> but the shallows in my long walk
>
> home, so I shook all the help
> my young right hand could use
> from the sand-crusted kelp
> of distant literatures.
>
> The frigate bird my phoenix,
> . . . .
> with one wing beat for scansion,
> that slowly levelling V
> made one with my horizon
> . . . .
> or the roofless pillars once
> sacred to Hercules.[22]

---

21. Walcott, *Selected Poems,* 51.
22. Walcott, *The Arkansas Testament,* 21, 24.

Language, rhythm, the example of admired predecessors, and an untrammeled world awaiting his pen, Walcott responds to the urge that has motivated humanistic poets of every age.

Fully conscious of the factional pressures of Euro-American traditionalists on one hand and Afro-Caribbean purists on the other, Walcott has attempted to maintain his birthright in both hemispheres. It is essential to keep this divided allegiance in mind while examining an adaptation such as *The Joker of Seville* (1974), rewritten to convey a New World perspective for Tirso de Molina's Spanish Golden-Age classic *El Burlador de Sevilla* (1630). While it is evident that he respects the achievements of metropolitan authorities, it is even more interesting to observe the extent to which he uses marginalized content and forms to challenge and revitalize accepted patterns. In the years since his move to the United States in the late 1970s, two poems and one play stand out as milestones on Walcott's journey toward *Omeros*, each one more directly focused on his eventual epic: "The Schooner *Flight*" from *The Star-Apple Kingdom* (1979), "The Light of the World" from *The Arkansas Testament* (1987), and the unpublished play "The Ghost Dance" (premiered 1989).

"The Schooner *Flight*" not only introduces the authentic "red nigger" poet-narrator Shabine who is capable of sustaining an extended narrative in island dialect, but it is a miniature sea odyssey that anticipates one of the primary plot lines of *Omeros*. As a racial hybrid and sailor who indulges in writing poetry, Shabine is a living contradiction. Much of the poem is an inventory of the factors that define his existence as a colonial derelict. Being of "Dutch, nigger, and English" extraction (as is Walcott), he puns that he has "no nation now but the imagination." Too black to suit his former white rulers yet too white to be accepted after the black revolution, he claims,

> I met History once, but he ain't recognize me,
> a parchment Creole, with warts . . .
> . . . .
> I confront him and shout, "Sir, is Shabine!
> They say I'se your grandson. You remember Grandma,
> your black cook, at all?" The bitch hawk and spat.
> A spit like that worth any number of words.
> But that's all them bastards have left us: words.

Lapsing into a hallucinatory dream, Shabine relives the arrival of famous admirals "Rodney, Nelson, de Grace," and the Middle Passage of his African ancestors. Upon awakening, he reflects that it is necessary to be a colonial to appreciate the pain of loving an inferior place that has been named by an alien culture. With his poetic sensibility he muses,

> . . . "Those casuarinas bend
> like cypresses, their hair hangs down in rain
> like sailors' wives. They're classic trees, and we,
> if we live like the names our masters please,
> by careful mimicry might become men."

Judging by history's unkind strokes, extermination of the Caribs, slavery, imperial subjugation, Shabine is led to conclude ironically that "Progress is history's dirty joke."[23] Nevertheless, he determines to go on living and writing about his personal dilemma.

Underlying the sociopolitical theme of "The Schooner *Flight*" is also Shabine's suspension between Maria Concepcion, the woman to whom he is passionately attached, and the wife and children to whom he is bound by love and duty. Although these divisions of the heart reflect the essence of the poem, the subject is not only his identity crisis but also the difficulty of expressing himself in words. Thus with Shabine, as with Walcott's assumed persona later in *Omeros,* the self-conscious author's relationship with his subject matter becomes an integral theme of the poem. Early in "The Schooner *Flight,*" Shabine addresses the reader directly to explain his chosen style.

> . . . When I write
> this poem, each phrase go be soaked in salt;
> I go draw and knot every line as tight
> as ropes in this rigging; in simple speech
> my common language go be the wind,
> my pages the sails of the schooner *Flight.*

By the end of the poem, he is equally explicit about his aesthetic intentions. It might well be the prayer of Homer's Odysseus, adrift between Troy and Ithaca over two thousand years ago.

---

23. Walcott, *The Star-Apple Kingdom,* 4, 8, 9, 12, 14.

> . . . I am satisfied
> if my hand gave voice to one people's grief.
> . . . .
> . . . I have only one theme:
>
> The bowsprit, the arrow, the longing, the lunging heart—
> the flight to a target whose aim we'll never know,
> vain search for one island that heals with its harbor
> and a guiltless horizon.[24]

Since he concedes that the aim of his heart is nebulous and his search for absolution is vain, emphasis must be placed on the meaningfulness of the voyage itself. In the struggle to formulate his problem, he engages in the process of defining the terms of his own existence.

The final poem to which I wish to refer appears in *The Arkansas Testament.* "The Light of the World" is unique in that Walcott mentions its direct connection with *Omeros.* During a 1990 interview, he explains to J. P. White that he had in mind a woman to represent St. Lucia as the Helen of the West Indies because of the wars fought among European powers to claim her. At that stage of writing, he planned to call her "Elena, a Black woman, much like the one on the bus in 'The Light of the World.'" Although her name is changed to Helen before publication of *Omeros,* she remains as emblematic as the woman who occupies his attention in "The Light of the World." Responding to her impact in the 1987 poem, he describes her as,

> . . . nothing else but heraldic . . .
> . . . .
> it was like a statue, like a black Delacroix's
> *Liberty Leading the People.*

As the poet observes her discreetly, he begins to regret all that he has lost by abandoning the earthy folk of St. Lucia to establish himself abroad as an artist. The sixteen-seater transport, precursor of Hector's speeding "Comet" in *Omeros,* picks up and deposits peasants after their day of work and shopping in the markets.

24. Ibid., 5, 19.

> I had left them on earth, I left them to sing
> Marley's songs of a sadness as real as the smell
> of rain on dry earth, or the smell of damp sand,
> and the bus felt warm with their neighbourliness,
> their consideration, and the polite partings.

When he reaches his stop opposite the ironically named Halcyon Hotel, he is driven to the verge of tears. The poem ends with his realization that in the fullness of their simple lives,

> There was nothing they wanted, nothing I could give them
> but this thing I have called "The Light of the World."[25]

There is genuine pathos in these closing lines and no hint of condescension.

It is tempting to reiterate that poverty and narrow existence are hardly components of materially rewarding lives. This consideration does not escape Walcott's attention. As a matter of fact, he spells out his attitude in an interview with Rebekah Presson for the *New Letters on the Air* series. Walcott asserts that while he does not want to glamorize the provincial lives of Caribbean fishermen, he is awed by the dangers of the sea they must face every day. He believes that what is accepted as ordinary among them must impress the outsider as heroic, worthy of admiration. Consciously avoiding patronization, he sees within the people qualities of "beauty and simplicity" that deserve to be celebrated. Ultimately this is the driving force behind the fictive characters of Achille and Hector who fight over their elusive Helen.[26]

Unfortunately, Walcott is never as explicit about his reasons for including the figure of Catherine Weldon in *Omeros*. What he has provided, however, is "The Ghost Dance" (1989), the unpublished play to which I have already alluded. In this case, "The Ghost Dance" also celebrates spiritual values, those of an actual person who is usually relegated to an obscure footnote in American history. One way to account for the role of Catherine Weldon in *Omeros* is to recognize the devotion of her life to the cause of North America's embattled Sioux Indians. They (as was the fate of their lost

25. Walcott, *The Arkansas Testament*, 48, 51.
26. Rebekah Presson, "Derek Walcott," audiotape interview with Derek Walcott.

Amerindian brothers the Arawak and Carib tribes of the West Indies) are
now on the verge of having their culture eradicated by white oppressors.
As Walcott dramatizes the story, Weldon has left her secure home in the
East to become private secretary to Chief Sitting Bull and a passionate
advocate of Native American rights. The Dakotas in the 1890s may be
far removed from Walcott's Caribbean, but there are parallel cultural
embroilments.

Weldon finds herself caught between the frontier military authorities and
the plight of her Indian friends. The dramatic crisis of the play centers on
the supernatural powers that are supposed to be released by the ceremonial
Ghost Dance. The army fears that if the Indians become convinced that
the dance will make them impervious to bullets, there will be a bloody
uprising. Considering both sides of the problem, Weldon asserts that as
new converts to Christianity the Sioux have merely embraced their faith
too boldly.

> First, we preach the resurrection and the life
> of a Second Coming, of a pale-faced Messiah
> whom we have crucified so he can redeem us,
> whom we must first murder to receive His pardon.
> That must be baffling enough to those savages
> who dare not presume to torture their gods.
> When they go a little further as all converts do
> . . . .
> You tell these converts that they believe too much
> That they exaggerate, they take belief too far.

By the end of the play, Sitting Bull has been murdered by a detachment of
Indian policemen and Weldon has to settle for spiritual consolation. In the
closing scene, she assures Dr. Beddoes,

> When History wins it doesn't mean God has lost.
> I feel a great victory in being on the losing side,
> in not having a heart as empty as that plain.
> I lived a rich and bountiful life out there,
> for all its losses. My ghosts are happy ones.

Although Sitting Bull, Kicking Bear, and their people are driven back to the
reservation, starved, abused, or killed, as Robert Bensen observes, much

of their narrative is conveyed through the eyes of Catherine Weldon.[27] In both "The Ghost Dance" and *Omeros,* Walcott is interested in the character of this woman who challenges the barriers of racial and cultural relations. Catherine Weldon loses her reputation, her fortune, and the life of her son in attempting to prevent genocide. The futility of her gesture makes it no less heroic than the unsung travails of the Achilles, Hectors, and Helens of the West Indies.

Because *Omeros* is largely an "establishment epic," in the sense that homecoming and the establishment of roots are paramount themes, it is to be expected that works such as Homer's *Odyssey* and Virgil's *Aeneid* would be fundamental points of departure. For example, although there is one major sea battle in Walcott's epic, *Omeros* is clearly more domestic than the *Iliad* and other national poems that emphasize the martial valor of a distinctly masculine prowess. The importance of this distinction is underscored two years after the publication of *Omeros* when Walcott once again draws from Homer's work to produce *The Odyssey* at Stratford-upon-Avon in 1992. Whatever parts of the *Odyssey* he may not have read at the time he wrote *Omeros,* he must have remedied that omission before writing this play; his narrative line derives from many of Homer's characters and episodes. Among the prominent revisions of the original, however, is his devaluation of the ancient code of heroism.

The ending of *The Odyssey* provides ample evidence of Walcott's appreciation of a less grandiose but nonetheless admirable form of valor for his protagonists. As with Homer's prototype, Walcott's Odysseus successfully exterminates all his wife's unwelcome suitors; but at that point, Penelope forcefully asserts her prerogatives as a woman who has remained faithfully at home throughout his twenty-year absence. Even after he had been presumed by many to be dead, she waited patiently, outmaneuvering numerous princes seeking her hand in marriage. Instead of blithely accepting his embrace after his palace massacre, she tests his authenticity by challenging him to move their marriage bed. Imposing this obstacle, Penelope not only legitimizes her own personal rights but also demonstrates her intellectual parity with Odysseus. Only after he reveals that he knows the bed cannot be moved because it is

27. Walcott, "The Ghost Dance," 2.5. pp. 22–23, 2.8. p. 31; Robert Bensen, "Catherine Weldon in *Omeros* and 'The Ghost Dance': Notes on Derek Walcott's Poetry and Drama," 119–20.

carved from a rooted olive tree will Penelope concede that he truly is her husband.

Walcott's rendition of Penelope's skepticism goes much further than Homer's comparatively simple reconciliation of man and wife. His kind of revision signals the difference between a simpler heroic ideal and our more relativistic modern values. Postmodern criticism has heightened our consciousness of authors' biased agendas so that we look for alternative readings. For example, in reexamining the traditionally masculine epic form of the *Iliad* and the *Odyssey* from a feminist perspective, Mihoko Suzuki argues, "At many points the *Odyssey* interrogates its epic predecessor." Citing as the most striking instance Achilles's denigration of earthly fame when he meets Odysseus in Hades, Suzuki argues that Achilles "implicitly repudiates the choice he perforce made in the *Iliad* of a short and glorious life over a long and obscure one." Walcott's Penelope exhibits similar reservations when she surveys the carnage in her palace. She protests that her home has been turned into an abattoir. To Odysseus's excuse that he killed for her, Penelope responds incredulously, "IT'S FOR THIS I KEPT MY THIGHS CROSSED FOR TWENTY YEARS?" Husband and wife are reconciled shortly thereafter, when Odysseus passes her bed test, as in the Greek original. The realignment of values exhibited in Walcott's version is borne out not only in the actions of his protagonists but also in the closing benediction sung by the blind poet "Billy Blue." This archetypal figure alludes to his Homeric lineage, but instead of adhering to the fabled themes of war and glorious exploits he celebrates home, a treasured woman, and peace:

> Since that first blind singer, others will sing down the ages
> Of the heart in its harbour, then long years after Troy, after Troy.
>
> And a house, happy for good, from a swallow's omen,
> Let the waves clap their hands and the surf whisper amen.
>
> For a rock, a rock, a rock, a rock-steady woman
> Let the waves clap their hands and the surf whisper amen.
> For that peace which, in their mercy, the gods allow men.[28]

28. Mihoko Suzuki, *Metamorphoses of Helen: Authority, Difference, and the Epic,* 58; Walcott, *The Odyssey,* 153, 160.

The action described in *The Odyssey* is a much closer parallel to its Greek source than *Omeros* attempts to be; nevertheless, in the years immediately following publication of his epic poem, Walcott continues to restructure the Homeric enterprise to conform to his West Indian frame of reference.

Hardly a year before the appearance of *Omeros,* Jeremy Ingalls anticipates the epic potential within third world contexts. One observation in *The Epic Tradition* (1989) now seems exceptionally prescient.

> By the nature of its motive and its resources epic composition always draws upon a long cross-cultural inheritance involving many peoples and coming in transit through many languages. . . . It seems wholly probable that epic narrative will increase rather than decrease in East Asia and India. It is also likely to emerge, if it is not already emergent, in Southeast Asia, in Africa, and among composers drawing upon compounded Amerindian as well as Old and New World resources in the Americas.

If disparate resources are necessary ingredients for an epic, the Caribbean provides the ideal situation. The various strands of racial and cultural material that Walcott assimilates and transforms in *Omeros* acquire all the more value as they cohere within a central defining core. Having truly become the "proprietor of the experience of the race," Walcott provides what Patrick Taylor calls a "narrative of liberation." He insists that, "[A]ny attempt to deny or negate human possibility, slavery and racism being primary Caribbean examples of such denial, is rejected by liberating narrative." Furthermore, Taylor elaborates,

> Telling a story in which all human beings can find themselves, Caribbean culture recreates the past, from the situation of the present, with a view to the future. Its challenge is to destroy myth without killing meaning, and this means creating art out of fantasy. A culture is formed that is national because it understands its own history, human because it is part of the universal quest for recognition, creative because it is a work without an end.

As may be seen by the intertwining of subplots in the larger story of *Omeros,* Walcott's strategy is inclusive rather than exclusionary. This is not to imply that he universalizes particulars into homogenized abstractions but that an order is posited which respects difference. In a 1975 interview,

Walcott remarks, "The more particular you get, the more universal you become," meaning that the more concretely such things as diction, plot, and characters are presented, the more readily available they become to outsiders.[29]

Beginning with his heavily Eurocentric youthful poems and plays—"Epitaph for the Young," *Henri Christophe, Drums and Colours*—Walcott has gradually transformed imitation of writers and genres into his own literary interpretation of reality. By no stretch of the imagination would I argue that he had for any length of time the idea of eventually writing a West Indian epic. For decades, nonetheless, he has been honing the requisite epic skills by developing a narrative voice and by defining the characters and themes that would be adequate to carry the burden of his multiethnic race. As he matures, he abandons "the yearning to be adopted" into "the mighty line of Marlowe, of Milton,"[30] and in the process he discovers exciting alternatives. Deeply indebted as Walcott is to Western tradition, he has not indulged in some of the more radical departures of postmodernist writers; nevertheless, he will occasionally venture into self-reflexive textuality to the extent that the writing process becomes an integral theme. By creative distortion of extant patterns and inventive use of native materials, Walcott generates his own malleable style. When it comes to *Omeros* itself, as I shall illustrate in successive chapters, vestiges of ideas and imagery long familiar in Walcott's career are drawn together into a polysemous, demotic narrative.

29. Jeremy Ingalls, *The Epic Tradition and Related Essays,* 29; Walcott, "Poetry—Enormously Complicated," 3; Patrick Taylor, *The Narrative of Liberation: Perspectives on Afro-Caribbean Literature, Popular Culture, and Politics,* 3, 228; Hamner, "Conversation with Derek Walcott," 412.
30. Walcott, "What the Twilight Says," 31.

2 Philoctete's Wound

Despite the explicit parallels and allusions linking *Omeros* with its numerous epic predecessors, Walcott insists on more than one occasion that he deliberately resists writing a traditional "heroic poem." This position may be traced at least as far back as "What the Twilight Says," his introduction to *Dream on Monkey Mountain and Other Plays,* wherein he asserts, "The last thing which the poor needed was the idealization of their poverty." Walcott is too traditional to undertake an anti-epic, yet his authorial intrusions and variations on conventional epic devices in *Omeros* interrogate conventional expectations. Anticipating publication early in 1990, Walcott informs interviewer J. P. White that regardless of his "Homeric line and Dantesque design," *Omeros* captures not the epic machinery of gods and endless battles but the "names of things and people in their own context. . . . Its the origin of the real Caribbean nouns that I'm after." Far from rewriting the *Odyssey* or the *Aeneid,* he confesses to White that he has read no more than excerpts from these two classics. A few months later he reiterates to D. J. R. Bruckner that while his poem may have one central battle (the Battle of the Saints) it lacks the requisite great wars and warriors of epic tradition. Another disclaimer leads off an interview with Rebekah Presson in 1992. "I think any work in which the narrator is almost central is not really an epic. It's not like a heroic epic. I guess . . . since I am in the book, I certainly don't see myself as a hero of an epic, when an epic generally has a hero of action and decision and destiny."[1] These cumulative reservations tend to focus on the ancient

---

1. Walcott, "What the Twilight Says," 19; White, "An Interview with Derek Walcott," 35–36; Bruckner, "Poem in Homage," 13; Presson, "Man," 9.

formula without allowing for innovations beginning as early as Dante, who first inserted himself as narrator into *The Divine Comedy.*

Nevertheless, Walcott concedes to Presson that there are characters in *Omeros* who possess heroic elements. As a matter of fact, in conversation with Bruckner, Walcott emphasizes the debt he owes to the neglected peasantry of his native St. Lucia.

> The whole book is an act of gratitude. It is a fantastic privilege to be in a place in which limbs, features, smells, the lineaments and presence of the people are so powerful. . . . And there is no history for the place. . . . One reason I don't like talking about an epic is that I think it is wrong to try to ennoble people, . . . And just to write history is wrong. History makes similes of people, but these people are their own nouns. . . . A noun is not a name you give something. It is something you watch becoming itself, and you have to have the patience to find out what it is. In the Caribbean, people come from everywhere, from Africa and Europe and the Mediterranean and the Middle East and the Orient. . . . There is a restless identity in the New World. The New World needs an identity without guilt or blame.

Walcott reveals in these lines not only the basis of his inspiration but also two of his fundamental themes. The islands await a historical treatment on their own terms, and his people deserve to be reified within their authentic context. This means that Walcott must walk a thin line between the immediacy of personal experience and the artificiality of literary form. In keeping with his respect for humble islanders, Walcott chooses to emulate the act of a man, "Homer the poet of the seven seas," rather than the valorized tradition that has accumulated around his work for more than two thousand years.[2] The distinction is significant enough that Walcott incorporates his image of a blind, outcast Omeros in a variety of guises throughout the poem. At the same time, he subverts nearly all of the conventional epic paraphernalia.

It is not as though there were no heroic material available to Walcott. In spite of the general opinion that nothing worthy of note had ever occurred in the West Indies, Walcott could have taken a cue from that imperial advocate James Anthony Froude and glorified European exploits in the New World. In the late 1800s Froude had predicted,

2. Bruckner, "Poem in Homage," 13.

> If ever the naval exploits of this country [Britain] are done into an
> epic poem—and since the *Iliad* there has been no subject better fitted
> for such treatment or better deserving it—the West Indies will be the
> scene of the most brilliant cantos. . . . At the supreme crisis in our
> history when America had revolted and Ireland was defiant, when the
> great powers of Europe had coalesced to crush us . . . Rodney struck
> a blow in the West Indies which sounded over the world and saved
> for Britain her ocean scepter.[3]

Although Walcott does include cantos on the justly famous Battle of the
Saints, he lays claim to another subject that is "better fitted for such
treatment and more deserving it" in the newly enfranchised citizens of that
receding empire. Rather than contribute another chapter to the European
saga of discovery and conquest, Walcott chooses to undertake a new legend:
the tale of his own sojourn, the struggle of his tribe.

Structurally, *Omeros* converts linear narrative development into incre-
mental loops of self-reflexive exposition. No matter how far the leading
characters may wander literally or imaginatively, their lives continually
revolve around each other; and much as they learn, they inevitably return
to their point of origin. Ironically, Walcott cites the examples of prose
writers Rudyard Kipling, Joseph Conrad, and Ernest Hemingway as major
influences on the poetry of *Omeros*. "I learned a lot in writing this poem,"
he tells Bruckner:

> I did not realize how much great prose I had absorbed into my nervous
> verse system. When I began to write in hexameter lines and in stanzas,
> well the structure is there in the architecture of the best turn-of-the-
> century prose, in Conrad and Kipling. And you find in them the wit
> of the paragraph; mentally, it keeps the rhythm up. . . .
>   . . . When I was writing this book, you might say I was thinking
> of the two great Caribbean artists, Hemingway and Homer. . . .
>   . . . It is a book for people, not a conundrum for scholars. It was
> as if I was learning to read Homer when I was writing it.

The result is a layered and essentially reciprocal complex of interrelated nar-
rative lines that uncannily approximates the subversive type of postcolonial
fiction described in Arun Mukherjee's *Towards an Aesthetic of Opposition*.

3. Froude, *The English in the West Indies*, 9–13.

> The new Commonwealth novelists, then, have had to build structures
> which allow them to capture the spider-web of relationships which
> constitute community life in the developing countries. These struc-
> tures may seem loose or episodic to the western critic, yet they have a
> coherence if judged in accordance with the forms of experience they
> set out to explore. These structures are political choices on the part of
> the new Commonwealth writers, a declaration that the metropolitan
> forms do not fit their needs. . . . Their use of parabolic structures,
> indigenous story telling conventions, folk tales, parodies of western
> and indigenous forms and rituals have not attracted adequate attention
> due to the critics' obsession with western categories.[4]

Due to the heavily narrative structure of the epic genre itself and Walcott's
admitted reliance on prose models, *Omeros* exhibits many of the episodic,
communal qualities enumerated by Mukherjee.

Natural and linguistic reciprocity emerge on every level throughout
Omeros. The process is often subtle and follows the geographic subdivisions
of the text. As I shall argue, although the book is thoroughly integrated
as a whole, there are discernible movements within the developing story
that lend themselves to separate treatment. Books one and two establish
the St. Lucian foundation by introducing characters and themes that will
be continually augmented. Books three through five retrace the Middle
Passage first to Africa, then to North America and Europe before returning
to the West Indies. Books six and seven round off the action back in St. Lucia
without suggesting a definitive conclusion. After all, self-discovery for an
individual as well as a people obviates stasis; it is an ongoing creative act of
becoming. From the outset, Walcott prepares for such an open conclusion.
It can be anticipated, for example, from both the initial scene of book
one and the foreshadowing vision that simultaneously ends book two and
prepares the stage for book three. It is ensured by the flexible, shifting
perspectives of a series of narrative voices.

Rather than begin with the pronouncement of a grand theme, invocation
of the muse, or even the introduction of his protagonist, Walcott launches
Omeros in medias res with the minor character Philoctete. As is the case with
his classical Greek namesake, Philoctete once sustained a painful, festering
wound that was offensive to everyone who came near. With just a hint

---

4. Bruckner, "Poem in Homage," 17; Arun Mukherjee, *Towards an Aesthetic of
Opposition: Essays on Literature, Criticism and Cultural Imperialism,* 17.

at antecedent information about a magical cure (that might be disclosed
for a price), Philoctete introduces the first narrative voice to be heard in
Omeros. Willing enough to provoke curiosity by displaying the unsightly
scar, he entertains tourists with a description of native fishermen felling
the trees that will be hewn into seagoing canoes. Folklore permeates the
scene as Philoctete, Hector, Achille, and their mates pay homage to the
spirits of the trees they must violate in order to secure their livelihoods.
Air, earth, fire, and water coalesce in Philoctete's poignant imagery. Not
only does the wind stirring the undergrowth evoke the sound and swell
of the restless ocean, but "the logs gathered that thirst / for the sea which
their own vined bodies were born with" (7). This is but the first suggestion
of nature's reciprocity; in this case we are reminded of the water cycle that
inextricably binds all the elements. Heat from the sun initiates evaporation
and provides the lifeblood of the trees in the first place. Then shipwrights
use fire to transform solid logs into the shells of canoes that hereafter float
in the element that once permeated their every fiber in the mountains.

In what may be no more than a salve to his conscience, Philoctete
projects into the logs the feeling that they do not feel "death inside them,
but use— / to roof the sea, to be hulls" (7). The spirituality of these earthy
peasants is underscored by their empathy with the natural environment
and the raw materials of their humble trades. The animistic flavor of their
Africanized Catholicism makes them respect not only living creatures but
also the ancestral ghosts of Aruac and Carib tribesmen who first called their
island " 'Iounalao,' 'Where the iguana is found' " (4). Significantly, when
Achille (pronounced "A-sheel" with only two syllables), the first of the
key protagonists, is introduced, his attention is drawn to the torn canopy
where the recently cut trees have created an opening to the sky. As Achille
gazes heavenward, a sea-swift crossing the gap elicits from him "a swift
sign of the cross" (6). Never one to overlook a pun or visual and verbal
correspondences, Walcott waits only a few stanzas to exploit the connection
between the sign of the cross and the image of the swift's outspread shape
among the clouds. Thus at the dedication of the new pirogues, Achille
notices that the priest makes "the swift's sign" of consecration.

The ceremony sets the occasion for one further semantic ploy. When
the priest sees humor in the misspelled name of Achille's canoe, *In God
We Troust*, Achille insists "Leave it! Is God' spelling and mine" (8). There
is more to Walcott's emphasis on a picturesque orthographic lapse here
than the fact of his actually having discovered this hand-painted epithet

Cutting the Gommier. Ink drawing by Derek Walcott (Larry Fink, photo).

on a local fisherman's pirogue. While Achille's slip in literacy might elicit a condescending smile, Walcott has come to view such misprision as cause for celebration. In his 1992 interview with Rebekah Presson, he confides that when he chanced upon the misspelled "Troust," it struck him as "interesting and personal, and perhaps more devout than the regular spelling." At a conference in Jamaica in 1988, he asserts the value of error in the creative process. In preparing his address for this audience, he confesses he accidentally typed "love" into his "Caligula's Horse" manuscript where he intended "life." Although he corrected himself, he editorialized, "to discover, through a typographical error, what is accidental but also true . . . That is one part of the poetic process, accident as illumination, error

Choosing "In God We Troust." Ink drawing by Derek Walcott (Larry Fink, photo).

as truth, typographical mistakes as revelation."[5] Even if Walcott had not made his position explicit, other characters within *Omeros* react to Achille's misspelling, and the appellation is repeated often enough to acquire a life of its own. Epithets on these indispensable pirogues reflect faith, as in *Praise Him,* or love of their homeland, as in *St. Lucia* and *Light of My Eyes* (the latter of which commemorates simultaneously the island and the blind

---

5. In a telephone conversation, September 6, 1996, Derek Walcott told me that he observed *In God We Troust* at Choc Bay, St. Lucia; Presson, "Man," 10; Walcott, "Caligula's Horse," 138.

saint for which it is named). Similar connotations are embedded in the descriptive terminology as well. When the newly launched vessels are first drawn upon the shore, Walcott refers to them ambiguously as staring like "myrmidons hauled up by the heels" (10). Were "Myrmidons" capitalized, the trope would be an apposite allusion to the Thessalian followers of Achilles against Troy. In the actual lower-case form, they are just as suitably cast as proficient instruments of their master's will. Inconsequential as many such details may appear to be at first reading, nearly all of them assume cumulative significance as they are woven into the rest of the poem: Philoctete's wound, the swift, *In God We Troust,* and the sea become motifs with thematic overtones.

Having established the setting and cultural atmosphere by the end of the opening chapter, the perspective shifts unobtrusively from Philoctete to a disembodied observer. At the same time, the narrative takes up the antecedent action of the first of three primary, interlocking plots. In the days when Philoctete's shin was still putrid from the cut of a rusty anchor, trouble arose between Achille and Hector. The first blows appear to be struck over a worthless tin can Achille took from Hector to bail out his canoe, but we learn that the real source of conflict runs much deeper: "The duel of these fishermen / was over a shadow and its name was Helen" (17). Associating these three classical names as he does, Walcott obviously invites comparison with the *Iliad.* While there may be irony in drawing parallels between superhuman warriors and these poor fishermen, Walcott adds more than a literary dimension to his work. Since slaveholders often borrowed names for their slaves from mythical and biblical sources, heroic names are perpetuated in contemporary West Indian society. The names already at hand, it remains only for Walcott to provide motive for his earthy characters to strive toward fulfillment of their more restricted dreams and aspirations. That motivation builds throughout the intricately sustained subplots of *Omeros.*

Walcott's lifelong commitment to drama is unmistakable in his distribution of conflicts. Undergirding the rising dramatic interest at all stages is the urge toward reconciliation and redemption in one form or another. For this reason the context of the struggle between Achille and Hector is as important as the contention itself. Multidimensional troubles radiate outward, affecting not only other characters but eliciting self-reflexive responses from the author as well. On the same fateful morning that Achille and Hector draw cutlasses over a bailing tin, we are introduced to blind old

St. Omere, "Seven Seas," who is Walcott's embodiment of the Homer figure.
In an apostrophe that comes as close to an invocation of the muse as Walcott
ever gets in *Omeros,* the modern poet acknowledges his indebtedness to
the ancient master.

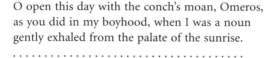

      O open this day with the conch's moan, Omeros,
      as you did in my boyhood, when I was a noun
      gently exhaled from the palate of the sunrise.
      . . . .
             . . . Only in you, across centuries
      of the sea's parchment atlas, can I catch the noise
      of the surf lines wandering like the shambling fleece

      of the lighthouse's flock, that Cyclops whose blind eye
      shut from the sunlight. Then the canoes were galleys
      over which a frigate sawed its scythed wings slowly.

Combined in these tercets are an invocation and a metaphorical confiscation
of imagery. Just as Homer is superimposed on St. Omere, Odysseus's
Cyclops (the shepherd Polyphemus in the *Odyssey*) becomes a one-eyed
lighthouse overlooking the white fleece of Caribbean surf; Greek galleys
become local fishermen's canoes; but the rhythms of waves, of the frigate
bird's flight and of poetry remain as they were thousands of years ago for
the poet of the Mediterranean.

From the beginning, some of Walcott's key images are protean in their
application and in their transmutations. Over the course of the epic the
blindness of Homer, of Seven Seas/Omeros, and of St. Lucia's patron saint
herself is symbolic of inner enlightenment as opposed to limited physical
vision. Eyes in turn are not only mentioned in connection with individual
characters, but are metaphorically elicited in association with cameras,
marble busts, statues, fish, drowned men, cyclones, lighthouses, telescopes,
birds, the novelist James Joyce, self-centered poets, and the sun. Perhaps
even more ubiquitous is the repetition of "O," which is not only the first
letter of *Omeros* but also the sound emitted from the blown conch shell
and by the dove. At one time or another, the figure is the oval shape of a
mouth, a throat, a vase, a cave, an island, and a circular journey.

In addition to the imagery, larger periods of time, scenes, and levels of
consciousness intermingle even further as Walcott's own persona emerges
from the page: "A wind turns the harbour's pages back to the voice / that

hummed in the vase of a girl's throat: 'Omeros' " (13). The ensuing stanzas
of chapter two are devoted to a brief interlude. In it the author recounts a
scene wherein a Greek sculptress teaches him the correct pronunciation of
"O-meros" and he pronounces its connotative etymology.[6]

> . . . I said, "Omeros,"

> and *O* was the conch-shell's invocation, *mer* was
> both mother and sea in our Antillean patois,
> *os,* a grey bone, and the white surf as it crashes

> and spreads its sibilant collar on a lace shore.
> Omeros was the crunch of dry leaves, and the washes
> that echoed from a cave-mouth when the tide has ebbed. (14)

Under the influence of this woman he calls Antigone, he moves from
the vibrations of a throat to other encircling enclosures (with all their
Freudian implications)—conch shells, cave mouths, vases, the parted lips
of a Homeric bust—and to the affective syllables of his own poetic title.
The interlude fades, as effortlessly as it begins, into the uproar surrounding
Hector and Achille fighting on the beach.

In addition to the physical altercation, Walcott makes clear that jealous
rage and shame have destroyed a brotherly closeness that tears at their
hearts. Ever-widening extensions of their spiritual malaise touch Philoctete
and Seven Seas as well, who spend their days isolated from normal human
activities because of their afflictions. While other tradesmen go about their
work, these two outcasts seek the cool shade of Ma Kilman's No Pain Cafe.
Ma Kilman provides yet another perspective and new insights into the
growing cast of characters. As the narrative detours through her mind, we
learn that St. Omere's sotto voce monologues are so unintelligible as to
be "Greek to her. Or old African babble" (18). The irony of juxtaposing
Greek and African tongues as equally alien may be hidden from her, but
the reader must weigh its implicit commentary on her uprooted existence.
That necessity is underscored as Ma Kilman commiserates with Philoctete
in his suffering. He interprets his wound as a racial affliction,

6. Derek Walcott, in a telephone conversation with the author on October 11, 1993,
asserted the authenticity of the encounter depicted here, claiming poetic license for the
name "Antigone" to enhance the mythical dimensions of the poem.

He believed the swelling came from the chained ankles
of his grandfathers. Or else why was there no cure?
That the cross he carried was not only the anchor's

but that of his race, for a village black and poor
as the pigs that rooted in its burning garbage,
then were hooked on the anchors of the abattoir.

At the same time, Ma Kilman searches her memory for an herbal remedy
her African grandmother could have prepared to draw out the poison.

It have a flower somewhere, a medicine, and ways
my grandmother would boil it. I used to watch ants
climbing her white flower-pot. But, God, in which place?

Where was this root? What senna, what tepid tisanes,
could clean the branched river of his corrupted blood,
whose sap was a wounded cedar's? . . . (19)

From this point, the symbolic ramifications of Philoctete's wound become
paramount, and Ma Kilman's quest must be to reestablish a connection
with her ancestors in order to help him.

Although Ma Kilman casually alludes to ants in passing, these insects
soon join the swift both as symbols and as potent links with the healing
forces of the natural world. The ants and the swift are on Philoctete's mind
as he limps from the No Pain Cafe to tend his yam patch in the mountains.
Passing the overturned ruins of an abandoned sugar plantation on the way,
he reflects bitterly that this is the only history left his black people, if their
detritus may be considered historical. As he sees it, they

. . . set out to found no cities; they were the found,
who were bound for no victories; they were the bound,
who levelled nothing before them; they were the ground. (22)

With these passing thoughts, Philoctete summarizes the historical vacuum
that leaves his people rootless and downtrodden. At the same time they
reveal the fissures, the fault lines in heroic tradition, that provide Walcott
the opening needed to experiment with the epic form. Neither the poet nor
his unassuming characters urge the necessity of recognizing their human
worth. That burden rests with the reader in experiencing the evolving

story. Much as we may appreciate Philoctete's righteous indignation as he
meditates on injustices of the past and present, for his own peace of mind,
he resolves to emulate a patient horse and endure his afflictions calmly.

On that contemplative note—Philoctete waiting, the conflict between
Hector and Achille on hold, the new element of social concern simmering
beneath the surface—Walcott abruptly shifts the narrative for the first
time away from the indigenous population of the island to introduce
an expatriate couple among his cast of characters: retired Major Dennis
Plunkett and his wife Maud. The Plunketts broaden the cultural spectrum,
but only slightly, having lived in St. Lucia, breeding pigs and orchids,
since the end of World War II. Despite their European origins (Dennis is
English, Maud Irish) and a longing especially on Maud's part to see the old
country again, they have adopted the island as their home. As a matter of
fact, offended by the "phony pukka tones" of their fellow expatriates, they
long ago turned their backs on the "middle-clarse farts" of the Victoria
Club (25). The traces of a Homeric parallel are hardly sufficient to warrant
extensive exploration; however, as a pig farmer existing on the outer fringes
of empire, the Major does resemble Odysseus's faithful swineherd, Eumaios.
Whereas Homer's swineherd is a generous host and indispensable assistant
in Odysseus's assault on Penelope's unwanted suitors, Walcott derives even
greater service out of the Major as a participating narrator.

The Plunketts' story complements the plot already underway. The Ma-
jor's military career gives him firsthand experience on the frontier of a wan-
ing empire and underlies his poignant regard for the annual ceremonies of
Remembrance Day (30).[7] Their background, the antecedent circumstances
that shape their perspective, includes Dennis's head-wound, suffered in the
British Eighth Army's Egyptian campaign (25–26); Maud's nursing him
to recovery (27); their marriage; and the dream of a new Eden unspoiled
by history, which led them to St. Lucia (28). The vital force that links the
Plunketts with Achille and Hector is Helen, who until recently served as
their housemaid. They reluctantly dismissed her when she began making
them feel like interlopers in their own home. It was as though Helen had
usurped their place, blithely going through Maud's clothes and jewelry as
she pleased. As ubiquitous as her yellow dress becomes through Walcott's

7. November 11 coincides with Armistice Day in Great Britain, Veteran's Day in the
United States, and Remembrance Day in Canada—to commemorate the end of World
War I, November 11, 1918.

repeated references to it, the Major never seems to settle finally within his own mind whether Helen stole or was given the frock by Maud (64).

Using a strategy that helps to extract the maximum impact from Helen as a person and as an image, Walcott suspends her actual entrance until the final line of chapter four. By then, our acquaintance with the men whose lives she dominates has prepared the way for her influence. Achille and Hector long for her physically; the Major just as passionately wishes to possess her as the veritable essence of the island itself. It is through the author's persona, however, that we first glimpse her effect on all observers. Her regal carriage evokes the image of a panther, or a mirage in a madras head-tie,

> but the head proud, although it was looking for work.
> I felt like standing in homage to a beauty
>
> that left, like a ship, widening eyes in its wake.
> "Who the hell is that?" a tourist near my table
> asked a waitress. The waitress said, "She? She too proud!"
>
> As the carved lids of the unimaginable
> ebony mask unwrapped from its cotton-wool cloud,
> the waitress sneered, "Helen." And all the rest followed. (23–24)

"All the rest" that follows may be taken quite literally. If Walcott risks thematic diffusion by scattering the narrative perspective, sharing the protagonist's role among a succession of voices and expanding the geographical and chronological boundaries to include distant continents and ancient Greece, the cohesive center of *Omeros* remains this figure of Helen.

Not only do separate characters reflect Helen's influence, but Walcott ensures that the reader must also step back and contemplate the terms of her existence. The first time he takes the reader into explicit confidence is shortly after introducing Dennis Plunkett.

> This wound I have stitched into Plunkett's character.
> He has to be wounded, affliction is one theme
> of this work, this fiction, since every "I" is a
>
> fiction finally. Phantom narrator, resume. (28)

When the "phantom" resumes, we find the Major committing himself to a grand scheme that will give purpose to his own life and immortalize Helen.

Plunkett's affliction that Walcott underscores for the poem as a whole, like
that of Philoctete, runs much deeper than its physical manifestation. The
Plunketts' union has proved to be barren, and the Major is not able to
accept the fact that his life will terminate without issue. At the same time,
it occurs to him that while he lacks personal immortality, Helen's existence
takes place in a historical void.

In one epiphanic flash he realizes that Helen needs a history and that
the subject is worthy of his complete dedication. The idea impresses him
in terms of historic and mythic hallucinations because of its overt Ithacan
connotations. Not only is she named Helen, but her island is often referred
to as "Helen," the "Gibraltar of the Caribbean," because of the European
powers who fought over her until she was finally ceded to England by
France through the 1814 Treaty of Paris. However, the Major insists he
must tell "Not his, but her story." He sees her village as another Troy,
the island's Pitons as her breasts, the Battle of the Saints as her Homeric
conflict (30–31). These people have no Parthenon, and Latin is replaced
by native dialect, but he can envision their athletic contests as Olympiads.
Thus Hector and Achille run marathons and wrestle not for victory's laurels
or shields but to win Helen.

Extending the Major's train of thought, Walcott's narrative cuts away to
Helen inquiring among the women for openings at the beach restaurant.
Pregnant and unsure of who is the father of her unborn child, she must
find a job. Despite the paucity of available work and her predicament,
she remains so much at peace with her situation that she can be heard
softly murmuring the Beatles's "Yesterday, all my troubles seem so far
away" (34), dialectically eliminating the past-tense marker from the verb
"seemed." Then as she passes through a cloud of smoke from burning
leaves, a second wave of classical associations arises, this time drawing a
sharp distinction between the Greek and this contemporary Helen. In the
moment of historical change, "white Helen died," and "her shadow ambles,
filly of Menelaus / while black piglets root the midden of Gros Îlet" (34).
The fact that this shadow is the darker impression of an original design is
clear enough in these lines. What is less apparent but perhaps even more
relevant than Walcott himself intended is the appearance of the piglets. Of
course their blackness is an obvious foil for the Greek's whiteness; but they
can be taken for much more than that. Not only are these rooting animals
as lowly as the inhabitants of Gros Îlet, but it is also worth noting that the

supernatural sign given to Aeneas, letting him know where he is to found his promised kingdom, is a white sow and her thirty offspring.[8]

Whatever Walcott's assorted reasons for mentioning these piglets (he may have intended no epic allusions), they conform to a pattern. Dennis Plunkett is associated with these animals because of the herd he maintains on his farm. Moreover, in a subsequent chapter we overhear the Major argue that the people of the island are not "resigned / to living with garbage" despite the fact that "Empires were swinish," and "History was Circe" with power to convert men to swine (63–64). Meanwhile as the Major is imagining the transformation of this black Helen, his new "filly of Menelaus" is suddenly joined by a stallion galloping down the smoke-shrouded beach. In one of Walcott's most elusively amorphous scenes, he builds on the lyrics of the Beatles' song we have just heard Helen singing. We are reminded that "yesterday" the horse was wooden, his thundering hooves were battle sounds, and this village was ravaged Troy, on the banks of Scamander (35). Once again, in the New World this time, Helen's troubles which "seem so far away" echo those of the heralded past, and her travail becomes our present story. What is most frustrating, however, in coming to that story is the fact that it can be told from such antithetical perspectives. The Major/narrator is so caught up in his classical atlas that Helen suddenly vanishes from his sight.

Helen's physical disappearance into the smoke of burning leaves signals a flashback that confronts us with yet another among the poem's myriad starting places. The next scene recreates the wrenching moment that drives Helen from Achille into Hector's arms. The demeaning incident involves nothing more significant than whether Helen or Achille should carry their basket of purchases home from the market. In the midst of the crowded produce stalls they exchange harsh words, then a flurry of blows. An embarrassed Achille is left to pick up the scattered fruit while Helen escapes in Hector's transport van. Hector is no Trojan Paris, yet he has just as effectively stolen Helen, and this new wound is opened. After Achille returns to his empty cottage, he relives the first painful moment when he began to doubt Helen. He had been diving illegally for conch shells, trying to make extra money, when there on the redoubt above the bay was Helen in her unmistakable yellow dress, meeting Hector. Looking back on the event, he

8. Virgil, *The Aeneid of Virgil*, translated by C. Day Lewis, 64, 167.

sleeps only to dream fitfully of their lovemaking in happier days. Impercep-
tibly, the dream merges into the author's reverie about an Adamic paradise
before corruption, "before it gaped into a wound, like Philoctete" (42).

Although Walcott's intrusion into Achille's libido is not as explicit as his
earlier claim to the Major's perspective, it is nonetheless evident that he
not only is present in *Omeros* in his own right as author but also is never
far beneath the surface of each of his invented characters. This unavoidable
feature of the narrative exposition should come as no surprise to anyone
who has become familiar with the autobiographical strain that is endemic
to Walcott's poetry and drama. He has drawn from his island background
for numerous characters. For example, forerunners of Achille, Hector, and
Philoctete are discernible in the resilient fisherman Afa from *The Sea at
Dauphin,* the misanthropic Chantal from *Malcochon,* and the visionary
charbonnier Makak in *Dream on Monkey Mountain.* Major Plunkett's quest
to identify himself with the island is prefigured by the crude machinations
of the title character in the unpublished *Franklin,* the ineffectual Harry
Trewe in *Pantomime,* and Clodia De La Fontaine in *The Last Carnival.*
Each of these earlier works contains indigenous villagers or colonists who
struggle to define their colonial roots. Walcott's personal attachment to
the islands is never far from the surface of the poetry as well. When asked
about the autobiographical facets of *Another Life,* he replied that "it would
be hard for one to leave out the details of a person's life in a book of that
kind. It is a particular experience. But in a sense it is a biography of an
'intelligence,' a West Indian intelligence."[9]

Among all the figures in *Omeros,* however, it is Helen herself who emerges
most directly from a sequence of informing sources. The name alone is
almost unavoidable since, as Walcott has pointed out, St. Lucia has been
called the Helen of the Caribbean. In the poetry the beauty of the island
and women are both frequently couched in terms of their power to seduce.
Although she bears little resemblance to Achille's Helen in *Omeros,* one of
her first manifestations serves as a classical comparison for a prostitute in
Another Life.

> Helen?
> Janie, the town's one clear-complexioned whore,

9. Hamner, "Conversation with Derek Walcott," 411.

> with two tow-headed children in her tow,
> she sleeps with sailors only, her black
> hair electrical
> as all that trouble over Troy,
> rolling broad-beamed she leaves
> a plump and pumping vacancy.

By 1987 in *The Arkansas Testament,* her image is equally sensual but far richer in its multifaceted applications through "The Villa Restaurant," "The Light of the World," and "Menelaus." The terra-cotta waitress described in "The Villa Restaurant" is not named; however, her slate irises and feminine curvature lead the poet to prefer her shapely "living vase" to sculpted stone, whether carved or fired. The message derived from his choice of the warm flesh over the cold marble is that "Your sea has its own *Iliads;*" therefore, she becomes his artistic ideal.

> the cracked ground in Mantegna
> is hers, the golden apple;
> the blue gesso behind her
> head is my Sistine Chapel.

Against a background of Renaissance masterpieces and the prize of Helen won by Paris in awarding the golden apple to Aphrodite, the poet admires this waitress dutifully tending her station:

> her beauty not her fault as
> her palm smooths the flaws
> of linen laid like altars
> with crumbs and today's flowers.

She remains anonymous when she appears again in "The Light of the World," the poem Walcott mentions to J. P. White as containing Elena, his prototype for the heroine of *Omeros* (35). Here he anticipates his feline imagery for Helen, as "a still panther." Under her spell, he wishes he could enter her home, lie beside her,

> tell her in silence
> that her hair was like a hill forest at night,
> that a trickle of rivers was in her armpits,

Helen. Watercolor by Derek Walcott (Larry Fink, photo).

> that I would buy her Benin if she wanted it,
> and never leave her on earth. But the others, too.

To do this, of course, he would have to become Achille. Yet his heart is in the right place. Impossible as it is to become one with her among the villagers of Gros Îlet, or to "buy her Benin," he captures the moment by creating for them all "The Light of the World." When it comes to "Menelaus" near the end of *The Arkansas Testament,* the mood is less accommodating. We encounter a disillusioned Menelaus who now sees Helen of Troy as white trash, who contemplates his "Ten years. Wasted in quarrel / for sea-grey eyes. A whore's."[10] Were this the final word, all we should have is the melancholy tragedy of the past. Obviously, this confined view is inadequate for Walcott. Three years later in *Omeros,* he determines to reclaim Helen as the centerpiece of a New World epic of survival. Discarding traditional forms of imperial heroism, he turns his attention to the equally vital if less spectacular saga of the dispossessed.

Chapter eight of the first book of *Omeros* departs briefly from Achille's painful loss of Helen to introduce the legend attached to an artifact in the island's small museum. It is a bottle encrusted with fool's gold that is said variously to be lost from a storm-driven galleon out of Cartagena or from the French flagship in the Battle of the Saints, the *Ville de Paris.* Local myth prefers to believe it spilled from the *Ville de Paris,* now an illusive wreck said to be guarded by an octopus-cyclops. The dream of sunken treasure that might win Helen back lures Achille to illegal diving along the reef. All he gets for his trouble is a startling vision of a hollow relic under the relentless gaze of a moon-eyed creature. When it occurs to him that it will be necessary to abandon all hope of ever locating the haunted wreck, he interprets it as a sign that he must also accept the fact that he may never get Helen back (46). The loss of Helen has a second dimension that is brought out by Philoctete. In spite of the bad blood between Hector and Achille, Philoctete undertakes the restoration of their severed friendship, arguing that their shared occupation as fishermen is enough to guarantee their fundamental brotherhood (47).

In the structural arrangement of the first two books, the low point of the narrative arrives during hurricane season. The inclement weather that drives fishermen to land also forces the Plunketts to sedentary pursuits in their study. Walcott uses the contrast between inner and outer weather to consolidate the status of his main characters before branching out in pursuit of three complementary subplots. Achille temporarily abandons his pirogue for the concrete feeding trough of Major Plunkett's farm. To Achille, who cowers alone in his shack, elements of the raging storm are personified as African and Greek deities. Shango, Erzulie, Ogun, Damballa, and Neptune are

---

10. Walcott, "Leaving School," 4; *Another Life,* 19; *The Arkansas Testament,* 26, 27; White, "An Interview with Derek Walcott," 35; Walcott, *The Arkansas Testament,* 48, 50, 51, 101.

holding a hurricane-party in their cloud-house,
and what brings the gods close is the thunderous weather,
where Ogun can fire one with his partner Zeus. (53)

While Achille imagines that Hector is safely comforted in Helen's arms,
his nemesis is engaged in a futile battle to save his canoe (51). His anchor
torn away, he is forced to dive into the raging sea and escape to the beach.
The lost anchor has thematic consequences beyond the moment, virtually
leaving him adrift for the rest of his life. Having lost his pirogue, Hector
abandons his calling as a fisherman to pursue the career of a taxi driver.

In the Plunkett household, Maud, preferring the seasonal regularity of
her Irish homeland to this tropical deluge (48), takes up the embroidery
of a tapestry representing all the birds of the Caribbean. Depressed by
the foul weather, the Major senses that Maud is slipping away, not just
transported melodiously by her *Airs from Erin,* but out of life.[11] Light does
break through the clouds, however, and in the aftermath of the baptismal
rain the world is refreshed. Achille gratefully bails out his canoe (54), while
the Plunketts set out in their Land Rover to tour the coastal mountains (57).

At the beginning of their drive, the Major returns to his interest in
history. For the first time the term "History" is capitalized in the middle of a
sentence, apparently in order to signify the imprimatur of official authority.
As the Major applies the capitalized version, he reacts against Eurocentric
marginalization. Preparing to write his own record of Helen's island ("Not
his, but her story," 30) Plunkett develops the practice of using the lower-case
"history" to designate his newly generated rendition of events. The Land
Rover trip provides more than an opportunity for epic cataloging of place
names—La Sorciere, Cul-de-Sac valley, Roseau, Anse La Raye, Canaries
(58–59). We learn that the folk name for the volcanic island's La Sorcière
is the same as that of the proprietress of the No Pain Cafe, Ma Kilman,
"because the village was darkened by their belief / in her as a *gardeuse,*
sybil, obeah-woman" (58). The open wounds of the sulfuric "Malebolge"
beneath the Pitons near Soufrière remind the Major of putrid Auschwitz
(59). Nearby, the imperial mining enterprise of speculators Bennett and

---

11. Although Walcott cites *Airs from Erin* on two occasions (56, 262), I have been
unable to obtain a copy of such a work. Thomas Moore, the composer of "Bendemeer's
Stream," also mentioned among Maud Plunkett's musical references (201), is credited
with a collection entitled *Airs of Old Erin* (New York: Edward B. Marks, 1936).

Ward had failed to convert the sulfur into English gold (60). Unlike the Plunketts, these exploiters failed back in 1836 and returned to their mother country. Observing these sights along the road leads the Major's train of thought to his own reasons for choosing St. Lucia over his birthplace.

> England seemed to him merely the place of his birth.
> How odd to prefer, over its pastoral sites—
> reasonable leaves shading reasonable earth—
>
> The loud-mouthed forests on their illiterate heights,
> these springs speaking a dialect that cooled his mind
> more than pastures with castles! To prefer the hush
>
> of a hazed Atlantic worried by the salt wind!
> Others could read it as "going back to the bush," but harbour
> after crescent harbour closed his wound. (61)

Here in brief are the stereotypical denominators of temperate and tropical climates that are supposed to divide light and dark races. In this subtle way, the Major justifies his chosen exile. Maud herself—who despises the humidity, pestilent insects, barefooted poor, religious converts with their "joy of sects," careering transports, and the merciless sun—much as she would like to see Ireland again, revels in the burgeoning flowers of her garden. As she recalls wryly the misspelling on Achille's *In God We Troust,* she reflects, "But then we all trust in Him, and that's why we know / the peace of a wandering heart when it is housed" (67).

Even as they pause to contemplate the Edenic quality of their life, the Major's thoughts are haunted by the butterfly-yellow of Helen's frock. Killing the engine of the Land Rover, he wonders whether her questionable acquisition of the dress could be exorcised by History, or whether she desires anyone's pardon. Without resolving that ethical issue, he concludes that since "All roots have their histories," (63) he would speak for Helen.

because she doesn't have one ha!!

> So Plunkett decided that what the place needed
> was its true place in history, that he'd spend hours
> for Helen's sake on research, so he proceeded
>
> to the whirr of enormous moths in the still house.
> Memory's engines. The butterfly dress was hers,
> at least her namesake's, in the Battle of the Saints. (64)

Having thus isolated two functions of history, those of legitimizing and generating narrative, Walcott has prepared the foundation for the three subplots that make up the remainder of books one and two. They involve, first, Walcott's exposition of his own attachment to the island; second, Major Plunkett's quest for historical fragments that may be assimilated into his and Helen's organic, written history; and third, the struggle of Philoctete, Achille, Hector, and other islanders to bear the political and social consequences of colonial independence.

Continuing the kaleidoscopic segmentation of his story, Walcott shifts easily from the Plunketts' intimate self-examination to his highly personal reveries in the twelfth chapter. The setting is his childhood home at 17 Chaussee Road in Castries, the house mentioned in his 1965 article "Leaving School" and lovingly described with its "carpenter's Gothic" trim surrounded with flowering bougainvillea and allamanda in the second chapter of *Another Life.*[12] When he returns in *Omeros,* the front porch is gone and his former residence has been converted to a printery. This visit may have begun with a touch of nostalgia, but while the presses roll out handbills on machines where cherished furniture once stood, the ghost of Warwick Walcott, his father, materializes.

This evocation of his father gives Walcott a useful vehicle for establishing literary roots uncannily deep in English tradition. Warwick not only is conveniently named after Shakespeare's home shire but also succumbed to an ear ailment (as Hamlet's father had) on the Bard's accepted April 23 date of birth. The father puns that his own "Will" to produce verse in Caribbean obscurity is his son's legacy, and that the explicit Shakespearean parallels have already afforded Walcott some peace: "Death imitating Art, eh?" (69). Warwick is the first to raise the issue of influence and the anomaly of their respective ages, an ironic point that Walcott will develop later himself.

> "In this pale notebook where you found my verses"—
> my father smiled—"I appeared to make your life's choice,
> and the calling that you practise both reverses
>
> and honours mine from the moment it blent with yours.
> Now that you are twice my age, which is the boy's,
> which the father's?"
>   "Sir"—I swallowed—"they are one voice." (68)

---

12. Walcott, "Leaving School," 6, 8; Walcott, *Another Life,* 10–14.

Walcott's birthplace, 17 Chaussee Road. Photo by Mary Love, Larry Fink, Roberts Studio.

His answer to Warwick's query effectively seals the continuity of their shared calling. In a scene reminiscent of Anchises guiding Aeneas through the underworld until he charges him with his mission in life, Warwick leads his son out of the house, down Grass Street toward the port of Castries. Unlike Virgil, however, who maintains the integrity of his closed narrative, Walcott reminds us of the fictive nature of his tour. He explains to the curious reader that he does not venture to inquire of the ghost about the life beyond death,

> because the white shadow I had made from my mind
>
> was vague in its origin and thin as belief,
> unsinged as an Easter lily, fresh as the wind,
> its whisper as soft as a pavement-scratching leaf. (70–71)

As this pair make their way toward the harbor, none of the individuals they pass is able to see the invisible father until they encounter the shade of Warwick's late barber. Referring to him as his chamberlain, Warwick fondly recalls quoting from his collection of *The World's Great Classics*,[13] prominently displayed on a varnished rack across from his elevated barber's chair.

Although the barber is one of the minor characters in the story, Walcott makes significant use of his appearance and repeatedly cites his collection of *The World's Great Classics*. As a Seventh Day Adventist and a follower of Marcus Garvey, the barber, a frustrated anarchist, had served two messiahs in life. Describing him to his son, Warwick says "The rock he lived on was nothing. Not a nation / or a people," and as a result of the curse of his birth, the "paradise" he proclaimed from his barber's throne was "a phantom Africa" (72). Because Warwick is determined that his son should not likewise set his eyes on some distant, mythical home, he shifts his attention away from the barber to the magnificent ocean liner anchored in the harbor. It is at this moment, poised literally on the corner of Bridge Street between an illusory past (whether of Christian or African origins) and a future geared to tourism, that Warwick most clearly emulates the role of Anchises, instructing his son about his destiny. Warwick prepares for an essential transition with a warning against the corruptive power of foreign values.

> Measure the days you have left. Do just that labour
> which marries your heart to your right hand: simplify
> your life to one emblem, a sail leaving harbour
>
> and a sail coming in. All corruption will cry
> to be taken aboard. Fame is that white liner
> at the end of your street, a city to itself,
>
> taller than the Fire Station, and much finer,
> with its brass-ringed portholes, mounting shelf after shelf,
> than anything Castries could ever hope to build." (72–73)

After these cautionary remarks, Warwick recalls the female colliers from his childhood who had trekked like ants down to this same harbor to fuel visiting ships.

13. *The World's Great Classics* (New York: Colonial Press, 1899–1901; Grolier, 1969 [in 50 vols.]).

Part of their curse is that these women drifted out of existence without leaving a record of their names. Warwick himself died too young to remedy that omission; however, he is convinced that their anonymity is not the equivalent of nothingness. Addressing his son as "O Thou, my Zero," he works one more variation on the "O" image. As he does so in this instance, he echoes the fool in *King Lear* who criticizes his powerless old master for having relinquished his identity in the process of abdicating his crown.[14] The major difference is that Lear is responsible for his own predicament, and it is history that has failed to do justice to the forgotten women of St. Lucia. Calling them "Helens from an earlier time," he extols their unrecorded labor.

> The carriers were women, not the fair, gentler sex.
> Instead, they were darker and stronger, and their gait
> was made beautiful by balance, in their ascending
>
> the narrow wooden ramp built steeply to the hull
> of a liner tall as a cloud . . ." (74)

Then, as a powerful climax to the first book of *Omeros,* Warwick charges his son with his sacred duty. Walcott's business is to follow in the footsteps of these women, using his pen as they had used their strong backs and feet.

> "Kneel to your load, then balance your staggering feet
> and walk up that coal ladder as they do in time,
> one bare foot after the next in ancestral rhyme. . . .
> . . . .
>
> keep to that narrow causeway without looking down,
> climbing in their footsteps, that slow, ancestral beat
> of those used to climbing roads; your own work owes them
>
> because the couplet of those multiplying feet
> made your first rhymes. Look, they climb, and no one knows
>   them;
> they take their copper pittances, and your duty
>
> from the time you watched them from your grandmother's house
> as a child wounded by their power and beauty
> is the chance you now have, to give those feet a voice." (75–76)

14. William Shakespeare, *King Lear,* Riverside edition, 1.6.192.

Situated as it is, emphatically at the end of book one, Warwick's challenge forms the central theme of *Omeros*. The meeting with the ghost of his father also sets the scene for Walcott to begin the crucial subplots that constitute most of book two, separate ancestral quests for Major Plunkett and Achille that eventually lead to their common St. Lucian identities.

3 The Battle over Helen

Book two begins in a Dutch port back in the 1700s. A young midshipman named Plunkett from aboard the *Marlborough* has been dispatched by Admiral Rodney to spy on shipping in the Lowlands. Intelligence gathered by young Plunkett proves useful in Rodney's fortifications in St. Lucia and in his preparations for the legendary Battle of the Saints. Thus, international intrigues link Holland with the distant Antilles. In another of Walcott's worker-ant similes, we encounter Achille's progenitor Afolabe among a gang of slaves laboring to hoist a cannon to the crest of the morne in St. Lucia. As a reward for his exertions, the Admiral himself renames Afolabe "Achilles," and this classically derived proper noun enters the annals of the island (83). At this point in the narrative, however, the focus is on the European strain of St. Lucia's history.

Chapter fifteen offers the first installment of Walcott's account of the Battle of the Saints, the only engagement in the poem that he thinks comparable to epic warfare.[1] Although historical records of the conflict show that Ródney's flagship *Formidable* attacked de Grasse's battle line from the lee quarter at 0930 hours on April 12, 1782, Walcott chooses to ignore the military and imperial significance proclaimed by James Anthony Froude in order to pursue his own poetic aims. The fact is that whether by design or instinct, Rodney allowed his Captain Charles Douglas to violate the sacrosanct "Fighting Instructions," which required ships to attack the enemy in strict parallel lines. When the winds shifted to favor

---

1. Various accounts of the Battle of the Saints mention its impact on British sea power. Several are listed in the bibliography: David Chandler, James Anthony Froude, Reginald Hargreaves, G. J. Marcus, Richard Natkiel, William Oliver Stevens.

the English at approximately 0930 hours on that fateful morning, Douglas of the *Formidable* and the captain of the *Bedford* seized the opportunity to penetrate the wavering French line in two columns. In the ensuing confusion, Rodney's forces managed to sink, disable, or drive off the entire French fleet. The result was not only the defeat and capture of De Grasse aboard his *Ville de Paris* at 1830 hours that day and immediate termination of French plans to invade Jamaica but also Rodney's precedent-setting maneuver of "breaking the line," which contributed significantly to British dominance at sea for decades.

The heroic proportions of these deeds prompt Froude's effusive call for epic treatment in *The English in the West Indies*.[2] The progress of empire, however, is not the primary concern of Walcott's epic of the dispossessed. Since his objective is to focus on the St. Lucian present, he uses this famous Anglo-French confrontation for his own evolving narrative. First, the Battle of the Saints is concrete evidence of the importance of St. Lucia in the European scheme for the New World; second, the introduction of a young Midshipman Plunkett makes available a predecessor for Dennis Plunkett; and third, a bottle washed overboard from the foundering *Ville de Paris* provides the local museum with a pyrite-encrusted artifact about which local legend can grow until it acquires mythical status.

Young seaman Plunkett and the wine bottle are Walcott's invention, but the *Marlborough* actually was heading the English fleet at the decisive moment when Rodney pierced the French line. Poetic revision alters events so that Plunkett's *Marlborough* directly confronts the mighty *Ville de Paris*. Unfortunately, young Plunkett, who has been ordered below to stand in reserve, meets his death when the *Marlborough* is rammed by the French vessel. Rushing madly to climb to the deck of his disabled ship, the midshipman is thrown fatally onto his own sword. In his dying moments he notices that wine bottles spill from the gaping hull of the *Ville de Paris* to join him at the bottom of the sea (86). It is one of these pyrite-coated bottles that is eventually recovered and displayed in the island's museum (43, 271). Young Plunkett fades from view in 1782, but his name on the ship's manifest lies in wait for the Major's research project.[3]

2. Froude, *The English in the West Indies*, 9–13.
3. For the Major's research project, Walcott has in mind the small museum near Gros Îlet, Pigeon Island National Park; telephone conversation with the author, September 6, 1996.

Chapters sixteen and seventeen depart from the unfolding battle to bridge intervening centuries. It is left for Dennis Plunkett to fill the blank spaces in both his family's and his island's history. Thus, he works simultaneously on his genealogical "ances-tree (his pun)" (87) and official records of shipping and armaments. One of his abiding regrets is that his marriage to Maud has proved barren, leaving them no heir. A typical evening with the Plunketts finds Dennis pouring over ledgers while Maud quietly sews images of birds into the silken quilt that will serve one day as her shroud. Prominent in her aviary is *"l'hirondelle des Antilles,"* the sea-swift, with its Latin tag dutifully appended. Watching her concentration, it occurs to Dennis that she is not long for this world, and he attempts to force his attention back to his notes. But his mind is full of reveries about his days in the service and his unfulfilled dreams. He had once planned to make a pilgrimage encompassing all the important outposts of the waning empire, undertaking what he calls "a masochistic odyssey," himself a journeying "I" (90). Now that this daydream has eluded his grasp, he feels the loss of that centralizing gesture. Instead he is left to complain that if there had only been a son he would have executed his ambitious plan.

Chapter seventeen is devoted to his immediate determination to redress Helen's wrong by giving her a history. From the vantage point of the fort overlooking the city, he contemplates the errors he has found in the tourist brochure provided by the local museum. When an iguana distracts him, he begins to reflect on the Indian names once attached to the island, where the iguana is found, "Iounalao" and "Hewanorra."[4]

> "Iounalo, eh? It's all folk-malarkey!"
> The grass was as long as his shorts. History was fact,
> History was a cannon, not a lizard; . . .
>
> . . . .
>   . . . Was the greatest battle
>
> in naval history, which put the French to rout,
> fought for a creature with a disposable tail
> and elbows like a goalie? For this a redoubt

---

4. Walcott uses variant spellings for both words: Iounalao (4, 229), Iounalo (92, Major Plunkett's misspelling); Hewannorra (229, incorrect lettering on a sign), Hewanorra (92).

was built? And his countrymen died? For a lizard
with an Aruac name? It will be rewritten
by black pamphleteers, History will be revised,

and we'll be its villians, fading from the map
(he said "villians" for "villains"). And when it's over
we'll be the bastards! . . . (92)

Walcott's insistence on the mispronunciation in the last stanza not only
exposes his sensitivity to vocal nuance but also recalls the flavor of Achille's
misspelling, *In God We Troust*. Insistence on the correctness of these
individual deviations underscores the human consciousness at the center of
his poem, and it reinforces Major Plunkett's reaction against the historian's
biased amnesia.

Despite his angry resentment toward those who would deny aspects
of the past that do not conform to their sanctioned version, the Major
perseveres in his assault on capitalized "History." And he is rewarded when
he least expects it with a discovery that serves to complete his life in a way
that he had long since given up hope of ever realizing. It is in the midst of his
reaction against the irony of bright red flowers being called immortelles
(when they are just as ephemeral as the regimental Redcoats buried on
the island) that he happens upon the registry entry for nineteen-year-
old Midshipman Plunkett. Suddenly, an impossible idea assumes concrete
embodiment, for "He had come far enough / to find a namesake and
a son" (94). Probably sensing that his inspiration might seem at least a
little overwrought, Plunkett decides not to share his discovery with Maud.
Nevertheless, he now has an essential blood-tie with St. Lucia, a young man
bearing his own name who gave his life defending the island.

Structural parallels also appear beneath the surface when we recall a
similar reversal of father-son chronologies in the twelfth chapter. Just
as Walcott makes a point of his being old enough to have fathered his
father Warwick (68), now Plunkett envisions himself as father to a son
who predates him by two centuries. The fact that both relationships are
inventions in no way undermines their effect as poetic images. In the
earlier example, Walcott makes explicit the irony of his narrative advantage,
molding an encounter with the ghost of his father to reinforce his vatic
calling. When he assumes the persona of the Major, he dramatically extends
the circumference of his poetic license. The crucial advantage rises to
the surface when in chapter eighteen the Major critically examines his

dissatisfaction with the dry historical data he has accumulated regarding the Battle of the Saints. It is not enough that native historians have cited Helen (the imperial desire to possess St. Lucia) as the principal cause. Nor does he find the mere factual details in the piles of books he has read to be adequate. His appreciation for Helen demands a great deal more. After all his meticulous research and calculation, he has concluded that the weight of classical parallels is too vast to be coincidental.

> He had no idea how time could be reworded,
> which is the historian's task. The factual fiction
> of textbooks, pamphlets, brochures, which he had loaded
>
> in a ziggurat from the library, had the affliction
> of impartiality; skirting emotion
> as a ship avoids a reef, they followed one chart
>
> dryly with pen and compass, flattening an ocean
> to paper diagrams, but his book-burdened heart
> found no joy in them except their love of events,
>
> and none noticed the Homeric repetition
> of details, their prophecy. That was the difference.
> He saw coincidence, they saw superstition. (95–96)

The difference Plunkett notes is between an attempt at objective reporting ("factual fiction") and an admittedly subjective response to a momentous event, a response that is as true as fact in that it is *in fact* his heartfelt reaction. In a pertinent article on origins and textual references, Nicolae Babuts comments on the evocative force of events, distant though they may be.

> A text is intended to communicate a view, a vision of the world. An epic is also meant to recapitulate a physically dead yet powerful past in order to reinvigorate a living but faltering present. . . .
> . . . And if we know very little about the primordial event, or if this event does not appear to break into the epic space in an objective form, we should not be surprised, nor should we be skeptical about the event's functional value. There is no neutrally objective past for an individual or a society. But the initial impetus for the creation of epic or any other kind of literary text is provided by real events and urgencies.[5]

5. Nicolae Babuts, "Text: Origins and Referencce," 68–69.

Clearly, because of his commitment to his image of Helen, Major Plunkett's version of events is not intended to be purely objective. Immediately following the passage just quoted from chapter eighteen of *Omeros,* the Major candidly admits that he could have accepted the official version if it were not for the fact that he had succumbed to Helen's magical influence. He recalls vividly the clandestine moment when he stood transfixed, looking into Helen's bold eyes as she brazenly tries on one of Maud's bracelets. Smelling her aroma, feeling the air stir from her passing, mesmerized by the serpentine grace of her body, he could do nothing but acknowledge her power.

Much as he would like to believe that he intends nothing but good for Helen, he is sufficiently alerted to the stereotypical master-slave implications of the situation to suspect his basic motives. Walcott makes the Major conscious of the type of Eurocentric hegemony that Edward Said warns against in *Culture and Imperialism.* "Only recently have Westerners become aware that what they have to say about the history and the cultures of 'subordinate' peoples is challengeable by the people themselves, people who a few years back were simply incorporated, culture, land, history, and all, into the great Western empires, and their disciplinary discourses."[6] Racing through Plunkett's mind as he gathers his thoughts are the names of other women who have been immortalized by the moving pen of History, beginning with Eve.

> . . . all History's appeal
>
> lies in this Judith from a different people,
> whose long arm is a sword, who has turned your head
> back to her past, her tribe; you live in the terror
>
> of age before beauty, the way that an elder
> longed for Helen on the parapets, or that bed.
> Like an elder trembling for Susanna, naked.
>
> He murmured to the mirror. No. My thoughts are pure.
> They're meant to help her people, ignorant and poor.
> But these, smiled the bracelet, are the vows of empire. (97)

The point of the catalog of names is that a pattern of conquest is latent within the Major's scheme for giving Helen a written legacy. Biblical, historical, and

6. Edward Said, *Culture and Imperialism,* 195.

Homeric references add a patina of allusiveness to his thoughts, but they do nothing to detract from the fact that his is a very personal quest. The ancient dumping-ground where he pursues his archaeological excavations cannot be mistaken for Carthage, Pompeii, or Troy; nevertheless, when he unearths two discarded French regimental buttons it is enough to bring a lump to his throat (99). Inspired by pride in the son he adopted from the glorious Battle of the Saints, he seizes upon another Homeric coincidence. The French *Ville de Paris* reminds him of Trojan Paris. In his analogical mind, the name inculcates the Judgment of Paris, Aphrodite's golden apple, the abduction of Helen, and ultimately the siege and conflagration at Troy. It is no great stretch of the imagination for the Major to see young Midshipman Plunkett as Paris; except that the approved Western code of heroism has long since replaced individual prowess with the ideal of social sacrifice. Unlike their Greek predecessors who sought earthly fame in battle, more recent warriors—the Mortimers and Glendowers recorded in Shakespeare, Plunkett's young midshipman, and Tumbly and Scott, his companions from the North African theater of World War II, had offered up their lives in answer to duty.

Reconciled to the inevitable subjectivity of his enterprise, Plunkett alternates between the use of established History and his history—his emerging narrative of experiences that would remain inconsequential by the reckoning of the greater world (103). The monomaniacal dimension of his commitment is graphically suggested by the "Cyclops eye" of the magnifying glass he uses at his desk. It occurs to him that the further he buries himself in his books, the more he betrays his wife, not so much for the obscure Battle of the Saints, but for Helen's black skin set off in Maud's lemon-colored frock. Deliberate ambiguity resides in his assertion that he has now "given *her* a son" (italics mine, 103). Midshipman Plunkett is the son, but since the female pronoun reference is indefinite, the reader must hold in balance Maud, Helen, and the island itself. The suspension of meaning is in perfect harmony with the Major's nostalgic contemplation of endless parallels and connections. Among his memories is a prize-winning essay on the Roman empire he once submitted in a formal history course. The thesis he vividly remembers is that "A few make History. The rest are witnesses" (104). Without acknowledging the application of the point to himself, the Major is an object lesson. Walcott is guiding the reader into weighing the narrator's role as witness to experience against his simultaneous role as creator of experience.

By design, the twentieth chapter plays with the noun "witnesses," using it adverbially this time in the first line, to describe the means by which Philoctete observes a political rally. Instead of having the Major relate the scene, Walcott more directly allows the action itself to unfold, as the son of Warwick's former barber leads his Marxists against Compton, representing the opposing Capitalist faction. Things become more immediate when both Hector and Philoctete decide to advance a third-party candidate, Maljo, a former "fisherman-mechanic" who claims to speak for the island's neglected poor. In shifting abruptly from the Major's quiet study to the mayhem of street politics, Walcott does more than simply dramatize the reality that Plunkett is attempting to weave into an orderly pattern. The device does effectively juxtapose island life with the Major's contemplation of it; but in addition, it involves us in the matter of the third subnarrative of this second book. As I have indicated earlier, Walcott is interested in showing us the rough process by which natives of St. Lucia handle their difficult struggle for political independence.

For all its raw friction, humor, and passion, the public exercise of democracy is no less serious than Achille's more private attempt to secure his identity. Maljo's speeches are a confusion of patois, cliché-laden rhetoric, and calypsonian satire. He enters a village in Hector's brightly decorated transport bus, the Comet, preceded by Philoctete, who hobbles along passing out pamphlets. Walcott plays up the parodistic comedy of Maljo's tactics, affecting MacArthur's corncob pipe and promise, "*Moi* shall return" (106), his exploitation of Philoctete's limp as an emblem of St. Lucian disabilities, his inept use of the microphone. His delivery is often so distorted over the speaker that people begin to refer to him as "Professor Static." As he gets absorbed in his own rhetoric, Maljo rails against the empty promises of established parties, the "fried chicanery" of their corruption. His own colonial education having touched him with the same classical germ that preoccupies Major Plunkett, he raises more comparisons between the Greek and Trojan parties contending for possession of Helen.

Despite the leavening of humor, the internecine struggle disturbs Philoctete. The "pane" of his wound (punning on the transport's windowpane through which he observes the divisive campaign) leads him to wonder why his fractious countrymen cannot love the island as he does, without rancor. He regrets that he is no more successful pulling the people of the island together than he has been in reconciling Hector and Achille over Helen. Maljo's resounding defeat at the polls is foreshadowed when his "Convention Blocko" extravaganza is washed out (109). Philoctete's anticlimactic duty is to clear away the soggy debris. The last we hear of Maljo, he has emigrated to work the Florida harvests.

Antiheroic as this facet of island development may be, it conforms to Walcott's humanizing agenda. The parodistic verve of Maljo's American-style campaign prevents him from taking himself too seriously while he mounts a grassroots effort to acquire power. Walcott seizes the opportunity to display characters who love street performance, who appreciate the distancing effect of role-playing even when it is not carnival season. Following the panorama of the race for public office, however, he turns once again to an intimate close-up of Helen and Achille. The time has apparently reverted to some point before their formal separation. We find that Helen can hardly wait to join the music, dancing, and excitement of Friday night's block fête. Achille, on the other hand, is withdrawn. He is suspicious of Helen, jealous and moody to the point that he refuses to participate in the freewheeling revelry.

In terms of the Homeric overtones, Achille's behavior resembles that of his Greek namesake. Achilles, nursing his wrath over the loss of Briseis, sulked in his tent rather than assist in the siege of Troy. Brooding in the darkness beside *In God We Troust*, it seems to Achille that Helen is determined to sell herself for the pleasure of gawking tourists just as the island "whored / away a simple life that would soon disappear" (111). Thus, despite its specific point of origin, Achille's jealousy gradually assumes a less personal dimension. He begins to reflect that Hector and Helen are both burning like comets across the horizon to become extinguished without notice in this unknown backwater. While Achille is contemplating the vastness of the night sky, not far away the Major is also gazing at the same array of stars. Only Plunkett is fascinated by the alternative patterns that lie before his inventive imagination. He passes over the dot-to-dot linkages of astrological constellations in favor of his own design for the webs of stars. Walcott's juxtaposition of these dissimilar thoughts from two men who share a common love for Helen places side by side the Major's philosophical and Achille's more physical yearnings.

When Helen returns from the party, Achille's passion forces him to challenge her behavior. Their breakup does not come immediately, but his inability to possess her completely is making it impossible for him to live peaceably with the woman he desperately loves. His jealous anger is slowly driving her into Hector's welcoming arms. A short time later she

Helen among Musicians. Watercolor by Derek Walcott (Larry Fink, photo).

packs all her belongings, leaving behind only a hairpin in a soap dish as evidence of her having lived in the house (116). Achille concludes with the encouragement of Ma Kilman that the hairpin is an omen that Helen will not be lost to him forever, that she will come back.

Hector, for his part, is unable to savor his victory because he senses that Helen remains in love with Achille. A further source of his misgivings is the outgrowth of his having chosen to abandon the fisherman's life in order to drive the sixteen-seat transport van he names the "Comet." Due to the reckless abandon with which he speeds along his routes with stereo blasting, he rapidly gains notoriety throughout the island. Even with Helen sitting beside him, his inner loneliness drives him mercilessly. With its imitation leopard-skin interior and flaming paint scheme on the outside, the Comet epitomizes the island's haunting schizophrenia.

> . . . Passengers
>
> crammed next to each other on its animal hide
> were sliding into two worlds without switching gears.
> One, atavistic, with its African emblem
>
> that slid on the plastic seats, wrinkling in a roll
> when the cloth bunched, and the other world that shot them
> to an Icarian future they could not control. (117)

With their accustomed appreciation for the ironies of such a fragmented world, Hector's passengers take the Comet in stride. An elderly woman noting the decorative flames wonders aloud if they are confronted with hell on earth. The predatory nature of the leopard-skin seats leads one passenger to joke, "So let us prey," punning in recognition of their need to "pray" for safe arrival. In the allusion to Icarus's imprudent flight too close to the sun, Hector's recklessness is given a classical thrust (117).

The social commentary of the Comet's imagery is obvious. It is worth recalling as well that on the autobiographical level, Helen would be the peasant woman Walcott once expressed a desire to accompany home in "The Light of the World."[7] In the earlier poem, her alluring face conjures up all that he is missing as an author isolated from his people. Her new appearance in Hector's Comet amplifies his personal feelings of disaffection. As a matter of fact, the tentativeness of human relations prevails throughout the concluding three chapters of this second book of *Omeros*. Hector's passengers risk their lives riding with him, Helen's heart is divided between the two men she loves, the Plunketts have yet to seal their bond with the island, and Achille's emotional pain is as acute as that of his wounded friend Philoctete.

To enhance the general focus of the picture, Walcott once again relies on the Major's perspective. As Plunkett continues his research, seasons pass and changes occur, but he muses over the fact that time's alterations do not always bring about material differences in the lives of the people.

---

7. White, "An Interview with Derek Walcott," 35.

The transition from imperial rule to independence places responsibility in the hands of local officials; however, the political change loses some of its significance when it fails to register materially. Following Maljo's ill-fated campaign, the island is left with,

> A government that made no difference to Philoctete,
>
> to Achille. That did not buy a bottle of white kerosene
> from Ma Kilman, a dusk that had no historical regret
> for the fishermen beating mackerel into their seine,
>
> only for Plunkett, in the pale orange glow of the wharf
> reddening the vendor's mangoes, alchemizing the bananas
> near the coal market, this town he had come to love. (119–20)

For the Major, as for Walcott, what is important is not the political apparatus or sources of power but the individuals who must struggle to make a life for themselves in spite of inaccessible government functionaries who touch their lives from great distances, whether geographic or social.

Several characters' personal problems tend to intersect in chapter twenty-three. The first to receive attention is Maud Plunkett. As Maud surveys their estate out toward the sea, a tiny canoe catches her eye as it beats toward the eastern horizon. We will learn later that the canoe is Achille's *In God We Troust,* but for the time being it merely causes Maud to speculate (with more accuracy than she has any way of knowing) that someone is headed for Africa. Significant as that observation will prove to be for Achille and for *Omeros* as a whole, it fades to the margins as Maud sights a passenger liner that represents contact with the Old World, the Ireland she will never see again because Dennis refuses her the money for passage. She is dwelling on this impossibility when she notices resentfully that Helen has appeared on the pathway leading up to the garden.

Not only does she find this beautiful woman's approach discomforting because of the question of her yellow dress, but Maud suspects some ulterior motive. As it turns out, she has guessed correctly because Helen's unwanted pregnancy has forced her to swallow her pride and seek money from her former employer. Maud is willing to give her five dollars, but when she inquires about how she expects to repay a loan since she has no employment and wonders why Hector or Achille is not providing for her, Helen serenely turns away empty-handed. In her frustration, Maud can only watch her stride arrogantly down the path toward the sea, as magnificent as the liner sailing from the harbor.

The third of the individual paths intersecting in chapter twenty-three becomes the exclusive focus of chapter twenty-four. Achille and his fishing mate occupy the small canoe Maud had spotted from her garden porch. A tantalizing reference to the day after a blocko gives us only the slightest hint of chronological awareness. The narrative is simply approaching its first interim climax. As the island recedes in the distance, Achille and his fishing mate still suffer from the previous night's bout of drinking. The mate jokes that his urine could intoxicate the fish, but Achille is preoccupied with the irretrievable loss of Helen. Then in the depths of his despair, he begins to pay attention to a tiny swift whose flight pattern suggests that she at first leads *In God We Troust* from ahead and then darts around to guide their pirogue from astern. Under the influence of the sun blazing down on his unprotected head, Achille succumbs to a hallucinatory trance.

It seems to him that the swift (tagged *l'hirondelle des Antilles* on Maud's quilt) who had flown over the ax-wielding boatwrights in the mountains, who had represented the crucifix at the priest's blessing ceremony, was now "the god's body torn from its hill" (126). Whether he means Christ or the spirit of the felled trees is not specified. It is certain, however, that the swift is tugging at Achille's heart, drawing him eastward toward Africa. He senses that *In God We Troust* is probably twenty miles out to sea, and that they are now floating above the very spot where the *Ville de Paris* sliced into Midshipman Plunkett's ship. Walcott describes the ritualistic way in which he lays the boat's oars together as though he were depositing a married couple in their coffin. Achille's actions strike the mate as so odd that he questions whether he is alright. He cannot respond, however, because a catalog is unfolding before his eyes. In addition to young Plunkett, he recognizes drowned fishermen whose names he had known and uncounted African slaves who died in the Middle Passage.

Stream-of-consciousness thought permits the figurative rush of the closing lines, though some of the images are more felicitous than others. There is slight awkwardness in comparing the sun to "a flat iron, singeing his cap with its smell" (128), but Achille's sunstroke excuses the frenetic pace as book two builds to its climax. As time whirls backward, we are prepared to accept the idea that Philoctete's wound bears tribal implications. As the mate literally hauls in fishing line, we understand that Walcott means for the reader to be cognizant of literal poetic lines as well.

> Time is the metre, memory the only plot.
>
> His shoulders are knobs of ebony. The back muscles
> can bulge like porpoises leaping out of this line
> from the gorge of our memory. (129)

When the mate ultimately hauls up the shrouded body of Achille's own father, we are reminded—by the self-reflexive text, the words themselves, and Walcott's earlier autobiographical comments regarding his involvement in the narrative (28)—that everything brought before us is his fictive invention. Without resolving the outstanding issues that have been raised, Walcott is deftly summarizing the journey he has traced up to this point. He is also setting the stage for the continuing odyssey of *Omeros*.

As I have intimated earlier in this chapter, Walcott is constantly moving forward by looping backward to advance the separate threads of his multiseamed narrative. Both Walcott as author and Major Plunkett as narrator have found parental links that evoke their respective pasts. What they will do with their discoveries remains to be seen. And Achille, who has more folk appeal and symbolic potential, has farther to search, a greater void to fill, than either of these other male characters. The instant Achille recognizes his father rising from the sea, his personal quest finds the direction it has always lacked. "Then for the first time, he asked himself who he was" (130). Immediately the sea-swift becomes a link to the past, an "engine / that shot ahead of each question like an answer," and the amnesia that is the curse of survivors of the Middle Passage comes under interrogation. "[O]nce Achille had questioned his name and its origin," the swift's trajectory "touched both worlds with her rainbow" (130). Drawn by the power of the swift, Achille believes that he is headed "home" (131).

Promising as that hopeful note may sound, the reader must beware of the deceptive certainty of simple answers in *Omeros*. There are latent flaws in both Major Plunkett's well-intentioned historical machinations and Achille's headlong voyage away from the island that must prove eventually to be his authentic home. For very good reason, Walcott has diligently stressed beginnings without allowing closure. Significantly, the recirculation of allusions, parallels, and parodies serves to underscore departures from origins because they make us conscious of alternatives to established patterns. The new pattern is in the process of becoming just as *Omeros* and its characters are filling out their dimensions.

4 The Middle Passage— Africa

Walcott maintains the continuity of *Omeros* on every level, from the prosody and underlying imagery to the various complementary narrative threads and interlocking themes. St. Lucia occupies center stage throughout the first two books; nevertheless, we are constantly reminded of the island's suspension in time and space. Achille's uprooted and transplanted people have inherited at best a synthesis of African, Asian, and Euro-American cultures. Even Dennis Plunkett, who emigrated voluntarily, struggles against the marginalizing forces of "History" and heredity to authenticate New World roots. Events in the first two books make it clear that simple possession of the island is insufficient. As St. Lucia is personified in the character of Helen, we have seen her slip from the grasp of both Achille and the Plunketts into Hector's uncertain hands. Moving in with Hector proves to be less than satisfactory, because his is only a Pyrrhic victory. First, he suffers from having abandoned the brotherhood of the sea to drive a van, and in his heart he senses that Helen really loves Achille. These lives intersect at crucial junctures, and Walcott emphasizes occasional parallels between their experiences and past events that have been commemorated through historical and literary texts: thus the presence of Admiral Rodney and Homer.

Also woven into this complex tapestry are autobiographical threads that constantly remind the reader of the author's active presence itself. Not satisfied with allowing the narrative to unfold as though it were merely a causal sequence, Walcott makes the process of composition one of his explicit subjects. As far back as a 1973 interview with Raoul Pantin, he was already convinced that "the most exciting part of poetry . . . is its craft." In that regard, he went on to underscore his consciousness of the impact that writing has on the writer. "In writing a poem, you know, . . . you are in a state of subdued astonishment. As you progress, subconsciously, you are astonishing not only yourself; the poem astonishes itself and then it finishes. . . . You're in a living language that's changing all the time. And that is where the poet keeps alive."[1] It is hardly surprising, then, to have Walcott emerge frequently from his own page in *Omeros,* or to realize that his poetic imagination is the vehicle that telescopes from intimate vignettes to surrealistic panoramas.

Having provided a succession of unifying devices throughout his kaleidoscopic narrative, Walcott still allows himself the latitude to range far beyond the St. Lucia of any one person's experience. Although books three, four, and five are extensions of the first two books, they constitute a far-ranging odyssey back into the ancestry of the New World. Book three traces the evolution of Negroes from tribal Africa to contemporary St. Lucia. Book four follows the author to the United States, where he delves into the tragic fate of Native Americans, then confronts his own feelings of personal and social alienation in the United States. Book five comprises a reverse Middle Passage back to cultural roots in metropolitan Europe. Despite the geographic distances and the generational leaps, subtle transitions lead from one section into the next—and they all lead back to St. Lucia.

Since Walcott has stressed the impact of history (or its absence) on the West Indian psyche from the beginning of *Omeros,* the successive journeys of the three central books into the pasts of Africa, the United States, and Europe are indispensable to the eventual resolution of this epic. Their importance may be gauged to some extent when we recall that he has insisted in the introduction to *Dream on Monkey Mountain and Other Plays,* "For imagination and body to move with original instinct, we must begin again from the bush." The same essay makes it clear that he intends no reversion to some primitive ideal. On the contrary, he ridicules the pseudo-folklore of African revivalists who lament the degradation of the present. "What is needed," he proclaims, "is not new names for old things, or old names for old things, but the faith of using the old names anew, so that mongrel as I am, something prickles in me when I see the word Ashanti as with the word Warwickshire, both separately intimating my grandfathers' roots, both baptising this neither proud nor ashamed bastard, this hybrid, this West

1. Raoul Pantin, "Any Revolution Based on Race Is Suicidal," 14.

Indian."[2] This might well serve as a definition for Creole culture; it certainly brings together the ingredients for an epic based on Walcott's dual heritage. In *Omeros,* as in the play *Dream on Monkey Mountain,* he takes a character to Africa, not as an end in itself, but to reclaim hereditary seeds that survived the Atlantic crossing, seeds that are now rooted in Caribbean soil.

Book three opens as the sea-swift Achille has followed in his dream disappears up an African river. The cry of the swift is the last contact he has with the world he has known. Watching the river "unreel," his first impression is that of the old films about Africa he had seen as a child— mangrove shallows, crocodiles and hippopotami emerging from the murky water. Fascinated as he is with the new environment, Achille is disturbed to realize the muddy river prevents him from seeing the shadow that he would have cast on the clear sands of home. A skeletal helmsman guides him as time flows backward by centuries until God's voice sounds in his ear, telling him that the sea-swift (his sign of the crucifix) was sent to bring him home—harking back to merge imagery of the crucifix (8) and the flying arrow (125). What strikes Achille as most eerie about the strange scene is its haunting familiarity. It seems to him that *In God We Troust* seeks out its own mooring stake at a settlement landing (135). When he steps ashore, he is welcomed by curious villagers who are intrigued by his Western attire.

Walcott's first overt intrusion is to remark that he is half with Achille on this African stream and half with Midshipman Plunkett by a Dutch canal (135). This hybrid consciousness mirrors the convergence of all the influences that permeate *Omeros.* The progenitor-progeny dichotomy already exploited between Major and Midshipman Plunkett and between Walcott and his father arises once again when Achille suddenly comes face to face with his paternal ancestor. Not only are their features virtual duplicates, but Achille is able to anticipate this father's every gesture and intention as though the two men are reflecting paired worlds. By this point, Walcott's insistence on a reversed temporal or spacial dialectic becomes an archetypal metaphor of self-discovery. The visual inversion of reflected scenery, fishermen, and mooring poles standing in the water is mentioned repeatedly. Each world sees itself in the other. After the formal exchange of names that takes place between Achille and his father, Afolabe

2. Walcott, "What the Twilight Says," 25–26, 10.

instructs his prodigal son regarding the essential relationship between each physical object and the unique shadow it casts. Equally significant, just as Aeneas's destiny is Virgil's Roman legacy in the *Aeneid*, Afolabe's future happens to be Achille's fragmented history. The effect is the juxtaposition of complementary opposites, two hemispheres of the same globe informing each other.

Since at least as early as *Another Life*, where he exulted in "Adam's task of giving things their names," Walcott has stressed the privilege of names and naming. In the poem "Names" from *Sea Grapes*, he laments the horizon that stands between his West Indian race and the nouns left behind in Benares, Canton, and Benin:

> Behind us all the sky folded,
> as history folds over a fishline,
> and the foam foreclosed
> with nothing in our hands
>
> but this stick
> to trace our names on the sand
> which the sea erased again, to our indifference.

Thus in the writing of *Omeros*, we find Walcott's determination to confront that indifference. "[W]hat this poem is doing, in part, is trying to hear the names of things and people in their own context, meaning everything named in a noun, and everything around a name."[3] Within the poem, Achille's visionary return to ancestral Africa is initiated when he first questions his identity. Afolabe's primary concern at their first meeting is to discover Achille's lost name. Within the tribe, each noun, each sound signifies a quality, a virtue that is associated with trees, a river, or a person. Without that connotation, Afolabe explains, a thing is meaningless, a person is nothing. The substantiality of the individual's name is such that it provides his shadow. When Achille can offer no etymological roots, Afolabe and the whole tribe sense the threat of oblivion (138). To combat Achille's amnesia, he is taught the ritual of the kola nut, to drink palm-wine, and the griot's litany of gods and men.

---

3. Walcott, *Another Life*, 152; Walcott, *Sea Grapes*, 41; White, "An Interview with Derek Walcott," 35.

Day by day, Achille regains the details of his lost genealogy until he makes the connection between the modern world he has inherited and the tribe's unknown future. He does not disclose the fate he knows awaits them, but the burden slowly turns to alienation. He appreciates the doubling effect of images in the water, his canoe, the tree line; however, the reflection of his face,

> swayed by the ochre ripples seemed homesick
> for the history ahead, as if its proper place
> lay in unsettlement. So, to Achille, it appeared
>
> they were not one reflection but separate men—
> one crouching at the edge of the spindly pierhead,
> one drowned under it, featureless in mien. (140–41)

Achille is realizing that although the experience he is gaining through racial memory is his birthright, Africa is no longer his personal home. He has been a rootless West Indian too long to deny the other components of his psyche. The morning after he first confronts the schizophrenia that separates him from his forebears, he joins a group of villagers in handling a communal fishnet.

Achille is hoping that the familiar activity will make him feel less estranged, but the net itself turns metaphorical—capturing fish the way his mind gathers memories; his wading into the river is shortly followed by a veritable baptismal dream. More properly, it is a vision within the ongoing dream of this third book. Under the hallucination of a fermented bark brew that he is given after he steps out of the river, Achille sees Philoctete hauling a net through seawater. The flashback sets the stage for an undersea journey that not only carries Achille from Africa to the New World but also transports him across the three centuries that separate his tribal beginnings from the present. Walking along the sandy bottom, he can see his shadow now floating overhead as he passes coral meadows, sunken galleons, bones of drowned men, rusted anchors, and lost treasures. Although we follow him until he emerges from the surf at Barrel of Beef in the Caribbean, Achille awakens from this truncated dream back in his African river settlement.[4] The illumination of his transatlantic

---

4. Barrel of Beef is a rock outcropping approximately a quarter of a mile off the southern tip of Rodney Bay, St. Lucia.

baptism dawns when he realizes that tribal ceremonies in the settlement are replicated in St. Lucian festivals to this day. There are the same plantain vestments, calabash masks, transvestite-female warriors, stick-fighters, and stilt walkers dancing to the same rhythms and familiar handcrafted musical instruments (143). Verifying that connection may not make him any more African, but he is comforted by the discovery of common roots.

Chapter twenty-seven takes a violent turn when the village is suddenly attacked by a band of slave traders. Achille is caught out in the open, but the raid flows around him as though the attackers are oblivious to his presence. By inserting this vicious assault into Achille's dream, Walcott is providing an antidote to a fallacy that he believes perpetuates the self-induced amnesia of African history. In his interview with Brown and Johnson, he complains that a pattern of segregating or "ghettoizing" the truth conveniently overlooks the tragic fact that slavery is founded on "Africans selling each other. . . . Black people capturing black people and selling them to the white man. That is the real beginning; that is what should be taught." Just as Walcott resists the temptation to ennoble the downtrodden peasant, he is determined not to rectify historical injustice by generating an equally inauthentic image of black virtue. The object is not to assign guilt or innocence, but to encourage responsible growth. Achille's faith must become large, encompassing both his African roots and the soil cleaving to them. His return to Africa is no more a pastoral escape than it had been for Makak and Lestrade in *Dream on Monkey Mountain*. In this play from the late 1960s, Walcott warns, "Once we have lost our wish to be white we develop a longing to become black, and those two may be different, but are still careers."[5] Portraying Achille's nightmare encounter with black slavers dramatically reinforces the pervasiveness of slavery's insidious web.

When the raid begins, Walcott relegates Achille to the role of helpless observer as the marauding tribe ensnares his ancestors. Once again the ant metaphor that describes the female colliers loading steamers in Castries harbor appears; it now applies to the file of chained captives being led away in the distance. In the abandoned village, Achille finds one starving dog, a lost child, and Seven Seas mournfully reciting the tribe's genealogy (145–46). When he looks again and discovers that even the dog and child have disappeared along with the bodies of the fallen warriors, he reaches

---

5. Brown and Johnson, "An Interview with Derek Walcott," 212; Walcott, "What the Twilight Says," 20.

the conclusion that they have all "vanished into their souls." He can change nothing, but Achille foresees ants in dark holds, disembarking at the far rim of the sea, climbing "pyramids of coal" (146). The sequence of events begins to elicit memories and leads to one of Walcott's most extended similes. When Achille notices the ancient griot pounding his hollow chest, he is reminded first of the decayed hulk of an old canoe in which he had played as a child; then it occurs to him that like the bilge of that overgrown wreck, the mind of Seven Seas must be equally choked with time-worn thoughts and words. Achille, who is also condemned to the knowledge of what the future holds for his ancestor (the tale of his own fate), nevertheless makes a futile attempt to cut off the retreating line of marauders.

Using the only weapon at hand, an oar, he manages to overtake and kill one straggler. When his victim dies "like a spear-gaffed fish," the comparison is appropriate to Achille's calling as a fisherman; however, it is also remarkably close to the epic simile Homer uses in the sixteenth book of the *Iliad* to describe Patroclus spearing Thestor and retrieving him the way an angler gaffs and lands a great fish. Despite the coincidental or deliberate similarities, the aesthetic and moral implications of the two episodes are quite different. Homer is enhancing Patroclus's stature before his impending death in heroic combat. When Achille kills the African warrior who had invaded his village, he subsequently grieves because it is as though he has murdered a brother. In fleeing the sight, he trips over the netted undergrowth, strikes his head and is transformed into the man he has just killed. Walcott's handling of this incident is in keeping with his "politically incorrect" but supportable argument that the origins of African slavery derive from internecine exploitation. This should not be misconstrued to suggest that the victim is being blamed for the crime. The interchangeability of Achille and the slave-trading native he killed dramatizes the fact that no race or class has a monopoly on oppression. Walcott simply does not wish to evade that sordid aspect of human rivalry and its aftermath into the twentieth century.

Chapter twenty-eight expands Achille's flexible identity even further, introducing the pronoun "we" to encompass the perspectives of the captives who are sold on the coast and transported across the ocean. Those who cannot complete the crossing float in the wake of slave ships like desiccated palm branches. Those who survive to cast shadows on foreign shores believe that the river gods follow in the form of sea currents, and they retain the seeds of their disrupted culture. The long quotation expressing their general perspective ends with the wish that contemporary society "remember us to the black waiter bringing the bill" (149). The sentiment links us to the present by gently hinting at the Plunketts' "Lawrence of St. Lucia," the waiter from the beach hotel in chapter four (23).

The descendants of those slaves may pursue menial callings among the tourist hotels of the islands, "But they crossed, they survived. There is the epical splendour. . . . / the grace born from subtraction" (149). Walcott's pronouncement might well serve as the thesis of book three. It is followed by a catalog of crafts that had to be adapted or lost in the environment of the New World: woodworkers, armorers, potters, painters who had to depend on fading memories for inspiration. In addition to their common loss of nationality and family, each individual suffers the absence of little things. Elsewhere Walcott has generalized from his own experience that

> the taste on the exile's tongue is the taste of his childhood. The taste cannot be washed away with a different wine, with the best sort of food, for beneath it all, the travel, the politics, the sociology, . . . there is an interior exile, however sublimated, in every writer who is not in his own territory . . . If you expand that into a wider sense of culture, this sickness increases in proportion to time, and obviously it must, because in the old idea of banishment for life, you find an unendurable idea.

In *Omeros,* the African diaspora has generated a nationality bound together primarily by the shared state of exile. As Shabine puts it in "The Schooner *Flight*" from *The Star-Apple Kingdom,* "I had no nation now but the imagination."[6] Since everything else has been subtracted, they are forced to begin again with their bare hands.

While Achille is reliving the evolution of West Indian dispossession in his African dream, chapter twenty-nine carries us back to the companions he has left behind in St. Lucia. Helen, who is hanging out sheets in Hector's yard, is disturbed by the cooing of doves. Rather than simply compare the sound to the "O" of an Aruac flute, Walcott's literary turn of mind forces him to insert an allusion to the noise coming from Agamemnon's "veined mesh." It should be pointed out that as far back as page fourteen, the "O" of a conch shell and the initial letter of Omeros's name first become

6. White, "An Interview with Derek Walcott," 20; Walcott, *The Star-Apple Kingdom,* 8.

the subject of discussion. In traditionally Freudian fashion, the shape as well as the sound is consistently associated with hollow objects: a woman's throat, a cave, a vase, anything that might suggest enclosure, completion. He goes on to claim that the "O" surrounds Helen, and the reader may be forgiven for recalling that Aeschylus's treatment of Agamemnon's death scene in the *Oresteia* is also touched with the net imagery that is becoming ubiquitous in *Omeros*.[7] Classical associations become more entangled when the waiting Helen is compared to Penelope. At first she may appear to have more in common with Clytaemnestra than the faithful Penelope, since she is presently living with Achille's rival Hector. In truth, however, Helen longs for Achille so that "a single noon was as long as ten years" (153). When she fantasizes about making love and brings herself to a sexual climax, her mind is on him, not Hector.

Philoctete, who is also worried that Achille has not returned with the other fishermen by nightfall, hobbles over to visit with Seven Seas, as is his custom on moonlit evenings. Seven Seas doesn't have to be told when his younger friend approaches, because of the odor of his wound. As a blind seer, he knows what is troubling Philoctete this night without having to ask. He not only assures Philoctete that Achille has undertaken a search for "his name and his soul" in Africa but also predicts that he will return soon. Philoctete's faith is in short supply; nevertheless, he weighs the fact that living on an obscure island named for a blind saint, and with little else to believe, he must settle for a blind man's vision or a miracle.

While these friends wait, Walcott prepares to retrieve Achille from his visionary African sojourn. In keeping with the intangibility of subconscious connections, Walcott's return to Achille is circuitous. He points up the interplay of dream and reality by shifting to a deliberately amorphous scene with an unidentified narrator in bed with Circe. Since Helen is demonstrably adept at mesmerizing men and the Major has previously compared her to Circe, it is reasonable to see her also as this mythological enchantress. The male figure is not so easily identified, however, since Walcott frequently interchanges his own persona with those of the Major, Achille, Hector, and even Philoctete. By leaving the perspective vague at this point, he manages a grotesque dramatization of all his male characters attempting to possess an unobtainable goddess—the embodiment in this

7. Aeschylus, *The Agamemnon*, 71.

poem of St. Lucia. Whoever the narrator may represent, he finds himself transformed into a repulsive swine. At first Circe spurns his embrace, but the nightmare resolves itself when she relents and draws him to her breast.

Abruptly, with no attempt to make the logical connection, the scene shifts to Achille, who is springing up from the floor of the sea. His ascent and his awakening carry him from the depths of unconsciousness through a catalog of past events until he surfaces in present reality. This latest reprise of three hundred years of history differs from the others he has experienced in his dream because this time he is not reliving the experience through his personal ancestors. Treaties are abrogated; governments and economies fluctuate; abolition follows manumission; a Jew flees the Inquisition to the New World; in a great sea battle, a midshipman (young Plunkett) meets his death; a rebellious Negro slave (Toussaint L'Ouverture) dies imprisoned in the Pyrenees; Victoria rules a vast empire; Wilberforce advocates emancipation; Darwin establishes the common ancestry of mankind; emigrants from India contribute an added strain to the mixture of Caribbean culture (155–56).

This brief list combines key events in the development of the New World with some of the subjects Walcott has touched on elsewhere. Not only has he already dealt with the Battle of the Saints in *Omeros,* but his interest in Toussaint is evident in *Henri Christophe* and his introduction to *Dream on Monkey Mountain and Other Plays;* the persecution of Jews, which has natural parallels with the African diaspora, figures not only in *Omeros* but in *Drums and Colours* and such poems as "North and South" and "The Fortunate Traveller" as well. In "North and South" he makes a candid admission that links the plight of Jews and blacks:

> . . . I remember once looking at my aunt's face,
> the wintry blue eyes, the rusty hair, and thinking
>
> maybe we are part Jewish, and felt a vein
> run through this earth and clench itself like a fist
> around an ancient root, and wanted the privilege
> to be yet another of the races they fear and hate
> instead of one of the haters and the afraid.

To his credit, this is a passing thought about which he is candid, and the emphasis in the poem is as much on the demise of empire as it is on the "paranoid anxiety of the victim."[8] Autobiographical traces and parallels between *Omeros* and external reality are inevitable since the author and his fictive characters bear the same historical burden. The conclusion of Walcott's catalog of names and events in chapter twenty-nine signals the end of Achille's Middle Passage.

As dawn breaks, Achille awakens cramped and wet from the morning drizzle. The swift that guided him to Africa has disappeared, but he concludes that the "ton" (idiomatic for a large kingfish) lying underfoot is responsible for drawing him back out of the depths. Introducing another variation on his circular emblems, Walcott focuses on the blind eye of the kingfish to reinforce Achille's return to conscious reality,

> . . . a globed window
> ringing with cold, its rim the circular river
>
> of the current that had carried him back, with the spoon
> bait in his jaw, the ton was his deliverer. (157)

Rather than accept Achille's explanation that he has spent the night in Africa, the mate attributes his hallucinations and unusually prolonged sleep to sunstroke.

Just as they sight land, both of them take pleasure in watching a frigate bird exploiting the labor of seagulls to obtain his breakfast. When Achille describes him as a black king with white slaves, the mate responds, "You Wish" (158). Welling with enthusiasm, Achille admires the frigate's beauty, and he exults in the name of Afolabe as he pronounces, "The king going home" (159). It is all he can do to refrain from shouting for joy, and Walcott seizes the moment to distinguish his epic from its predecessors.

> This was the shout on which each odyssey pivots,
> that silent cry for a reef, or familiar bird,
> not the outcry of battle, not the tangled plots
>
> of a fishnet, but when a wave rhymes with one's grave,
> a canoe with a coffin, once that parallel
> is crossed, and cancels the line of master and slave.

8. Walcott, *The Fortunate Traveller*, 15.

Then an uplifted oar is stronger than marble
Caesar's arresting palm, and a swift outrigger
fleeter than his galleys in its skittering bliss.

And I'm homing with him, Homeros, my nigger,
my captain, his breastplates bursting with happiness! (159)

This passage advances the theme propounded earlier (150–51) when Walcott enumerates the little things that anchor the exile's heart to his native land. Without the intricacies of a convention-laden tradition, simple people can appreciate the sea and a worthy canoe. Once life is reduced to its most basic essentials, the oar that brings a man home is more meaningful than the authority commemorated in an *Augustus of Primaporta*. For these reasons Achille finds happiness, not in Africa, but in his accustomed island. This is also why Walcott celebrates his earthy "Homeros" rather than some glorified military or civil hero (159).

With nothing more spectacular than the muted praise of beloved details, the homecoming scene is almost anticlimactic. Tending his yam patch on the hillside, Philoctete hears the conch announcing Achille's arrival and is moved to repent his previous doubts. Seven Seas knows of the boat's arrival before his dog can even sense it. Much as she had been concerned about Achille's safety, Helen appears to be content merely seeing him approach the shore. Although she is near enough to speak, the time of reconciliation has not arrived and she chooses to walk away without saying a word. At least, Achille is not forced to assume the disguise of a beggar as Odysseus is when he returns after twenty years to Ithaca.

The subdued tone continues through the concluding two chapters of this third book. Strategically, chapters thirty-one and thirty-two round off the African phase of Achille's quest for self-knowledge, but since *Omeros* is not an African but a West Indian tale, a broader epic of the dispossessed, these chapters are also transitional. They lay the groundwork for the expanding geography of successive books. The thirty-first chapter opens on Saturday morning in the aftermath of a riotous blockorama. We find Achille washing his canoe and beating out the reggae rhythm of Bob Marley's "Buffalo Soldier." Engrossed in the tune, he envisions a black soldier in the American West sighting a red enemy with his rifle, the venerable oar-weapon turned into a firearm. Moving in for a closer look, we discern the features of Achille as he becomes a buffalo soldier, pretending to aim and fire his oar; with each discharge another palm tree crumples until he imagines a shore littered with fallen savages, "like Aruacs / falling to the muskets of the Conquistador" (162). At the time Walcott makes no more of the scene, but Achille's pantomime links the fates of Amerindians throughout the Americas and it foreshadows the central passages of book four that are set in the United States.

More immediately, his targeting of palm trees leads into the next scene, where Seven Seas hires Achille to rake and burn pomme-Arac, banana, and coconut branches that are cluttering his yard. The chore turns into an educational experience as Seven Seas explains that the patois "pomme-Arac" signifies the apple of the Aruac (Arawak) Indians. Then as Achille unearths an artifact with his rake, he comes face to face with "History" in the form of a glowering petroglyph. No archaeologist, Achille hurls the totem aside in superstitious fear, but Seven Seas, who possesses the wisdom and experience of the ages, is there to connect him with the past. He is able to bridge the distance from Carib and Arawak to Sioux through the elegiac fate they have in common with fallen leaves. Furthermore, when Seven Seas claims that he had once been a ghost dancer among the snowy mountains of an alien climate, Walcott is preparing a veiled autobiographical link as well (164). Beginning in the late 1970s, his own career choices have resulted in a dual residence, spending much of each year fulfilling academic and professional commitments in metropolitan centers such as Boston, returning to his native archipelago as often as possible.[9]

Before shifting the scene from St. Lucia to the United States in book four, Walcott reserves his thirty-second chapter for a delicately wrought leave-taking. Just as he closes book one bidding farewell to his father Warwick (chapter thirteen), he ends book three with a visit to his mother, Alix, in the island's Marian rest home. She must struggle to remember the son who is now older than the husband she lost many years ago. As the past flits through their minds, they recount family names and his lost childhood floods back. When he walks away from the Marian Home, an overheard snatch of patois reminds him of the life he has missed. Although he inhabits

9. An account of Walcott's resignation from the Trinidad Theatre Workshop (November 15, 1977) and his subsequent residence in the United States is covered in Bruce King, *Derek Walcott and West Indian Drama*, 259–64. Since leaving Boston University in the summer of 1995, Walcott now owns an estate in the northern Gros Îlet Quarter of St. Lucia.

"In God We Troust" on Choc Bay. Ink, chalk, and oil, Jared Hamner
(Ken Roberts, photo).

a skin that needs no translation here, it takes the sound of patois to open his
ears, break his amnesia, and restore a whole continent of experience (167).
To underscore Walcott's flight northward the following day as an extension
rather than a departure from Achille's African odyssey, we are treated to

another form of reflected imagery. From the plane above, we are able to look down on Achille's lateen-rigged canoe sailing toward Gros Îlet. As the shadow of the plane flitters across the lilac hue of coral ledges outlined against the emerald lagoon, a window catches the glare of sunlight so that Achille looks up to watch it pass. From the helm of *In God We Troust,* the plane resembles a minnow gliding "into cloud-coral over the horned island" (168). Obviously the two perspectives coalesce and move forward in the poet's imagination.

5 The Middle Passage— North America

Certain portions of the fourth book are conspicuously autobiographical, dramatizing Walcott's marital difficulties and personal responses to the cultural environment of Boston and the United States. Nevertheless, this is an essential facet of his multivalent odyssey. By transporting his Afro-Caribbean experience northward, he is able to confront powerful geographic and historical influences at their metropolitan source. Walcott is St. Lucian by birth, yet as he makes clear in his 1974 article "The Caribbean: Culture or Mimicry," the West Indies are too thoroughly integrated into the context of the Americas to be comprehended in isolation.

> . . . we were American even while we were British, if only in the geographical sense, and now that the shadow of the British Empire has passed through and over us in the Caribbean, we ask ourselves if, in the spiritual or cultural sense, we must become American. . . . In the case of my own identity, or my realness if you like, it is an absurdity that I can live with; being both American and West Indian is an ambiguity without a crisis, for I find that the more West Indian I become, the more I can accept my dependence on America as a professional writer, not because America owes me a living from historical guilt, nor that it needs my presence, but because we share this part of the world, and have shared it for centuries now, even as conqueror and victim, as exploiter and exploited. . . . and we can absorb it because we know that America is black, that so much of its labor, its speech, its music, its very style of living is generated by . . . "black" culture, that what is most original in it has come out of its ghettos, its river-cultures, its

plantations. Power itself is ephemeral, unstable. It is the least important aspect of any culture, who rules.[1]

Regardless of the technicalities of citizenship, Walcott asserts his genetic, historic, and geographic right to a larger New World identity. This passage also indicates his reasons for concentrating on the narrative of the dispossessed rather than prolonging the annals of the great and powerful in *Omeros*.

Chapter thirty-three serves to establish the melancholy opening of book four.

> From the provincial edge of an atlas, from the hem
> of a frayed empire, a man stops. Not for another anthem
> trembling over the water—he has learnt three of them—
>
> but for that faint sidereal drone interrupted by the air
> gusting over black water, or so that he can hear
> the surf in the pores of wet sand wince and pucker (170).

Since he mentions Long Island and New London in his "new empire," we know the coastline he is contemplating and we can surmise that the "Star-Spangled Banner" or "America the Beautiful" might be the third anthem he would be adding to national scores from St. Lucia and England.

The location becomes very specific when he describes living in Brookline, a suburb of Boston, as though he were a hermitic Japanese soldier left behind after World War II, or harboring an offensive wound like Philoctete. Because of his loneliness, he fears that strangers will be aware that he has become a casualty in the war of love (171). No precise dates are given, but his period of seclusion would coincide with the breakup of his third marriage. Although he is landlocked in his Brookline home, he maintains the sea imagery that has dominated the poem from the beginning. He is a shipwrecked castaway, his bed a raft and the telephone his single oar. The vacancy of the house is exacerbated by the missing domestic sounds, another ghostly *Marie Celeste* all the more startling because of its inexplicable tranquility.[2]

---

1. Derek Walcott, "The Caribbean: Culture or Mimicry?" 3–4.
2. His third marriage was to actress/dancer Norline Metivier, former member of Walcott's Trinidad Theatre Workshop: married 1982, now divorced.

Out in the streets, he follows a woman whose silhouette reminds him of his wife. He loses her, ironically, "in the aisles of Vallombrosa / drugged by the perfume of flowers I didn't need" (172). The irony is that the flowers are useless because he no longer has anyone to whom he can give them as a love token. The reference to Vallombrosa (shady valley), located near Florence, Italy, comes from Milton's *Paradise Lost*. In the first book of Milton's epic, Satan takes stock of his prostrate legions on the shore of Hell's flaming lake, "Thick as Autumnal Leaves that strow the Brooks / In *Vallombrosa*."[3] It would be quite a stretch to compare a desperate lover to Satan's lot; however, this is not the first time Walcott has drawn on the conventional metaphor of fallen leaves to symbolize dead or discarded souls. It may be that the association of profuse leaves with the overpowering aroma of useless flowers is sufficient to explain the allusion in this particular case. What is clear is the prevailing vulnerability.

Following the allusion, he bemoans the fact that he is lost with only an empty enclosure to call home. The idea is immediately reinforced by the insertion of seventeen rhymed iambic tetrameter couplets wherein the word "house" is conspicuously repeated eighteen times and "home" appears only once as the last rhyme. Although this is not Walcott's only variation in prosody, it is such an emphatic departure from the prevailing longer verse pattern that it demands special attention. The sequence is almost incantatory in its repetitive simplicity. By enumerating little things that make a dwelling a home—toothbrushes, stains on sheets, shadows that conjure memories—the inventory highlights the intimate concreteness of his personal alienation. The vacancy surrounding the abandoned mate amplifies his loneliness. Haunted by creaking sounds, sinister external noises, he resorts to Onan, masturbating just as Helen does in her longing for Achille. At this point the narrator is centered in a space that has lost the essence of home. As might be expected, Walcott's persona reverses the figure by internalizing it imaginatively.

> I do not live in you, I bear
> my house inside me, everywhere

The American brig the *Marie Celeste* was found drifting in the North Atlantic on December 5, 1872; the lifeboats and crew disappeared without a trace, and there was no evidence of difficulty on board.

3. John Milton, *Paradise Lost*, in *The Complete Poems and Major Prose*, 1.303–304.

until your winters grow more kind
by the dancing firelight of mind (174)

Just as mirrors and water give back another picture of the world in which we live, mental reflections on reality acclimatize the individual as perceptions are molded into meaningful order. The subject is as basic as the rhythm of these couplets and it underscores the central theme of *Omeros*.

As a matter of fact, the implications of this sequence of couplets is a miniature of the overlapping actions affecting the narrator and all the protagonists. In order to convert a house, a colony, or a nation into a home, the individual must confront inner as well as external sources of alienation. Philoctete's festering racial wound prevents his integration into the life of his community. Achille journeys to Africa in search of his original name. Helen, suspended between two men (not counting Dennis Plunkett), is uncertain whether Achille or Hector is father of her expected child. Heirless Major Plunkett, fearing that he and the neglected island he has adopted will fade into oblivion along with the disappearing British empire, is determined that he and St. Lucia are to share a common historical legacy. The narrator, suffering through divorce in the racist climate of Boston, is forced to seek new means of regeneration.

Immediately following these intensely autobiographical verses, Walcott unexpectedly makes his most radical narrative shift within the entire poem. Even though his own change of residence to the United States in the late 1970s makes the geographic move to Boston explicable, and he has casually planted the idea of buffalo soldiers and Sioux Ghost Dancers through Achille and Seven Seas in chapter thirty-one, his dramatic leap in chapter thirty-four to the American Dakotas is exceptionally abrupt. Suddenly we are presented with a Crow horseman observing the narrator's plane flying high over Colorado. What follows is a reprise of the aerial views offered through plexiglass as recently as five pages earlier in *Omeros* (168) and farther back in the title poem of *The Gulf* and "Over Colorado" from *Sea Grapes*.[4] Indians appear in the latter of these earlier poems, but both ironically juxtapose the "American Dream" with its concomitant history of genocide, slavery, and violence.

4. Walcott, *The Gulf*, 58–62; Walcott, *Sea Grapes*, 56.

Walcott's flight this time over the American landscape takes on the added dimension of self-reflexive intertextuality because he makes a point that his invented Crow horseman becomes an image on his page. With that conscious notation he also begins a catalog of events that lay the groundwork for a major portion of book four.

> Clouds whitened the Crow horseman and I let him pass
> into the page, and I saw the white waggons move
>
> across it, with printed ruts, then the railroad track
> and the arrowing interstate, as a lost love
> narrowed from epic to epigram. Our contracts
> were torn like the clouds, like treaties with the Indians
> but with mutual treachery. Through the window,
> the breakers burst like the spray on Pacific pines,
>
> and Manifest Destiny was behind me now.
> My face frozen in the ice-cream paradiso
> of the American dream, like the Sioux in the snow. (175)

Within these lines, which do double duty as ruts on his page, Walcott combines the theme of personal and political treachery in the image of torn contracts burying unfulfilled promises.

In keeping with the broad conceits, wide-ranging parallels, and word play characteristic of the rest of *Omeros,* this simile is hardly remarkable; however, a number of critics have seriously questioned the thematic and aesthetic value of broaching the plight of native Americans in a West Indian epic. Nevertheless, aside from the audacity of undertaking a modern verse epic in the first place, this is probably the most precarious experiment in the poem's overall narrative structure. When Christopher Benfey considers *Omeros* to be a "sort of fantasy on Homeric themes," he succumbs to the temptation Walcott anticipated from the beginning. With his attention distracted by classical models of structural cohesiveness, it is understandable that Benfey should find some of Walcott's "imaginative journeys" to be "misguided—for example, the bathetic trips to the American West and South." Brad Leithauser regards the Great Plains section as "not only narratively peripheral but thematically superfluous." Sean O'Brien wonders whether the excursions to Ireland and parts of the American West are "fully meshed with the poem as a whole"; David Mason goes so far as to call them "a narrative red herring."[5]

In *Derek Walcott's Poetry: American Mimicry* (the first book-length study of Walcott since his receipt of the Nobel prize), Rei Terada evades the question of the appropriateness of the Amerindian element of *Omeros* by simply using the terms "America" and "New World" generically to apply to the entire Western hemisphere. While this ploy is defensible on the grounds that she is following Walcott's own sweeping definition and that she is making a special case for the species of New World mimeses that represents the "nonoriginality" of the reality it imitates, it is outside the purview of her analysis to justify the introduction of the Crow and Sioux tribes into Walcott's epic.[6] It is worth noting that neither of these terms warrants mention in Terada's index.

In contrast with these negative opinions, expressed or implied, Patricia Ismond believes that the American section of *Omeros* "engages the fullest and most searching response." Indeed, Ismond contends that Walcott's development of the "native Indian past . . . in the mid-Western landscape of the Dakota Plains," rather than the New England Pilgrims, "makes a truly revolutionary gesture in inviting America to relocate the heartland in these beginnings." In support of her argument, Ismond could have noted that as early as "A Village Life" (from *The Castaway*), Walcott expresses a healthy preference for the American heartland as opposed to the hectic pace of New York City. Describing himself,

> I was a frightened cat in that grey city. . . .
> . . . .
> of walking, running the rat race,
> locked in a system, ridden by its rail,
> within a life where no one dares to fail . . .

he has reason to look elsewhere for the country's essence and goes on to express a yearning for "Montana, Minnesota, your real / America, lost in tall grass, serene Idyll." From *The Castaway*'s "Lines in New England," we

---

5. Christopher Benfey, "Coming Home," 38; Leithauser, "Ancestral Rhyme," 92; Sean O'Brien, "In Terms of the Ocean," 977; David Mason, review of *Omeros*, 514.
6. Rei Terada, *Derek Walcott's Poetry: American Mimicry*, 226, 1.

also discover that Walcott is apprehensive about living in New England. A tropical outsider in this winter-bound northern city, Walcott contemplates his status in the place where immigrant pioneers annihilated the original inhabitants, and bequeathed the irony of "separate but equal." He asks himself

> Why am I so far north,
> who dread these stripped trees' polar
> iron, and fear fall,
> cinders and brimstone of
> the pilgrim's prophesy? . . .
> . . . .
> where I imagine a crazed, single, deer-
> skinned quarry drinking, the last
> Mohican. Redcoat, redman, their thirst-
> ing, autumn battle-ground,
> its savage lacerations healed
> by salt white spire and green field.[7]

Nevertheless, a conscientious critic may accept the fact that Walcott uses the term "American" in its broadest sense, may appreciate his boldness in focusing on abused and neglected native American tribes without conceding that the material carries its own weight in *Omeros.*

The argument I wish to advance is that while Walcott's insertion of Sitting Bull, the Sioux Ghost Dance, and Catherine Weldon into his epic requires more explanation than the earlier African excursion, it has thematic purpose. In its function as an epic of the dispossessed, *Omeros* encompasses precisely those individuals who are traditionally peripheral in standard classics. By design, the heroic formula concentrates on the prowess of demigods and warriors who tower above common men, touching only occasionally on representatives of the larger community. The hospitable swineherd who assists Odysseus in regaining his throne may live in reduced circumstances, yet Eumaios boasts the lineage of a king. Rather than turn his back on the heroic ideal, Walcott resorts to a more democratic level of human endeavor. The aboriginals of Africa, North America, and the West

---

7. Patricia Ismond, "Walcott's *Omeros*—a Complex, Ambitious Work," 10; Derek Walcott, "A Village Life," in *The Castaway,* 16–17; Walcott, "Lines in New England," in *The Castaway,* 48–49.

Indies—Aruac, Ashanti, Carib, Crow, Ibo, Mandingo, and Sioux alike—
are among the first, most obvious victims of post-Columbian imperialism.
To do justice to that broader story, it is necessary that Walcott illustrate
historical as well as contemporary vestiges of dispossession on the fringes of
waning empire. As an exceptionally talented, biracial repository of several
cultures that converge in the New World, he sets himself the task of pulling
together the disparate threads of a unique narrative that obtains mythic
proportions.

Such inclusiveness obviously threatens the integrity of the central nar-
rative. As many critics have already complained, Walcott's attempts to
incorporate the disparate stories of North American natives and then
Europeans are the least defensible aspects of the poem. The American
segment has at least both the common historical thread of imperial genocide
and the author's personal associations with Boston. When Walcott crosses
the Atlantic to take up the European sources of imperialism, his experiment
becomes much less supportable.

The linkage between the Dakota Sioux and Walcott's autobiographical
evolution depends heavily on imaginative parallels. Thus, through the
abruptness with which book four juxtaposes personal divorce and the
failure of the American Dream, Walcott exposes himself to charges of self-
aggrandizement. Obviously the breakup of marriage, tragic as it may be
to an individual, falls short of the effects of tribal genocide. Nevertheless,
Omeros pursues a multifaceted narrative that alternates between intimate
portrait and social consciousness. In the aftermath of divorce, Walcott's
persona strives to express his desolation metaphorically. Indulging in self-
pity, the poet/narrator considers both Achille's despair after the loss of
Helen and the devastation of the Sioux when the last Union Pacific spike
was driven into the heart of their land, linking the white man's East and
West Coasts.

Through his authorial persona, Walcott confesses toward the end of the
thirty-fifth chapter that he determined to mitigate his own marital troubles
by focusing on someone else's pain.

> so Catherine Weldon rose in high relief
>
> through the thin page of a cloud, making a fiction
> of my own loss. I was searching for characters,
> and in her shawled voice I heard the snow that would be blown

when the wind covered the tracks of the Dakotas,
the Sioux, and the Crows; my sorrow had been replaced.
Like a swift over water, her pen's shadow raced. (181)

In these lines, Walcott strikes a note of candor in explaining his motivation
for selecting an actual woman as a model for this character, but Weldon,
an attractive, financially independent widow from Brooklyn, New York,
who became secretary to Chief Sitting Bull in 1889, is as much a literary
embodiment of symbolic values as Helen is for St. Lucia. Although Walcott
has Weldon assert that she has admired Indians since she first worked
with them as a hired hand in Colonel Bill Cody's western show, there is
no verification for such a connection in biographical materials relating
to Mrs. Weldon.[8] It may be that Walcott extrapolates from Sitting Bull's
two actual tours with Colonel Cody's troupe (1884, 1885) to provide a
colorful explanation for the origin of Weldon's devotion to the Indian
cause.

At Weldon's first appearance on the Parkin's farm in the Dakotas in
chapter thirty-four, she has already lost her son Christie to lockjaw, she is
disillusioned over the government's genocidal Indian policy, and because
of her friendship with Sitting Bull, she is ostracized by her own race.
Walcott presents her in medias res, then with a flashback gives us essential
background details. Antecedent to the present scene is the infamous "Trail
of Tears" leading westward from Georgia (177). No more likely than Major
Plunkett to allow coincidence to escape notice, Walcott seizes upon key
parallels—Greek revival architecture gracing mansions in the Deep South;
cities named Athens, Sparta, and Troy; descendants of slaves who had been
called Hector or Achille living in rustic shacks; Afolabes lynched under
silk-cotton trees—to invoke vestiges of his native colonial background.
The Southern states and the West Indies share the historical institution of
slavery, and Walcott reminds us that the same kind of brutality would have
condemned Seven Seas to the "Trail of Tears."

---

8. Walcott associates Weldon with William "Buffalo Bill" Cody (1846–1917) on
two separate occasions (179, 216). While Catherine Weldon is a relatively minor
historical figure, information about her presence among the Sioux and examples from
her correspondence are available: Dorothy Johnson, *Some Went West,* 129–36; Rex
Allen Smith, *Moon of Popping Trees,* 101–10; and Stanley Vestal, *New Sources of Indian
History,* 92–115. The fullest treatment of Walcott's characterization of Weldon is in
Bensen, "Catherine Weldon in *Omeros* and the 'Ghost Dance.'"

From Georgia to Oklahoma and then the Dakotas is another visionary odyssey for Walcott's poetic imagination. It is even simpler for him to elide Weldon's Brooklyn, New York, and his Brookline, Massachusetts, as well when he adopts her persona: the names of these two eastern cities are virtually duplicate in spelling and pronunciation. In linking her fate with his own, he literally substitutes his Brookline residence for her actual home in New York, and introduces altered versions of her authentic letters into his terza rima stanzas. When he writes the line, "Like a swift over water, her pen's shadow raced," he can inscribe his page with her sentiments because he literally "shadows" her by emulating her act of putting feelings on paper. The loss of her child and his wife, the abrogation of contracts whether pertaining to Indian treaties or to marriage and the sense of living in a hostile environment, all coalesce in their combined story.

Certainly, Walcott is interested in the plight of the Plains Indians in the Dakotas section of *Omeros,* just as he has focused on Africans in the Caribbean; but his choice of Catherine Weldon as a narrative center ensures a second, broader emphasis. Weldon embodies the same feminine presence as Helen in the St. Lucia setting, but her complexion raises the same obstacle that confronts British Major Plunkett. Because Weldon, like the Major, is now without an heir since the death of her only son, she too must look beyond bloodlines for posterity. Both of these representatives of white imperialism reject the trappings of hegemony in favor of people who are traditionally victimized as racially inferior. The price of their decision becomes another form of dispossession. They may not be forcibly detained or transported to alien soil, but their allegiances leave them suspended between the people to whom they have dedicated their lives and their blood ties. As residents of the New World along with the descendants of Indians and slaves, they too engage in "Adam's task of giving things their names."[9] Rather than slip into didacticism and make this point explicitly, Walcott allows character and action to reveal meaning.

Perhaps as a result of his own dual racial heritage, Walcott concerns himself with internal as well as external aspects of dispossession. He shows Catherine Weldon contemplating the evaporation of her trust while treaties as changeable as clouds are inked on paper and then abrogated. Whether in the Dakotas or Versailles, "History" records the broken trust as wars

9. Walcott, *Another Life,* 152.

are settled only to be renegotiated over and over again at conference tables (180). Building on his paper/cloud imagery, Walcott incorporates the threads of narrative into his authorial voice.

> The clouds turned blank pages, the book I was reading[10]
> was like Plunkett charting the Battle of the Saints.
> The New World was wide enough for a new Eden
>
> of various Adams. A smell of innocence
> like that of the first heavy snow came off the page
> as I inhaled the spine. She walked past the lanterns
>
> where some bark canoes were moored to the landing stage,
> then paused to look at the waltzers in their ghost dance,
> then stood at the window clapping transparent hands. (181)

Since the Old World's dream of a New World Eden has failed so often, it is understandable that the downtrodden should become susceptible to chimerical promises. One of these, African Zionism, Walcott examines in *Dream on Monkey Mountain.* Another arises among the Sioux in the form of the Ghost Dance.

The purpose of this mystical ceremony (which fascinates Walcott so much that he not only conceived "The Ghost Dance" in 1989 but also worked it into *Omeros* a year later) is to conjure up the reincarnation of all the buffalo and Indian ancestors who have been wiped out by rapacious white men. The Paiute holy man Wovoka arose to prophesy that faithful warriors could become invisible by wearing magically sewn clothing and that the Ghost Dance would eliminate their white nemesis. This is the uneasy state of affairs prompting Weldon's "final letter to the Indian agent" (who would be Major James McLaughlin in 1890). She has been ostracized and maligned by her frightened white neighbors, and in protesting Wovoka's incendiary teachings she also has been estranged from her beloved Indians.[11] Walcott's transcription of her thoughts into terza

---

10. On October 11, 1993, Walcott informed me that he was reading Rex Allen Smith's *Moon of Popping Trees* as part of his research for "The Ghost Dance," which had been commissioned by Hartwick College in Oneonta, New York (premier November 9, 1989).

11. Examples of malicious rumors that were being printed in contemporary newspapers may be seen in Smith, *Moon of Popping Trees,* 101; and Vestal, *New Sources of Indian History,* 96–98. Both articles cited mistakenly call her C. Wilder, and the Bismarck paper gives New Jersey as her home.

rima stresses the common ground of human doubt and faith, instead of the differences standing between the Sioux and the army's "wheat-headed soldiers." Arguing that "[d]oubt isn't the privilege of one complexion," Weldon presses the similarities between the Indian and the Christian versions of paradise (182). If the resurrection preached within the church applies to Indians as well as Europeans, then we share a common desire for an Edenic home. On that note of faith, Walcott leaves her momentarily as he had introduced her, by referring to her shadow, illuminated this time against the translucent wall of an army tent.

After briefly sharing his sense of alienation vicariously with Catherine Weldon, a somewhat restored Walcott returns in chapter thirty-six to his adopted environs of Boston. Putting aside his marital woes for the time being, his concerns now incline toward the social and aesthetic. He is reminded as he wanders through a museum that the imprimatur of "Art" with its capitalized authority has the same stifling effect as official "History." To escape "its whiff of formaldehyde" and to reclaim the living breath of reality, he steps outside (182–83). In the open air, he contrasts "the Bayeux of ivy," and "calligraphy / of swallows" with the reverential hush of the museum, where visitors behave as though they have entered an imposing bank or a hospital's terminal ward. It would certainly be disingenuous for Walcott the poet/painter to denigrate artistic expression itself, especially since he is fully conscious of the extent to which art shapes his own perception. Nevertheless, he seizes this opportunity to liberate the revered "Art" object from its sanctified medium (be it marble or canvas) and reassert its roots in vital experience.

Walcott brings the work of art and reality together, in keeping with his practice throughout *Omeros*—reflexively—by juxtaposing two complementary observations. First (echoing once again Malraux's anecdote from *Psychology of Art* which prefaces *Another Life*), Walcott reiterates the power of art collections to teach us how to see the mundane world, "till every view is a postcard signed by great names: / that sky Canaletto's, that empty bench Van Gogh's" (183).[12] Then after he summons up the courage to walk back into the oppressive museum, he encounters a painting that sharply reverses the equation. The shock of recognition is so great when

---

12. As an epigraph for *Another Life,* Walcott quotes Malraux's *Psychology of Art:* "it is never the sheep that inspire a Giotto with the love of painting: but, rather, his first sight of the paintings of such a man as Cimabue," *Another Life,* 1.

Gulf Stream. Oil painting by Winslow Homer. (Courtesy of the Metropolitan Museum of Art.)

he happens upon the Negro sailor depicted in Winslow Homer's *The Gulf Stream* that he exclaims, "Achille! My main man, my nigger!" (183). What gives the moment its power is his awakening to the subject of his own experience in Homer's work. He is not finding something in nature to be aesthetically pleasing because it has been captured by art; quite the opposite, he is discovering the artistic potential in his most familiar reality.

Walcott's fleeting description of *The Gulf Stream*'s lone derelict stranded aboard a dismasted boat "between our island / and the coast of Guinea" merely hints at this painting's relevance to the immediate narrative (183–84). There is not only the correspondence between the Greek and American names—Omeros and Winslow Homer—but also this painter who was born in Walcott's adopted city of Boston shares his love of seascapes and humble subject matter. When Winslow Homer depicts military themes, he concentrates on the human side of camp life rather than the heroism of pageantry and battle—*In Front of the Guard House* (1863), *Home Sweet Home* (1863), *The Briarwood Pipe* (1864). His paintings of former slaves in the 1870s reflect appreciation for the dignity of these ambivalent, marginalized men and women—*The Cotton Pickers* (1876), *A Visit from the Old Mistress* (1876), and *Dressing for the Carnival* (1877). Many of his coastlines and seascapes other than *The Gulf Stream* (1899) are just as expressive of the majesty and danger confronting Walcott's humble fishermen. The fact that the Gulf Stream itself forms in the western Caribbean, flows northward through the Straits of Florida up the eastern seaboard of the United States, and joins other Atlantic currents is highly relevant to *Omeros*, since it links the vital points of Walcott's epic compass: the Americas, Europe, and Africa. Coincidence abets fortuity when he considers that in *The Gulf Stream*, "another Homer's hand" has depicted an individual like himself who is adrift in a hostile environment. A waterspout threatens from starboard; sharks hungrily roil foreground waters between the viewer and the damaged craft; and rescue from the trimaster on the distant horizon seems beyond reach. The derelict sailor Walcott has named Achille looks stoically away from danger and potential succor alike. Perhaps taking his cue from this black seaman's resolution, Walcott scornfully dismisses any futile hope of mercy from white sails or the implacable sea. In fact, the very whiteness of the sail triggers a sarcastic response to Melville's *Moby Dick*.

> Heah's Cap'n Melville on de whiteness ob de whale—
> *"Having for the imperial colour the same imperial hue . . .*
>
> *giving the white man ideal mastership over every dusky tribe."*
> Lawd, Lawd, Massa Melville, what could a nigger do
> but go down dem steps in de dusk you done describe? (184)

If God could inform Achille in patois that it was he who sent the swift to guide him to Africa, then Walcott's expressive narrator should certainly be allowed this vent to his frustration.

When the narrator walks out of the museum nursing his anger, Walcott's taste for satire dictates that his attention be drawn to further edifices and monuments dedicated to Boston's storied past. He notices in particular Saint-Gaudens's *Shaw Memorial* on Beacon Hill, the frieze commemorating Colonel Shaw with his black troops from the Civil War. Thus the scene that begins with "Museums endure; but sic transit gloria" (182) descends to "Sic transit taxi" (184) due to the poet's inability to hail a taxi as darkness gathers. The ironic humor is that after more than a hundred years and thousands of lost lives a black man in this city continues to endure discrimination. As a matter of fact, he concludes on the basis of his own experience of living for years in Boston that the city is extraordinarily prejudiced.[13]

---

13. White, "An Interview with Derek Walcott," 28.

Alluding to Melville once more, he feels as though he is going through
Queequeg's harpooning motion, heaving a futile call after Ahab's departing
cab (184). The wall of complexion separating him from the white majority is
reinforced when he catches a woman's startled expression as he approaches
a lighted bus stop.

Book four closes with a stroll along the beach at Marblehead that again
evokes Winslow Homer's deft brush. The autumn wind chills Walcott so
that tears blur his vision. At that moment, the spirit of his young father
appears before him, dressed in white drill, impervious to the weather.
Alluding once again to the expanding distance between their respective ages,
Walcott protests that he has grown too old to be meeting outside. Warwick
jokes ambiguously about seeking a warmer destination, but quickly insists
he has nothing more infernal in mind than an Edenic island. As with
Warwick's first appearance, he has returned to guide his son's further
poetic development. Drawing from his own truncated career, he confirms
the necessity of returning to St. Lucia; but first he directs Walcott to visit
some of the great cities of the world that are codified in *The World's Great
Classics*. Never having realized his dream of casting his shadow on streets
immortalized by "History," Warwick confesses that he had experienced
self-contempt, felt diminished; nevertheless, he realized great pleasure in
creating works for his wife and their circle of friends. In their constricted
world, he had enjoyed God's perspective, feeling "like the 'I' that looks down
on an island, / the way that a crested palm looks down from its ridge" (187).

Warwick's reincarnation at the conclusion of book four is structurally
critical for at least three reasons. First, he interrupts the bout of depression
that Walcott suffers as a result both of ongoing racial ostracism and
his recent divorce. Second, the nature of the message he delivers to his
son explicitly validates northern American and European locations in the
narrative. Additionally, since Walcott has now moved away from the island,
Warwick comes back to reaffirm St. Lucia's centrality in the poem both
psychologically and aesthetically. Warwick spells out their mutual priorities:

> "Once you have seen everything and gone everywhere,
> cherish our island for its green simplicities,
> enthrone yourself, if your sheet is a barber-chair,
>
> a sail leaving harbour and a sail coming in,
> the shadows of grape-leaves on sunlit verandahs
> made me content. The sea-swift vanishes in rain,

and yet in its travelling all that the sea-swift does
it does in a circular pattern. Remember that, son." (187–88)

Clearly, the sea-swift has been one of the dominant motifs in the poem. Its natural flight pattern now becomes symbolic of the recirculating imagery of narratives that revolve around the island.

These are the kinds of "simplicities" Walcott cites as being worth preservation as opposed to the grand scale of traditional epics; yet, he is really tapping sources close to the foundations of life. In *Milton's Epic Voice*, Anne Ferry enumerates the fundamental imagery of Adam and Eve's morning hymn in praise of creation's "Perpetual Circle." She argues that no man-made rhetorical devices can equal the unifying power of nature's rhythms. "The 'Rising or Falling' of waters, the ascent of birds imitate the cyclical order of the world. The principle of hierarchy, the scale of nature, becomes one with the principle of unity. Both are expressed in the figure of the circle, no rhetorical image invented by man for the purposes of his poetry, but a description of the actual arrangement of creation." Given the scope of Walcott's segmented narrative as it encompasses hundreds of years and crisscrosses the Atlantic and various national boundaries, it is evident that he does not depend on linear discourse to hold *Omeros* together. As a native of a small island surrounded by the immensity of the sea, he has no faith in the rigidly logical dictates of historians. He describes to J. P. White his perspective as an islander,

> [T]he strength of the sea gives you an idea of time that makes history absurd. . . . History is a very, very minor statement; it's not even an intrusion, it is an insignificant speck on the rim of that horizon. And by history I mean a direction that is progressive and linear. With the sea, you can travel the horizon in any direction, you can go from left to right or from right to left. It doesn't proceed from A to B to C to D and so on. It is not a rational line. It's a circle, and that's what you feel.[14]

Reacting against the inhibitions of linear interpretation, he offers an open pattern of variations on underlying themes (such as the relationships

---

14. Anne Davidson Ferry, *Milton's Epic Voice*, 158. Milton's "Perpetual Circle" occurs in *Paradise Lost*, 5.182; White, "An Interview with Derek Walcott," 21.

between fathers and sons) and interconnected imagery (such as birds and nets) so that meanings build incrementally without intermediate closure.

The circle that he describes to White is echoed in *Omeros* by all the enclosures he celebrates—the "O" of Omeros, the cave, the vase, a woman's throat, the eye, the conch shell, the swift's circular flight, the island surrounded by ocean. The essence of the Walcott circle, however, what makes it exceptional, is its macrocosmic permeability, not its exclusion of otherness. The same ocean that isolates his St. Lucian home also serves as the watery crossroad for all the extraneous cultures that have influenced his life. Gaston Bachelard's succinct description of the way an individual grounds his *weltanschauung* fits Walcott's autobiographical treatment of St. Lucia perfectly: "[e]very universe is enclosed in curves, every universe is concentrated in a nucleus, a spore, a dynamized center. And this center is powerful, because it is an imagined center. . . . This nucleizing nucleus is a world in itself. The miniature deploys to the dimensions of a universe."[15] Walcott's is an expansive universe, but no matter how far he stretches its parameters, it centers in his controlling imagination. While St. Lucia remains the anchor, his consciousness of the island's colonial history never allows him to forget racial and cultural origins across the sea.

Following the second encounter with the ghost of his father, it remains for Walcott to pursue the trajectory of his odyssey across the Atlantic once more, this time to the birthplace of his Anglo-Saxon grandsires. To the extent that the New World reaps the legacy of Old World dreams and nightmares, this second transmeridian crossing necessarily complements the polarized orientation of *Omeros*. Preparation for this European terminus of Walcott's Middle Passage begins when immigrants Maud and Dennis Plunkett are first introduced; it is implied in the current of Winslow Homer's Gulf Stream; and it receives the impetus of Warwick Walcott's charge in the fourth book's closing scene.

---

15. Gaston Bachelard, *The Poetics of Space*, 157.

6 The Middle Passage— Europe

To signify his personal dividedness as well as geographic and temporal demarcations between the New and Old Worlds, Walcott opens the fifth book of *Omeros* by saying "I crossed *my* meridian" (189, italics added). I am indebted to Rei Terada's cogent discussion of Walcott's varied use of the meridian's ineffable nature, "for the meridian is as amorphous as it is definite." Her observations are in keeping with Walcott's own comments on the nature of colonial schizophrenia and the mutability of a person's horizons. In his interview with J. P. White, Walcott defines a permanent affliction of the colonial mentality that he calls schizophrenia: "a shadow, a kind of meridian, a crossing that has to be examined." The memory of slavery, for example, "can always be a shadow ahead of us if we continue to think of the past as something like a light behind us by which we move. What happens in the Third World in the colonial imagination is acceptance of the idea of history as a moral force." Years earlier in "The Muse of History," Walcott asserts that the "truly tough aesthetic of the New World neither explains nor forgives history. It refuses to recognize [history] as a creative or culpable force." In his more recent conversation with White, he refers to the example of the sea as an alternative to history's lineal rationalism: "with the sea you can travel the horizon in any direction."[1] A key advantage to this outlook is that the visually finite horizon (meridian) is relative to the individual's position; therefore, it changes with the viewer as he or she moves in any direction.

1. Terada, *Derek Walcott's Poetry*, 39; White, "An Interview with Derek Walcott," 18–19, 21; Derek Walcott, "The Muse of History: An Essay," 2.

Having already transcended longitudinal axes to encompass his African forebears and latitudinal axes to engage the influence of North America, he reverses time and space once again by recrossing the meridians separating the Americas from their European ancestry.

In keeping with those critics who question the inclusion of Euro-American scenes in what is ostensibly a West Indian epic, I must agree that these scenes disrupt the general texture of the narrative. Moving farther and father away from his initial circle of characters to establish residence in Boston, Walcott undertakes a highly personal journey to the Old World—devoting single chapters to Portugal, England, Ireland, and the Mediterranean in succession. Perhaps the most that can be said is that each of these places represents a significant facet in his colonial background. As important as the autobiographical aspect of *Omeros* may be, book five may simply reflect Walcott's lifelong fascination with European culture. Europe's position as one of the hubs of the triangular trade route linking Africa with the Americas hardly mitigates the fact that this side trip is not thoroughly integrated into the poem. It helps only marginally to observe that in the famous cities Walcott visits, dispossession remains an essential thematic concern. The decline of power in such places as Lisbon, London, and Dublin is part of the imperial equation; but their present difficulties are hardly equivalent to the history of racist domination over former colonial possessions.

For his own reasons, Walcott chooses to pursue the origins of colonial power back to their source in metropolitan countries. Portents of his intentions in this regard may be found early in *Omeros* itself. Incorporation of expatriate settlers Dennis and Maud Plunkett from the outset was less a dissolution of focus than an authentic distribution of vision. Derek Walcott's personal identity as a citizen of the Americas derives from a bifurcated heritage. As early as "A Far Cry from Africa" he wonders,

> Where shall I turn, divided to the vein?
> I who have cursed
> The drunken officer of British rule, how choose
> Between this Africa and the English tongue I love?[2]

Nationalists and racial purists may spurn adulterated blood and culture, but Walcott celebrates his creole legacy. To a large extent his career revolves

---

2. Walcott, *In a Green Night,* 18.

around a core of assimilative consciousness. In *Omeros,* the result is a centripetal force pulling disparate elements into Walcott's St. Lucian center. It admits the Plunketts among native islanders and evokes not only Achille's entranced return to Africa but ultimately the poet/narrator's solitary journeys to North America and Europe. Tangential as these latter foreign excursions may be to the essential St. Lucian material, they augment the context within which Walcott perceives his birthplace.

When he takes us to Europe in book five, Walcott's decision to visit Lisbon first seems at least historically appropriate. In the early 1400s, Portugal was the first European nation to use its incursions along the Western coast of Africa to exploit the trade in black slaves. In 1493, the conflicting demands of Portugal and Spain led Pope Alexander VI to draw an invisible line (meridian) authorizing hegemonic domination: Portugal over Africa and Spain over the New World. Given Walcott's interest in names, the Portuguese capital of "Ulissibona" has the added attraction of a popular, if unlikely, etymology that depends on the city's apocryphal founding by Ulysses. Traversing meridia backward reverses time the way an hourglass is inverted; the crossed pattern of rising swifts repeats the hourglass's X; horizon succeeds horizon with the rotation of the earth, and the church clock spins back to an earlier age. A cobblestone lane crawls from the shore toward the ancient buildings with the patience of a tortoise. As the narrator reads the clouds backward, bells are muffled in their towers. The surreality of Lisbon's wharf on the opposite side of Walcott's familiar ocean is personified as Sunday, dressed similar to the ghost of his father, in an ice-cream suit. Correspondences suddenly reproduce Lisbon in far-off Port of Spain, and when Sunday rewinds his watch the static scene bursts to life. Here mulatto clerks and black stevedores and drivers curse and work among the din until overlapping centuries recede into earlier sugar and slave markets.

The collage of scenes reflecting each other underscores the similarities between opposite hemispheres. It also resurrects a perennial theme running through a number of Walcott's individual poems over three decades: "Ruins of·a Great House" (*In a Green Night,* 1962), "The Bright Field" (*Sea Grapes,* 1976), and sections of *Midsummer* (1984). Pope Alexander's decree politically divided the globe, but swifts on either side fly and sound the same; the sand on opposite coastlines is perfectly interchangeable; trade goods pass through wharves at both ends of their journeys. After he has made his Atlantic crossing in *Omeros,* Walcott recalls what is left behind, but he is struck by the familiarity of this "antipodal wharf."

> My shadow had preceded me. How else could it recognize
> that light to which it was attached, this port where Europe
> rose with its terrors and terraces, slope after slope? (191)

Racial memory similar to that which flooded over Achille in Afolabe's African settlement seems to inform the shadow image in this scene. Walcott is quick to distinguish his shadow from those of religious pilgrims who might have come to this port to venerate columned majesty. When he complains that his "throat was scarred / from a horizon that linked me to others," he means the leveling chain of slavery. The humble predecessors with whom he shares a colonized horizon were herded from Lisbon's docks with "our eyes / lowered to the cobbles that climbed to the castle yard" (191). As ship hands or cargo themselves, they bore the physical and psychological marks of imperial trade.

Chapter thirty-seven builds on the contrasts between a hemisphere of monuments and one that has no heroic ruins. On the one hand, imperial plazas vaunt bronze equestrian conquerors gazing seaward and marble admirals bearing gifts of Indians or slaves. On the opposite shore,

> . . . Above us, no stallions paw
> the sky's pavement to strike stars from the stones,
> no sword is pointed to recapture the port of Genoa.
>
> There the past is an infinite Sunday. It's hot, or it rains;
> the sun lifts the sheets of the rain, and the gutters
> run out. For those to whom history is the presence
>
> of ruins, there is a green nothing. (192)

The ennui of tropical Sundays seems to militate against the belligerence that might turn the tables and "threaten the port of Genoa." That Genoa should offer a hypothetical target of acquisition may have been suggested by the fact that it is the birthplace of Christopher Columbus. As is indicated by the lower-case "history" in these lines, a land unable to boast respectable ruins is saddled with low expectations if not an inferiority complex. The result is that "We think of the past / as better forgotten than fixed with stony regret" (192). Ironically, however, in spite of the fact that a Pope once awarded half the world to Spain and half to Portugal, Lisbon's "past dryly grieves / from the O's of a Roman aqueduct" (192). Leaves of the olive trees, which Walcott seems to associate with southern Europe, are reversible as imperial fortunes, silver and green by turn as the wind stirs. The New World narrator sees the castle overlooking the contemporary harbor from the leafy mountainside as the city's tombstone. His personified Sunday afternoon passes vacant cafes, with their curtain-beads "hanging like rosaries" (193). We leave the scene to the doleful strain of fado mandolins.

Since England and France succeeded the Portugal-Spain rivalry for imperial dominance in the seventeenth century, the setting of chapter thirty-eight in London follows chronologically. England has particular significance for Walcott as well, because Admiral Rodney's victory in the Battle of the Saints eventually secured his French-Creole, Catholic island of St. Lucia for the British Empire and gave him his language. The opening scene presents us with an old black bargeman who emerges from the London Underground at Charring Cross. This ragged old seaman, who turns out to be Omeros himself, staggers off toward the National Gallery clutching the manuscript of his dog-eared *Odyssey* wrapped in brown paper. His erratic course takes him through queues of impatient people, past double-decker buses giving tourists chartered metropolitan views. It is tempting to read the "chartered" nature of the city's attractions in light of Blake's famous condemnatory "London" (1794), especially since Walcott capitalizes "Chartered Tour" four pages later in a highly derogatory passage damning vestiges of capitalist materialism (197). Omeros makes his way as far as St. Martin-in-the-Fields before collapsing on the steps. The incongruity of his unkempt presence among the imposing edifices of Trafalgar Square is first registered by the decorative gryphons snarling down from their sandstone perches. Their uncharitable attitude is reinforced when "suddenly, a raging sparrow / of a church-warden bobbed down the steps" to prod and kick the derelict on his way. When old Seven Seas points out the framed statement of "this Sunday's lesson / in charity," the warden is unfazed by the irony (194). He sees that the intruder is well on his way before reentering the sanctuary.

Although Walcott does not indicate whether the National Gallery is Seven Seas' actual destination or merely a point of reference, simply alluding to this institution reminds us of its treasury of cultural holdings. After a second bastion of tradition, the church, sends its minion of authority to drive Omeros away, Walcott uses nautical terminology to describe his course down to the nearby Thames Embankment: "The bargeman tacked towards his estuary / of light. It was summer. London rustled with pride" (195). Evidently, Seven Seas has eyesight at this point in life, because he is able to see the filth and grime coating all the statuary, the ginkgo leaves, spires, bridges, and

> he saw the tugs chirring up a devalued empire
>
> as the coins of their wake passed the Houses of Parliament.
> But the shadows keep multiplying from the Outer
> Provinces, their dialects light as the ginkgo's leaf, their
>
> fingers plucking their saris as wind picks at water,
> and the statues raising objections; he sees a wide river
> with its landing of pier-stakes flooding Westminster's
>
> flagstones, and traces the wake of dugouts in the frieze
> of a bank's running cornice, and whenever the ginkgo stirs
> the wash of far navies settles in the bargeman's eyes. (195–96)

The scene may be Walcott's, but the atmosphere echoes that of Conrad's opening for *The Heart of Darkness*. The same river Marlow calls "a waterway leading to the uttermost ends of the earth,"[3] Walcott ironically refers to as an "estuary of light." Both authors use chiaroscuro, drawing upon conventional associations of sunlight and shadow with good and evil, to comment on the imperial enterprise. Their narrators are equally concerned with the human toll of the rise and fall of colonial powers. Refuting the anachronistic adage that the "sun never sets on the British Empire," Walcott mentions that "the sunflower sets after all, retracting its irises" (196). And as fog closes in, he counts down from London to Rome to Greece, a catalog of faded glories. Seven Seas imagines the extended hand of a statue reflected upside down in the river to be responding to a question raised in Parliament. The lapping of the water and the rustling leaves serve as applause from the benches. Because of its great ships, and the legislation decided on its banks, the Thames was once the gleaming hub of international commerce and sovereign might.

    The closing section of the London chapter questions the faceless arbiters of power as to the source and extent of their authority. Recognizing that he cannot address responsible parties or historical events directly, Walcott puts his questions to specific emblems of fame and influence: what amounts to

---

3. Joseph Conrad, *Heart of Darkness*, 4.

a catalog of buildings and landmarks around London that have acquired
renown or notoriety. In the process of creating the list, he also wonders
who will draw attention to the equally deserving but neglected and unsung
people who have been marginalized within the imperial narrative. The
first question concerns the Prime Meridian running through the borough
of Greenwich. Since Greenwich anchors the invisible line that marks the
beginning point for global time and longitudinal orientation, Walcott asks
who decides the greatness of an epoch or the direction of hope. To prevent
his question from being purely rhetorical, he lists prominent landmarks
as potential sources of authority. He mentions "sinister Shoreditch," the
district where Edward IV's unfortunate mistress Jane Shore died in poverty
(1527); the area within hearing of Big Ben, near the houses of Parliament;
the Thames, where barges are "chained like our islands"; Westminster
Abbey, where graves of honored artists and statesmen lie commemorated in
stone; or St. Martin-in-the-Fields, noted for its elegant music. His disbelief
in any adequate material center is reflected in the inequality of these
suggestions.

Perhaps giving up on each of these alternatives, the voice becomes
palpably embittered at this point. The question now becomes, "Within
whose palatable vault / will echo the Saints' litany of our island people?"
He offers the possibility of "St. Paul's salt shaker," but only "when we are
worth their salt" (196). For a more realistic possibility he mentions the
"tilted crosses" of Maud Plunkett's Glen-da-Lough. Having raised the issue
of his people's worth, he thinks of the Corn Exchange, wondering what price
might be offered for his countrymen. "Who invests in their happiness?"
he asks. By way of answer he singles out the ubiquitous "Chartered Tour."
The double-decker buses show off the "Bloody Tower" of London, but he
queries, "Who will teach us a history of which we too are capable?" It
disturbs him that the swans plying the Serpentine lake in Hyde Park are
royally protected while no one seems responsible for "the black crusts of
our children." The tirade culminates in a passage beginning

> Where is the light of the world? In the National Gallery.
> In Palladian Wren. In the City that can buy and sell us
> the packets of tea stirred with our crystals of sweat.

and ending with reference to the underprivileged suburb of Brixton's—
"Dark future down darker street" (197). It should be noted that in Walcott's

departing glance at London are embedded three allusions. "The Light of
the World" repeats the title of the poem he considers seminal to *Omeros;*
the daring conflation of drying sweat and sugar crystals evokes an entire
history of slave economics; his reference to Brixton recalls also the scene
of alley riots he mentioned in that district of London from poem "XXIII"
of *Midsummer.* Thus the National Gallery with its horde of great works
and Christopher Wren's magnificent architecture are juxtaposed with the
progeny of dispossessed Calibans struggling for mere survival.

The Irish or Joyce chapter, chapter thirty-nine, grows out of the preceding
scene because it merely shifts from the treatment of one type of marginalized
people to another: from London's second-class citizens to a bifurcated
former colony whose people are still torn apart by internecine strife. Before
Ireland's independence in 1949, Dublin had been subject to English rule
from the time of the Normans. In addition to this political similarity to his
own background, Walcott has long felt a particular affinity for the Emerald
Isle. He expresses this feeling in his 1970 article entitled "Meanings":

> There is another strange thing for me about the island of Saint Lucia;
> its whole topography is weird—very conical, with volcanic mountains
> and such—giving rise to all sorts of superstitions. Rather like what
> Ireland was for Yeats and the early Irish poets—another insular culture.
>   . . . I think that is why a lot of my plays remain set in Saint Lucia,
> because there is a mystery there that is with me from childhood, that
> surrounds the whole feeling of the island.

If the colonial environment of the islands were not enough to encourage
Walcott's inclusion of Irish material, it should be remembered that for a
time during his secondary education, St. Mary's College in Castries was run
by the Irish Brothers of the Presentation. In "Leaving School," he fondly
remembers the classroom atmosphere and values he developed under their
tutelage:

> . . . admiration for Synge and Yeats, for Pearse, and even for Joyce,
> an atmosphere, fortified by those martial Irish tunes that the school
> choir was taught, . . . an atmosphere that summoned that of my
> current hero, the blasphemous, arrogant Stephen Daedalus. . . . a new
> cynicism for the Empire and a passion for . . . Fergus and Cuchulain
> and in the struggle and wrestling with my mind to find out who I was,
> I was discovering the art of bitterness. . . . Like Stephen, . . . I was a

knot of paradoxes: hating the Church and loving her rituals, learning
to hate England as I worshipped her language.

The Irish influence that led him to imitate Synge's *Riders to the Sea* in *The
Sea at Dauphin* (1954) and Joyce's *Portrait of the Artist* in "Epitaph for
the Young" (1949), that enters into the character of his Maud Plunkett,
culminates now in the thirty-ninth chapter of *Omeros*.[4]
     Just as personified Sunday exemplifies the ennui of Lisbon and Seven
Seas/Omeros represents the disenfranchised of London, James Joyce may be
said to embody the spirit of Walcott's Dublin. In addition to open allusions
to specific works and characters and Joycean verbal play, Walcott names
him "our age's Omeros, undimmed Master / and true tenor of the place"
(200). The opening landscape could well grace an emblematic postcard;
not only do gravestones front a decrepit abbey at the end of a monk's
footpath and a brook "talk the old language of Ireland," but also the very
nouns and adjectives double as religious icons: hymn, Celtic cross, wafer,
missal, encircling power, vertiginous Latin. The narrator looking on feels
"The weight of the place, its handle, its ancient name," Glen-da-Lough,
and attempts its translation—" 'wood with a lake,' or 'abbey with hooded
hills' " (198–99). No matter how picturesque, the place

> . . . echoed the old shame
> of disenfranchisement. I had no oasis,
>
> no pebbled language to drink from like a calm horse
> or pilgrim lapping up soul-watering places. (199)

The source of alienation is found once again in capitalized "History." It is a
nation that finds itself divided along internecine lines, ironically, by faith.
Streets are wreathed in barbed wire, hearses wait in the rain, and snipers
take their deadly toll.
     In his first obvious borrowing from *Finnegans Wake*, Walcott character-
izes the bloodletting as "splitting heirs, dividing a Shem from a Shaun, / an
Ireland no wiser as it got older" (199). The pun on hairs/heirs introduces two
figures from Joyce's novel who are so intertwined as to represent opposite

---

4. Walcott, "Meanings," 50; Walcott, "Leaving School," 12–13.
     Walcott's indebtedness to Synge and Joyce for *The Sea at Dauphin* and "Epitaph for
the Young" is documented in Robert Hamner, *Derek Walcott, Updated Edition,* 22, 38–39.

sides of the central character, their father, H.C.E. This aggregate protagonist, like his creator who suffered eye problems, also sports an eye patch on occasion. Among the myriad critics who have assayed the autobiographical traces in Joyce's works, John Gordon for one has commented on the similarities between the complementary aspects of H.C.E. that correspond with the personalities of James and his father, John Joyce. Gordon's argument, if I may simplify for my purposes here, finds that repeated Shaun/John/Kevin associations lean toward domestic traits of "the archetypal old man" and Shem's repeated associations with James/Jacob/Jerry suggest the usurper, the exile.[5] Needless to say, the schizophrenic person, especially including a father-son dichotomy, conforms perfectly with other familial pairings in *Omeros*. In fact, this splitting of Irish "heirs" conforms with a formidable catalog of divisiveness. Walcott, who from some of his earliest poetry sees himself as "divided to the vein," constructs *Omeros* on the foundation of his mixed heritage. He emphasizes the longitudinal and latitudinal axes that collectively immesh the whole world in a net but individually divide space and time—north from south, east from west, and old from new. The European and American hemispheres have been divided from each other by an ocean and a Pope; St. Lucia is divided by race and class just as Ireland is split along religious and class lines. It is not difficult to see the attraction of James Joyce and his protagonists, who exemplify the same internal and external alienation that characterizes the personae in *Omeros*.

Before moving into the city of Dublin proper, the narrator surveys the Wicklow countryside once more by the orange glow of the sunset. Aside from its descriptive function, the short, three-stanza passage contains two suspiciously tantalizing half-references. The color orange, for example, may be no more than the sunset hue; yet in light of Ireland's religious turmoil, it is too conveniently reminiscent of the British past. William of Orange succeeded to the throne as a result of the Protestant victory over Catholicism in the "Glorious Revolution" (1688); two years later, his Orangemen at the momentous Battle of the Boyne (1690) secured English sovereignty over Ireland. In contrast to the elaborate flight of fancy required to follow the connotations of an orange sunset, his description of the moon is a simple metaphor evocative of Ireland's ubiquitous ecclesiastical bearings: the moon

---

5. John Gordon, *Finnegans Wake: A Plot Summary*, 93–95; Walcott, *In a Green Night*, 18.

"in its wax-collar" mounts "the green pulpit of Sugar Loaf Mountain." Then there is possibly an ephemeral allusion to van Gogh in the first half of the line, "The wick of the cypress charred. Glen-da-Lough's tower" (200). If Walcott intended such an association, he certainly stretches a metaphysical conceit by drawing upon this artist's known mental turmoil and expressive painting style. Although the flaming cypress dominating the lower-left foreground of van Gogh's *The Starry Night* (1889) comes to mind, Walcott seems merely to be enriching the imagery of spiritual devastation that permeates his reading of Glen-da-Lough.

Tentative as the preceding tropes may be, when the narrator stands on the banks of Dublin's river Liffey in the closing segment of the thirty-ninth chapter, his invocation of James Joyce is unequivocal. Many of the allusions and parallels in this section along with less obvious references throughout the poem have been duly recognized by critics and reviewers. Rei Terada illuminates many of the Joycean influences, and Sidney Burris singles out *Ulysses* as "the most generous sponsor of *Omeros*."[6] While the literary traces are undeniable, I perceive Joyce to be more useful to Walcott in the same capacity as Homer, not so much as traditional literary fodder but as examples of men who draw inspiration from their immediate surroundings and record them assiduously. He shares with Joyce the ambiguous experience of colonialism, an interest in common people with ordinary pursuits, and a fascination with language. There is precedent also in Joyce's loose, stream-of-consciousness narrative line and introverted (Stephen Dedalus, Leopold Bloom), permutating (H.C.E., Anna Livia) characters for Walcott's shifting scenes and perspectives in *Omeros*.

When Walcott says, "I blest myself in his voice," the narrator acknowledges a debt to his "undimmed Master" and at the same time obliquely refers to the fact that some of his language is borrowed from Joyce's physical appearance and writings. For example, Walcott puns on the name of the protagonists of *Ulysses,* Leopold and Molly Bloom, when he imagines that Joyce "bloomed" before him. "Joycespeak" is stretched to the depths of equivocation when he calls Joyce "the Master / and true tenor of the place!"—that is, if Joyce's known tenor register is counted in his capacity as singer (voice) of Dublin; furthermore, "true tenor" may be taken to affirm the authenticity of the Dublin he recreates in his fictional characters and

6. Terada, *Derek Walcott's Poetry,* 186–87; Sidney Burris, "An Empire of Battles," 561.

events. Walcott not only imagines the novelist himself "with eye-patch and tilted hat, / rakish cane on one shoulder" but also Joyce's personification of the Liffey, Anna Livia Plurabelle, rushes by "in black cloche hat and coat." In *Finnegans Wake*, ALP serves Joyce as everywoman, "Anna was, Livia is, and Plurabelle's to be."[7] Walcott sees Anna Livia as the "Muse of our age's Omeros" (200) in the same way that Helen inspires his St. Lucian poetry.

Walcott displays an excellent example of what may be called Joycean poetic economy in two of his three-line stanzas near the end of this chapter.

> The Dead were singing in fringed shawls, the wick-low shade
> leapt high and rouged their cold cheeks with vermilion
> round the pub piano, the air Maud Plunkett played,
>
> rowing her with felt hammer-strokes from my island
> to one with bright doors and cobbles, and then Mr. Joyce
> led us all, as gently as Howth when it drizzles, (201)

In the opening line of this quotation, Walcott subtly juxtaposes the title of Joyce's famous short story, "The Dead" (without quotation marks), with a pun on Maud Plunkett's home county of Wicklow. There is equal concision in the use of music to reintroduce Maud Plunkett's name for the first time since book three and to assert what Walcott conceives to be a physical link between Ireland and his St. Lucia. A note of immediacy is inserted when he feigns uncertainty about the author of the piece Maud is playing. The line he once referred to as "some tripe / about 'Bendemeer's stream'" (56) is now quoted in full and tentatively attributed to Moore. "There's a bower of roses by Bendemeer's stream" (201) is actually taken from the second part of Thomas Moore's exotic romance, *Lalla Rookh* (1817).[8]

Readers of Joyce are likely to recognize the place-name "Howth" as the pleasant hillside in *Ulysses* where Leopold and Molly Bloom once exchanged a bite of masticated seedcake in the heat of youthful intercourse. Using aural imagery reminiscent of Joyce, Walcott converts the sound of the name into onomatopoeia as he has a dog barking "Howth! Howth!" This last location, within sight of Dublin Bay, leads to the Martello Tower and "one-eyed Ulysses / . . . watching the mail-packet / butting past the Head,

---

7. James Joyce, *Finnegans Wake*, 215.
8. Moore's words have been set to music: "Bendemeer's Stream," in *Folk Songs of Many Peoples*, edited by Florence Hudson, vol. 2, 112–13.

its wake glittering like keys" (201). The monocular observer is the author of *Ulysses,* of course, as well as an addition to the series of one-eyed figures in *Omeros* (camera, Cyclops, lighthouse, telescope, etc.); and the Martello is the coastal guard tower immortalized in *Ulysses,* where Stephen Dedalus shares bachelors' quarters with Buck Mulligan and Haines. In the closing scene as we look seaward, the glittering keys of the waves reflect backward on Maud's piano while the departing mail-packet draws us away from Ireland for the next phase of Walcott's odyssey.

Chapter forty emerges as a palimpsest initially because the packet departing Dublin becomes a snail nibbling "the Aegean coast, its wake a caterpillar's / accordion" (201). The Irish sea gives way, and time rolls back to the ancient columns, cracked plaster walls, and alabaster statues of the ancient Mediterranean. Aimlessly adrift beneath the blistering sun, Odysseus's restive crew watch their captain peel layers of sun-burned skin. His feigned detachment belies the fact that his heart "in its ribs, thuds like the galley-slaves' drum" (202). Then, as they speak to him, a second layer of Walcott's palimpsest materializes. Their captain and Helen are white, their destination is supposed to be Ithaca, and a "cloud-eyed singer" composes their story; but in this incarnation their gods are African and their language is Caribbean.

> Hunched on their oars, they smile, "This is we Calypso,
> Captain, who treat we like swine, you ain't seeing shore.
> Let this sun burn you black and blister your lips so
>
> it hurt them to give orders, fuck you and your war." (202–3)

Thus, Irish Sea gives way to Aegean and Aegean to Caribbean as successive ages have fought the elements and pursued their respective goals. Odysseus has his beckoning sea-swift just as Achille does, and an "ant" breeze caresses his brow as he steers homeward. The layering effect of this chapter continues as Walcott has Odysseus and a black crew longing for familiar landmarks.

> . . . They knew the drifting
> Caribbean currents from Andros to Castries
> might drag them to Margarita or Curaçao,
>
> that the nearer home, the deeper our fears increase,
> that no house might come to meet us on our own shore,
> and fishermen fear this as much as Ulysses

> until they see the single eye of the lighthouse
> winking at them. Then the strokes match heartbeat to oar,
> their blistered palms weeping for palms or olive trees. (204)

The overlay of repeated homecomings is carried through the subtle shift from Ithacan Odysseus to Roman Ulysses and on to the biological pun in the closing tercet. Mediterranean and Caribbean seamen long for the familiar landmark, the native vegetation, whether olive or palm, they have known since childhood.

The short catalog of West Indian place-names in the preceding lines reestablishes Walcott's primary orientation after his lengthy sojourn in the Old World. One consequence of the recapitulation of overlapping themes within chapter forty is that it serves very effectively as a pivotal turn or a transitional device for retracing Walcott's steps back to his beginning point of book four in the United States. He turns away from Istanbul and Venice with all their fabled attractions, admitting to himself that it is not their "statues but the bird in the statue's hair" that he prefers (204). Signaling his growing independence from the past, he catalogs some of the European masters whom he and his father had treasured. This time he registers his objection to the manner in which art is manipulated by the power elite.

> . . . What my father
>
> spiritedly spoke of was that other Europe
> of mausoleum museums, the barber's shelf
> of *The World's Great Classics,* with a vanity whose
>
> spires and the bells punctually pardoned itself
> in the absolution of fountains and statues, . . .
> . . . .
> Tell that to a slave from the outer regions
> of their fraying empires, what power lay in the work
> of forgiving fountains with naiads and lions. (205)

It is not the art itself to which Walcott objects in these lines, but a nation's penchant for exonerating itself, for elevating and propagating its culture through exclusionary power.

Walcott's own adherence to epic paraphernalia makes *Omeros* subject to this very same condemnation. Since he shares with Major Plunkett the goal of immortalizing Helen, they have both participated in the age-old tradition of imperialists everywhere to record their exploits in monolithic script. From the outset, they have sought to provide Helen with the recognition denied her by "History." Noble as the sentiment may be, unfortunately, the humanity of the woman is in danger of being absorbed by the artifice. It is not enough that Walcott acknowledges the fictional nature of his invented voices and occasionally draws attention to the fact that he is manipulating images and ink on pages. Here in this fortieth chapter he candidly tests the relationship between art and the world it signifies. In the process, he eventually interrogates the aesthetic assumptions and classical correspondences that permeate his text. He does not refute the preceding influences, but from this point to the end of the poem, he explores with heightened awareness the relationship between artistic aims and human experience.

Examples are not far to seek: the catalog proceeding from traditional representationalism to the eclectic expressionism of Marcel Duchamp. First is Spanish painter Velazquez, whose "creamy strokes" immortalize "the idiot dukes" on whom his patronage depends. In our century, from among concentration camp ovens beautiful strains of Schubert can be heard rising incongruously with the charnel smoke. Walcott wonders rhetorically, and somewhat ambiguously, whether Dada anticipated "the future of Celan and Max Jacob / as part of the cosmic midden" (205). Since Celan narrowly escaped the holocaust that claimed his Jewish parents, and Jacob died in Drancy concentration camp, Walcott leaves us to contemplate the Dadaistic "cosmic midden" on two levels: on the one hand is their surreal experience of Nazism, on the other is the irrational genius of their creative works. Paul Celan (Romanian Jewish poet Paul Antschel, 1920–1970) and Max Jacob (French Jewish poet-painter, 1876–1944) are both noted for their surreal fantasy and self-exploration. Citing the only specific artwork in this short list, Marcel Duchamp's *The Bride Stripped Bare by Her Bachelors, Even* (or the *Large Glass*), Walcott draws attention to the anti-art self-consciousness of his own work. The *Large Glass* carries special significance because Duchamp's symbolic representation of machines and sex on a transparent surface leaves the viewer with problems similar to those facing Walcott's reader.[9]

9. Extensive imaginative criticism is available on Duchamp to substantiate the metaphysical philosophy surrounding the *Large Glass* (1915–23). Richard Hamilton's highly readable "The Large Glass," in *Marcel Duchamp*, edited by Anne D'Harnoncourt

There is the subject matter itself, which is open to complex interpretation since both Duchamp and Walcott derive abstract figures from the real and imaginary life around them. In painting on glass, Duchamp employs a medium that makes it possible for the viewer to see through and between images on the glass to objects and persons who might chance to pass on the opposite side. By the same token, an opposed viewer simultaneously takes in his counterpart, and both viewers become elements within the field of vision. From a certain angle, the surface of the glass reflects other images that add to the observable material. Walcott has similarly inserted himself as an observer in *Omeros*. Frequently, the reader is placed in the position of having to sort out the figurative representations of the author's persona and his permutations within characters throughout his text. Duchamp and Walcott appreciate randomness and the "fortunate flaw" that can intervene in the process of artistic creation. Walcott pointedly refers to the accidentally cracked glass that Duchamp accepted as an integral part of his work (205). In one of his essays, Walcott expresses his particular delight in "errors" that reveal insights of their own;[10] now in *Omeros*, he sustains a partially fragmented and elliptical narrative with strategic fissures that invite incremental interpretation. It is no wonder that, in his reconfiguration of epic tradition, Walcott should single out this particular work by Duchamp; among other things, *The Bride Stripped Bare by Her Bachelors, Even* is a carnivalesque parody on the disintegration of European cultural hegemony.

Walcott, of course, is one descendant of a "slave from the outer regions / of their fraying empires" (205) who now challenges the centralizing power that has historically controlled access to and interpretation of the arts. This theme extends into the first section of the forty-first chapter, reminding us that the Romans imported enslaved Greeks to teach their children aesthetics. Unfortunately, military conquest did not guarantee quality of life. A major difference between the two cases is that the Romans began without vital Athenian imagination and substituted authoritarian power where they lacked creativity. The result of their materialism and prejudice,

---

and Kynaston McShine, includes a labeled diagram and front and back reproductions of *The Large Glass,* 57–67; Craig E. Adcock's *Marcel Duchamp's Notes from the Large Glass: An N-Dimensional Analysis* looks meticulously at both the work and the copious notes provided by Duchamp himself.

10. Walcott, "Caligula's Horse," 138.

as Walcott indicates in the blink of two millennia, lives on in the legacy of the Old South:

> corrupting the blue-veined marble with its disease,
> stillborn as a corpse, for all those ideals went cold
> in the heat of its hate. And not only in tense
>
> Southern towns and plantations, where it often killed
> the slaves it gave Roman names for dumb insolence,
> small squares with Athenian principles and pillars
>
> maintained by convicts and emigrants who had fled
> persecution and gave themselves *fasces* with laws
> to persecute slaves. A wedding-cake Republic. (206)

It is not that the contribution of these slaves, convicts, and emigrants is unappreciated, but as these lines indicate, mainstream society has difficulty accommodating these useful undesirables. Significantly, Walcott begins this forty-first chapter with the single-word sentence "Service," emphasizing the same dedication Major Plunkett praises as the redeeming quality of unsung soldiers he remembers from the North African campaign and the motivation of his adopted son, Midshipman Plunkett (101). The irony in the Roman names for slaves is echoed in the fact that the forced labor of these people built the "wedding-cake Republic," and now their masters wish them to disappear like leaves, as the Indians have drifted out of sight.

Having crossed his meridian eastward, visiting the famous cities and treading the Old World soil his father never lived to see, Walcott retraces his journey to the "reversible world" of North America. Recalling an earlier scene in which Achille notices his inverted image in the African river, Walcott now sees himself "split / along the same line of reflection that halved Achille" (207). It is his European half that comes presently to be scrutinized, just as his African heritage has informed the Afolabe chapters. Unlike inanimate chess pieces, human beings, regardless of their color, cannot be moved about with impunity; furthermore, they lack the instinctive ability of chameleons to adopt the coloring of any immediate background. Much as Walcott insists on the virtues of the West Indian's ability to mimic creatively in "The Caribbean: Culture or Mimicry?" he now stresses the essential residuum of the individual's native soil. From Walcott's bifocal perspective, that sword cuts two ways. Once settled in

the New World, Pilgrims uprooted the Indians, and the result was the
destruction of their culture. Wielding the Bible and building churches as
they cleared the forests, they became instruments of a historical pattern,
"[a]ll over again, / diaspora, exodus" (207). The tragedy he sees on the
reservations in the Dakotas is the loss of "the art of mimicry, and then,
where the trees were, / the fir, the palm, the olive, the cedar," nothing
remains but a barren desert (208). Walcott traces this lesson from Caesar
to King George down to the rebellion of the American colonies. In Africa,
Walcott accepted the guilt of his black, slave-trading ancestors; now that
he is back in Boston, he resumes the persona of Catherine Weldon to share
his white racial burden.

> This was the groan of the autumn wind in the tamaracks
> which I shared through Catherine's body, coming in waves
> through the leaves of the Shawmut, the ochre hands of the Aruacs[11]
> . . . .
> The Shot heard round the world entered the foliage
> of Plunkett's redoubt, when the arc of an empire was
> flung over both colonies, wider than the seine
>
> a fisherman hurls over a bay at sunrise,
> but all colonies inherit their empire's sin,
> and these, who broke free of the net, enmeshed a race. (208)

Continually telescoping experience, Walcott succinctly draws strands of
his American narrative together once again. The same arc of empire that
closes around the Indian and the Negro slave encompasses the Weldons
and Plunketts, who inherit their own version of alienation by resisting the
imperial center.

  In adopting his Weldon persona, Walcott relates the less sympathetic
side in the imperial equation. Although she is white and he is black, he can
sympathize with her refusal to be constrained by the prevalent ostracism of
Native Americans. With Weldon, he is offended by the sober New England
psyche whose Ahabs could "hurl the roped lance in the heart of Jehovah"
(209), the Transcendentalists whose statues cast shadows longer than the
benefactors they are erected to commemorate. In keeping with the sepia
and ochre leaves falling in the October chill, the Indians to whom Weldon

11. Shawmut peninsula, on which the city of Boston is situated.

dedicates her life are disappearing. Affording himself the perspective of the privileged race through Weldon, Walcott finds no relief from the confines of history.

> Privileges did not separate me, instead
> they linked me closer to them by that mental chain
> whose eyes interlocked with mine, as if we all stood
>
> at a lectern or auction block. Their condition
> the same, without manacles. The chains were subtler,
> but they were still hammered out of the white-hot forge
>
> that made every captor a blacksmith. (210)

This chapter ends with Walcott comparing these metaphysical bonds with the vision Achille had of his ancestral artisans idled in their chains (150).

An encounter with a Polish emigrant waitress in a Toronto hotel dining room occupies the bulk of the forty-second chapter. Watching her go about her work conjures up images of her grim, occupied country:

> that other servitude Nina Something was born into,
> where under gun-barrel chimneys the smoke holds its voice
> till it rises with hers. Zagajewski. Herbert. Milosz. (212)

Despite the mild humor in Walcott's inability to pronounce her name, the episode adds another ring to the expanding parameters of dispossession. Nina is not alone in having fled in search of a better life, and the three Polish writers she calls to mind have each found means to resist oppression in one form or another—Nazi, Stalinist, racist, religious.[12]

The bleakness of the mood is underscored as the months flow from October into November and the bright red of fall yields to the white snows of winter (209–13). The "ghost dance" of the floury snow begins to filter along the Charles River in Boston, and it is replicated in the glass sphere

12. Zbigniew Herbert (1924): poet, dramatist with classical affinities; served in underground resistance during World War II, and endured Stalinism in quiet, isolated opposition. Czeslaw Milosz (1911): poet, novelist, critic who received Nobel Prize for Literature, 1980; also in the Warsaw underground, later broke with Communist government. Adam Zagajewski (1945): poet; he felt it necessary to escape oppression in Poland by emigrating to France in 1981.

that fascinates Catherine Weldon years after she has left the Parkin farm in the frozen Dakotas. As she shakes the toy crystal, a white flurry obscures the miniature cottage and trees nestled in the globe, just as the relentless snow outside falls on the starving but proud Sioux. In her mind's eye an old scene comes to life: the lances of pine trees riding against the cavalry's rifles and cannons, the muffled reports and the avalanche of carnage among the warriors who placed their faith in the Ghost Dance.

> and she had been taught the meek inherit the earth.
> The flour kept falling. Inedible manna
> fell on their children's tongues, from dribbling sacks
>
> condemned by the army. The crow's flapping banner
> flew over the homes of the Braves. They stood like stakes
> without wires: the Crows, the Sioux, the Dakotas.
>
> The snow blew in their wincing faces like papers
> from another treaty which a blind shaman tears
> to bits in the wind. . . .
> . . . .
> The flour basting their corpses on the white fields.
> The absence that settled over the Dakotas
> was contained in the globe. Its pines, its tiny house. (214–15)

Within this scene-within-a-scene, Weldon gazes into her crystal ball and foresees the destruction of the people she ventured west to save. Prevented from feeding and housing themselves, the tribes suffer the ignominy of faithless treaties as well as inadequate food, clothing, and shelter. It is no wonder that they became susceptible to the futile promises of the Ghost Dance.

It is easy to discern the image of Seven Seas/Omeros in the blind shaman tearing up useless treaties. Walcott has not forgotten him, nor has he lost sight of the unifying thread of his far-ranging narrative. In fact this unobtrusive reference to a shaman might pass without comment were it not for the emphatic recapitulation of the following scene. On pages 215–16, Walcott virtually repeats the abandoned village sequence from pages 145–46. This time, instead of Achille walking the empty lanes between vacant huts, it is Catherine Weldon riding her horse among uninhabited tepees. Instead of captive black ants being led away, she sees men like red ants chained in single file. A papoose replaces Achille's lone black child, but the mongrel is in both versions of the scene, and Weldon also discovers Omeros, seemingly deaf as well as blind in his inexpressible grief. As impotent as Achille had been in his dream, Weldon is left to stand "like a Helen among their dead warriors" (216).

Reinforcing the explicit parallels, as Major Plunkett insists on stressing the poignancy of fateful coincidence, Walcott follows up with a polyphonic commentary. He begins the closing section of the last chapter of book five thinly veiled behind Weldon's voice but enclosing within it Omeros's summation.

> "This was history. I had no power to change it.
> And yet I still felt that this had happened before.
> I knew it would happen again, but how strange it
>
> was to have seen it in Boston, in the hearth-fire.
> I was a leaf in the whirlwind of the Ordained.
> Then Omeros's voice came from the mouth of the tent:
>
> 'We galloped towards death swept by the exaltation
> of meeting ourselves in a place just like this one:
> The Ghost Dance has tied the tribes into one nation.' " (217)

The duplication of detail and now the explicit remark point to the common plight of the dispossessed of all places and all ages. Catherine has lived through the experience, but it has weathered her into "a carved / totem" (217).

Of course, she is Walcott's "totem," and in order to fold her back into the fabric of his autobiographical text, he bids her peaceful retirement in Boston one year after the winter of the Ghost Dance. Winter signals another of his lines of division; this time, not only splitting a year in half but also confirming Walcott's return to the real present in a climate that, unlike his native tropics, has sharply contrasting seasons. Turning self-reflexive once again, he also derives further advantage out of the blanketing snow:

> Turn the page. Blank winter. The obliteration
> of nouns fading into echoes, the alphabet
> of scribbling branches. . . . (218)

The specific obliteration in this instance is his forgetting the address of the studio belonging to the Greek woman who had initially corrected his pronunciation of Omeros at the beginning of his poem. As this fifth book winds down, he gazes from frosted trolley windows as he searches unfamiliar streets with strange doors that no longer extend their welcome. In terms of his island upbringing, he begins to see houses as wharves and the passing trolleys as hulls sliding through snowy combers. Thus on this subdued note he finds at the end of his journey to North America traces of his beginnings. The itinerary of his Odyssean exile incorporates the cultural roots of the New World: in his own persona and through Achille, Catherine Weldon, Warwick Walcott, and Seven Seas, he has experienced Africa, the United States, Lisbon, London, Dublin, and the Mediterranean. The time has come for him to comply with his father's exhortation, complete the circle, and return to his beloved islands.

7   The Healing

The geographic expanse and restless movement of the central chapters of *Omeros* fill out the panoramic background of Walcott's West Indian epic. As diffuse as his narrative has been in encompassing Africa, Europe, and North America, he has not wandered from the bloodlines that converge in him and in his native islands. Whether speaking as his own persona or through various protagonists who enact his multivalent story, from Achille to Dennis Plunkett or Catherine Weldon to Seven Seas, he elicits the experience of characters who must carve lives for themselves out of the detritus of alien civilizations. This is the essence of Walcott's epic of the dispossessed.

When Walcott accepted his Nobel prize for literature in 1992, he delivered a paean to the spirit that makes it possible for the descendants of slaves and indentured servants to generate a culture of their own. In the process, however, he also warns against the mistaken historical tendency to elegize the quaint practices of marginalized peoples who do not conform to established patterns. At the beginning of "The Antilles: Fragments of Epic Memory," he recounts his own inability to participate in the East Indian *Ramleela* festival in Trinidad. Nevertheless, instead of simply noting the irony of his familiarity with the Greek *Odyssey* as compared to his ignorance of the Asian and African mythology that is more integral to Caribbean societies, he ties these disparate strands together.[1]

Rather than accept an image of the Caribbean as a marginalized vestige of distant continents, Walcott in "The Antilles" looks to imaginative

---

1. Derek Walcott, "The Antilles: Fragments of Epic Memory," 26. Ramleela (Rāmlilās): a cycle of plays performed annually and dedicated to Rāma.

127

predecessors who are not intimidated by the weight of "History"—a method of accounting that "can alter the eye and the moving hand to conform to a view of itself; it can rename places for the nostalgia in an echo; it can temper the glare of tropical light to elegiac monotony in prose, the tone of judgment in Conrad, in the travel journals of Froude." Instead, Walcott finds both Alexis Leger (Saint-John Perse) and Aimé Césaire—the first of French and the second of African ancestry—to be equally inspiring despite the vagaries of divisive history: "There is a force of exultation, a celebration of luck, when a writer finds himself a witness to the early morning of a culture that is defining itself, branch by branch, leaf by leaf, in that self-defining dawn." Thus, rather than deny either white or black origins in "Antilles," he declares,

> Antillean art is this restoration of our shattered histories, our shards of vocabulary, our archipelago becoming a synonym for pieces broken off from the original continent. . . . The stripped man is driven back to that self-astonishing elemental force, his mind. That is the basis of the Antillean experience, this shipwreck of fragments, these echoes, these shards of a huge tribal vocabulary, these partially remembered customs, and they are not decayed but strong.

And having been born into this unformed society, his task is to interpret his people's milieu, "the island's life, illiterate in the way leaves are illiterate; they do not read, they are there to be read, and if they are properly read, they create their own literature."[2]

Apposed, then, to the romantic nostalgia of a historical perspective, to the Edenic advertisement for the consumption of tourists, and to the aspersions of disillusioned exiles, Walcott offers his creole reality: a new whole reassembled from broken fragments. Although he concludes that life in "the Caribbean is not an idyll," the local people "draw their working strength from it organically, like trees, like the sea almond or the spice laurel of the heights. Its peasantry and its fishermen are not there to be loved or even photographed; they are trees who sweat, and whose bark is filmed with salt." In his imaginary and physical journeys away from St. Lucia in quest of ancestral roots, he often strays great distances, but through his succession of transplanted characters in *Omeros,* he delineates the homing

2. Walcott, "Antilles," 30, 31, 28, 32.

instinct of a modern Odysseus. "The traveler cannot love, since love is stasis and travel is motion. If he returns to what he loved in a landscape and stays there, he is no longer a traveler but in stasis and concentration, a lover of that particular part of earth, a native."[3]

After the wide chronological and geographic expanse of the middle section of *Omeros,* the two closing books reconfirm the Caribbean essence of Walcott's vision. Complementing the opening books, which reify the creole-folk foundations of modern St. Lucian culture, the sixth and seventh books amplify the narrator's cosmopolitan perspective and his self-reflexive text. The "stasis and concentration" he cites in "Antilles" fulfills his father's ghostly prediction earlier in *Omeros* that the swift's flight is circular (188).

Book six opens with an interlude, a refreshing January dawn back in the islands. While St. Lucia is clearly identified as "home" for Walcott, he telescopes the term in the initial scene to embrace the broader Caribbean. By citing San Fernando (Trinidad) and Mayaguez (Puerto Rico) in the first line, he marks the extent of the Windward and Leeward Antilles. Having lived for periods in both Jamaica and Trinidad before his years in the United States, it is as though Walcott wishes to establish the fact that while St. Lucia is at the heart of *Omeros,* the island symbolizes the West Indianness of his identity. The sensual evocation of the opening scene is as palpable to the narrator as the texture of his evolving poem when a gentle breeze and soft rain stir the cane leaves on the hillside above the savannah in Port of Spain. Below his French windows (perhaps overlooking the Queen's Park racecourse), Walcott watches a groom exercising a "skittish stallion" (221).

Inspired by the nostalgic morning light, he recalls scenes from the past, and in the blink of an eye we are transported back to St. Lucia. The January morning carries over from the initial scene as Walcott flashes back to his characters from the village of Gros Îlet. A brief review projects Achille forlorn on his mattress, Hector urgently struggling to save his canoe, and Walcott's own first vision of Helen. Drawn to the window by the familiar odor of rain on asphalt and jackfish cooking nearby, he glimpses a sail, "like a sail towards Ithaca" (223). Because that ship could be coming or going, he reflects on the dual visage of Janus, god of his birth month, whose gaze takes in simultaneously the degradations of the past and the elation of the dawning year. In addition to this reference to January's doubling

3. Ibid., 32, 30.

effect and a narrative that draws attention to its own textuality, synesthesia underscores the metaphysical aspect of his perspective, "I smelt with my eyes, I could see with my nostrils" (224).

Transcending the physical present, we witness Hector's last run through the mountains. The time is cool December; his Comet hurtles around hairpin turns of precipitous roads overlooking Atlantic combers that have completed their crossing from Africa. With its stereo blaring a lively *zouk* on this fateful day, the transport swerves wildly to avoid a stray piglet and arches through space to crash into the trees below. For one suspended moment, the sight of the wandering piglet reminds Hector that Major Plunkett had cautioned him about his reckless speed. What is a flashback for Hector, at this point in the story, is foreshadowing of an altercation between Plunkett and Hector that Walcott has yet to recount for the reader. In this section of *Omeros,* the intermingling of past, present, and future combined with the superimposition of authorial presence over narrative action generates yet another palimpsest of discourses. Rather than resembling a steadily flowing stream, the narrative may be more fittingly compared to the motion of waves surging and ebbing with the tide. Successive episodes replace their predecessors, seamlessly complementing, finishing, and initiating another action that grows out of itself.

Chapter forty-five affords a typical mixture of overlapping perspectives. Embedded in the violent scene of Hector's death are references to his guilt over having abandoned the sea and over his broken friendship with Achille. In the silent aftermath, the Comet's dashboard statuette of a *Madonna of the Rocks* signs her benediction over Hector's bowed corpse. One of the protagonists may be dead; however, his impact on the story continues because of his influence both on other characters and on the narrator. It is significant that the scene of Hector's death is immediately followed by the description of Walcott returning to visit St. Lucia. The juxtaposition is all the more emphatic because the anonymous transport driver who picks him up at the airport insists on stopping to show him the very spot where the Comet plunged to its destruction.

Despite his subtle attempt to remain aloof, Walcott's persona finds himself drawn into the loquacious driver's friendly banter. When his guide declares that the modernization taking place around the island is "all to the good," he verbally concurs, but he silently inventories his reservations. The returning writer in him grudgingly admits nostalgia for the obsolescent

colonial past that is being converted into the postcard views of hotels and
marinas. Reflecting that his craft demands the same archaic skills as the
outmoded carpenter, he questions the efficacy of his own vision:

> . . . Didn't I want the poor
> to stay in the same light so that I could transfix
> them in amber, the afterglow of an empire,
> . . . .
> . . . Had they waited for me
>
> to develop my craft? Why hallow that pretence
> of preserving what they left, the hypocrisy
> of loving them from hotels, a biscuit-tin fence
>
> smothered in love-vines, scenes to which I was attached
> as blindly as Plunkett with his remorseful research?
> Art is History's nostalgia, it prefers a thatched
>
> roof to a concrete factory, and the huge church
> above a bleached village. The gap between the driver
> and me increased when he said:
> "The place changing, eh?" (227–28)

Self-doubt arises when he contemplates the inauthentic souvenirs that are
now proffered at generic curio shops from Greece to Hawaii. Given the
grace and beauty of the local people, he realizes that his art is rendered
superfluous by their daily struggle for endurance.

Reaching the airy heights above Micoud on the Atlantic coast, Walcott's
guide pulls to the shoulder of the road to show his passenger the precipice
where Hector careened to his death. As the driver casually urinates in the
undergrowth, his sympathetic commentary on the accident savors of an
earthy camaraderie. He sees his lost friend as a road-warrior who may have
been a little "Crazy, but / a gentle fellow anyway, with a very good brain"
(230). In the seconds it takes us to assimilate this simple testimonial, Walcott
capitalizes on the sentiment to launch a cinematic reprise of Hector's story.
In the five rhymed tercets following the driver's assessment, Walcott uses the
word "cut" eight times to frame allusive scenes with an invisible camera: a
leopard galloping across the Serengeti (matching the seat covers of Hector's
Comet); a stallion on the banks of the Scamander (recalling the horse

spraying surf in the sixth chapter, 35); a woman clutching hands to her mouth (as Catherine Weldon helplessly watches her beloved Sioux freezing in the snow, 216); spiked chariot hubcaps (a second reference to Hector's Comet); the set of an angry jaw (conflict with Achille over a bailing tin, 15–16); a girl whispering "Omeros" (Walcott's Greek lover, 14); the silver shield of a hubcap (a third intimation of Hector's status as a warrior); "myrmidons gathering by a village river";[4] an ocean "surpliced," "droning its missal," evoking the island's sacramental orientation; and finally, the crane that retrieves the wrecked Comet becomes a metaphorical horse, "shuddering its neck" (230). The climactic image for this flickering montage is particularly fitting when we recall that one of Homer's favorite epithets for Hector's Trojan namesake was "breaker of horses."

Hector's modern counterpart also suffers a comparable ignominy in death. Whereas Grecian Achilles drags his defeated Trojan enemy through the dirt behind his chariot, the St. Lucian Hector has sold his birthright as a fisherman in shameful pursuit of the tourist's dollar. Neither the lights of the city, his flaming Comet, nor possession of Helen prove sufficient consolation for abandoning his true calling. Reiterating the adage first derived from "O-mer-os" early in the epic, Walcott summarizes Hector's sin:

> A man who cursed the sea had cursed his own mother.
> *Mer* was both mother and sea. (231)

In the aftermath of his violent death, however, it becomes evident that Walcott considers Hector's months of living torment to have partially expiated his guilt.

Hector's body is laid to rest in a pitch-pine coffin, his burial canoe, near the beach where he and Achille had come to blows over Helen and a rusty bailing tin. Philoctete blows his death knell through a conch, and shells are mounded over the closed furrow. In final tribute, a subdued Achille produces the disputed tin. He also lays down the oar that he refers to as Hector's spear, and voices his respect for such an admirable rival. In death, all animosity dissipates as Achille recalls Hector's masculine grace

---

4. "Myrmidons" were not only tribesmen following Achilles at the battle of Troy but also the noun is a simile Walcott employs three times in *Omeros*: first, in book one to describe fishermen's beached canoes (10); second, when Plunkett observes Helen moving among sunbathing tourists (31); and now it is applied to a gathering of villagers (230).

and his kindness to Helen, the woman who spans the breach between them. As for Helen, radiant in pregnancy, grief merely ennobles her remarkable beauty. With a few strokes of his authorial brush, Walcott limns the funereal landscape by describing the reversal of land and sea imagery as sea sounds emanate among the dry plantains of Philoctete's garden and misty columns rise from the surf like wood smoke. While the quarter-moon becomes the crooked neck of a heron over Hector's grave, the nail heads of raindrops glitter on the roof of the sea. Harkening back to the island's African roots, it seems that the breeze rustling through dry straw suggests "a chorus of aged / ancestors," enclosing each village dwelling (235).

As Walcott closes off Hector's portion of the narrative in chapter forty-six, he draws our attention once again to Philoctete's ongoing agony. We are reminded that his festering wound, like Hector's spiritual anomie, runs deeper than its physical manifestation. Thus the groundwork is prepared for chapters forty-seven through forty-nine—the story within the story— wherein Ma Kilman retrieves the herbal ingredients that will finally cure Philoctete's sickness. The episode begins with the description of a lost "sibylline cure" involving bay leaves, a sprig of lime, and a particular spray of thorn: the fruit of a seed transported across the Atlantic in the belly of an African swift. In effect, the account of Ma Kilman's journey into the hills and back becomes a miniature quest.

Wearing a new wig and attired in formal black for five o'clock mass, this Sunday morning Ma Kilman appears to be the model of Catholic propriety. From the outset, however, her attachment to the earth is manifest. Not only is her black hat fringed with berries but also the predawn humidity already has her sweating beneath her uncomfortable clothes. The painful grip of stockings biting into her calves reminds her of Philoctete's daily suffering, and she fingers the "berries" of her rosaries. A flood of associations then pervades her litany of Hail Marys and sets her mind on a catalog of floral herbs. Mary leads to marigolds, then anemone,

> and clear watercress, the sacred heart of Jesus
> pierced like the anthurium, the thorns of logwood,
> called the tree of life, the aloe good for seizures,
>
> the hole in the daisy's palm, with its drying blood
> that was the hole in the fisherman's shin since he was
> pierced by a hook; there was the pale, roadside tisane

of her malarial childhood. There was this one
for easing a birth-breach, that one for a love-bath,
before the buds of green sugar-apples in the sun

ripened like her nipples in girlhood. But what path
led through nettles to the cure, the furious sibyl
couldn't remember. (236–37)

Such a mixture of Christian belief and folk remedies exemplifies those
"rites of the island . . . simplified by its elements" (234) that are eulogized
just two pages earlier in Walcott's treatment of Hector's burial. Given the
juxtaposition of disparate elements that constitute Ma Kilman's faith, it is
evident that her religious practices are "simple" only in the sense that they
are based on natural intuition rather than sophisticated abstractions.

Pervading Ma Kilman's thoughts this morning are the subliminal vestiges
of ancestral knowledge. In back of childhood experience is the storehouse
of racial memory, based on homeopathic or imitative magic. She senses
that, if she can recall it, there is a pronged flower (shaped like the anchor
on which Philoctete cut his shin) that holds the restorative ingredient she
needs. In this heightened state of awareness, the telltale odor of the unknown
plant begins to register on her senses. The foul aroma itself reminds her
of the gangrenous stench of Philoctete's flowering sore. Once its bitterness
filters into her nostrils, she attempts to screen the smell with a cologned
handkerchief, but she instinctively follows the wind-borne scent out of the
village along goat paths into the hills.

As soon as her quest is undertaken, its magical impetus is enhanced by
animistic overtones. Suddenly, she not only becomes aware of a line of ants
that lead into the distance ahead but also realizes that they follow all along
the course she has been pursuing. These creatures of the earth are drawn
toward the same objective that leads Ma Kilman to the inland heights. They
serve as one more link in an organic chain: the African plant in St. Lucia
sprung from a seed dropped by a migrant swift lures Ma Kilman and an
army of ants back to the healing earth. The transatlantic odyssey cost the
swift its life,

but the vine grew its own wings, out of the ocean

it climbed like the ants, the ancestors of Achille,
the women carrying coals after the dark door
slid over the hold. As the weed grew in odour

so did its strength at the damp root of the cedar,
where the flower was anchored at the mottled root
as a lizard crawled upwards, foot by sallow foot. (239)

With poetic efficiency, in summarizing the flight of the swift, Walcott en-
capsulates the Middle Passage, the menial labor of his enslaved forefathers,
and the growth of the secret plant here in Iounalao, the land of the iguana.

While Walcott leaves Ma Kilman following the scent of the vine, he uses
the time by focusing our attention on a parable about fictive beetles who live
by devouring their mates. The faux-parable turns autobiographical when he
admits that, although there is no such race of mutually destructive beetles
living under the mold of the forest, there is a species of two-legged creatures
who drive their mates to hysteria. Personal experience is unmistakable as
he recounts the story of betrayal, reconciliation, tears of love and hate that
result in self-contempt, the "fatherless wanderings of my own sons," and
"marriages dissolved like sand through the fingers" (241).[5] Regret lingers in
the aftermath as vividly as Helen's memorable hairpin remains in Achille's
crusted soap dish. Lest the aside appear overly indulgent, Walcott deftly
turns his insight into a multivalent lesson in human relationships. As it
applies to himself, he confesses,

the love I was good at seemed to have been only

the love of my craft and nature; yes, I was kind,
but with such certitude it made others lonely,
and with such bent industry it had made me blind.

It was a cry that called from the rock, some water
that the sea-swift crossed alone, and the calling stayed
like the hoarse echo in the conch; it called me from daughter

and son, it called me from my bed at dawn in darkness
like a fisherman walking towards the white noise
of paper, then in its hollow craft sets his oars. (241)

He goes on to assert that recognition of this wrong-headed love has dawned
on him as painfully as it struck Achille in Helen's absence. Each in his own

5. Although Walcott uses the plural "sons" here, he has one son (Peter) and two
daughters (Anna and Elizabeth) from his first two marriages.

way, like Philoctete, needs healing reconciliation, Ma Kilman's cleansing seawater bath.

Ma Kilman, in the meantime, is struggling to reconnect the supernatural powers of Christ and Mary with the long-forgotten gods of Africa. She senses them among the rustling vegetation, but their names are obscure shadows in her blood rather than solid nouns. Without knowing them, she is vaguely aware of such figures as Erzulie, Shango, and Ogun.[6] Since these deities had been suppressed for three centuries, Ma Kilman must purge herself of doubt before she can solicit their help. Waving her arms and calling them namelessly, she begins to feel their net stitching into her nerves. As the incantation begins to take effect, Walcott compares her to Virgil's "caverned prophetess," the sibyl who guides Aeneas through the Latin underworld.

Just as Aeneas complies with Roman ideals, Ma Kilman is now delineated in compliance with her Afro-Caribbean setting. In order to restore her connection with the natural forces, she removes her berry-fringed hat and horsehair wig and presses her forehead to the ground, communing with the ants. Wordless language makes them one as she remembers the worker-ant generations of her predecessors who carried coal into the holds of ocean vessels. Like an animal herself, she bays at the canopy of leaves, prays that the infection be lifted from Philoctete, and sprinkles soil into her wild hair. Her open mouth becomes a metaphor for the original sibyl's prophetic cave and her howl reverberates within Philoctete, although he is well beyond the sound of her voice. Generations coalesce in her image as Walcott invites us to witness her mystical apotheosis.

> See her there, my mother, my grandmother, my great-great-
> grandmother. See the black ants of their sons,
> their coal-carrying mothers. Feel the shame, the self-hate
>
> draining from all our bodies in the exhausted sleeping
> of a rumshop closed Sunday. There was no difference
> between me and Philoctete. One wound gibbers in the weeping
>
> mouth of the sibyl, the obeah-woman, in the swell
> of the huge white satin belly, the dark gust that bent her
> limbs till she was a tree of snakes, the spidery sibyl

6. Erzulie (or Ezili) is the beautiful wife of Dambala, the powerful voodoo spirit typically seen as a great snake whose coils delineate the paths of the sun, earth, and stars. Shango (or Sango), god of thunder, and Ogun, god of war and iron, are drawn from Yoruba mythology.

hanging in a sack from the cave at Cumae, the obeah
that possessed her that the priests considered evil
in their white satin frocks, because ants had lent her

their language, the flower that withered on the floor
of moss smelt sweet and spread its antipodal odour
from the seed of the swift. (245)

With the assistance of the ants and her neglected gods, Ma Kilman has
delved to the root of her people's degraded souls. The sacred herb that will
heal Philoctete's physical sore is also symbolic of the restorative baptism
that awaits all his countrymen.

It is worth noting that in this sweeping gesture Walcott emulates Homer's
treatment of the abandoned master-bowman Philoctētēs. Before the Greek
forces will be able to defeat the besieged Trojans, it is necessary that they
return to the island of Lemnos where they had exiled Philoctētēs. Only after
they have welcomed him back into their company, despite his offensive
wound, will they achieve military victory. In his own way, Walcott has
now made Philoctete's recovery essential to the self-validation of creole St.
Lucia's culture. Having procured the requisite flower, Ma Kilman completes
the cycle of her journey, walking back into the social fold of the quiet village.

Ma Kilman heats up her batch of herbs in an old sugar-mill cauldron
full of seawater and sulfur. The cauldron itself is yet another gaping "O:
the scream of centuries," onomatopoeia for both pain and the language
of utterance. Immersed in the steaming concoction, Philoctete breaks into
a cold sweat as putrefaction drains from his afflicted shin. Giving him a
violent scrubbing, Ma Kilman restrains him in the cauldron while both
the illness and the shame are leeched out of his body. As Philoctete soaks
in his baptismal ablution, Walcott launches into a veritable catalog of its
restorative virtues. The warrior's bow springs back into his grip; his muscles,
bone, and heart are rejuvenated; as a hand wraps around a familiar oar,
his mouth forms his lost African name; centuries of tribal loss and shame
are absolved in cathartic tears until he is born anew.

as he stood like a boy in his bath with the first clay's
innocent prick! So she threw Adam a towel.
And the yard was Eden. And its light the first day's. (248)

While Philoctete's rebirth might be a sufficient conclusion for Ma
Kilman's sibylline quest, Walcott's larger context requires that it be woven

back into the ongoing epic scheme. For this reason, her beneficent influence extends to the author himself in the closing section of the forty-ninth chapter. We find the narrator as we had last seen him in the second section of book six, musing on a balcony. This time, however, he contemplates a city square in his native St. Lucia. Having taken us through Philoctete's cure, he now feels restored faith in his native island. His personal renewal is presented in terms of a changing form of love. The "wrong love" he rejects seems to hark back to the artist's preference for archaic quaintness, "History's nostalgia," mentioned a few pages earlier (228). In turn is reborn a deeper, more authentic appreciation for the bubbling Malebolge near Soufrière, the rain-washed village rooftops: physical places and actual people. In his elation, he celebrates the parallels between his personification of the island as Helen and the departed Greek Circe who had given him the pronunciation of Omeros (14). Unlike Philoctete, who limped among the highland furrows in his yam patch, Walcott has been looking down on his island from the elevated balcony of art. The quality of his new perspective registers in a series of earthy metaphors and similes, beginning with the line, "My love was common as dirt; brown sheep bayed at it," and continues repeating the pronoun "it" sixteen times in six consecutive stanzas. Significantly, the central metaphor in this list compares the poet's new love to Helen's unborn baby, and for the first time unequivocally identifies Hector as the child's father.

Strands of *Omeros* continue to weave together complete segments of the open design. Now that Hector is buried, Philoctete is restored to health, and the narrator has been purged of his adulterated vision of St. Lucia, a flashback recreates for us the disillusioning visit the Plunketts had last made to England. As chapter fifty opens, Maud criticizes Dennis for refusing to honor her wish to make one more trip back to the British Isles. Contrary to her assessment of his parsimony, the Major actually resists because he despises the tourist trap of ruined gentility that London has become. By the time of their previous journey to London, postwar cubes of glass and steel had filled in the old bomb sites, and prices at the *Rodney* hotel prompted him to rename it the "Admiral / Rob-me" (251). The ubiquitous statues of lions drew tears when they reminded him of his faithful tomcat; but above all, he missed the surf-inflected dialect of the West Indies. In the absence of that familiar intonation, his own voice took on a strident edge; he could never strike the appropriate key between a request and an order. His departure from England was an escape, and he was grateful to return to St. Lucia.

Although Maud continually pesters him for one more trip back to Ireland, she abides by his decision. Their commitment to the island long settled, she eventually grows to prefer her garden to empires (254). One day while working among her flowers, Maud receives her first premonition of impending death. She is not frightened, but she realizes she grows easily exhausted and she wishes for a little more time. With her death in abeyance, Walcott introduces another flashback to indicate the degree to which this couple jealously defend their right of St. Lucian citizenship. Their latent sensitivity to this issue becomes overt one morning as Hector's speeding transport nearly forces them off the road on their way to five o'clock Mass. It is more than the Major can tolerate when a voice from the careering Comet taunts, "Move your ass, honky!" Slamming on his brakes, he stalks back to where the transport has stopped to take on more passengers. Borrowing a line from Kipling's "Mandalay," Walcott toys with Plunkett's martial air when he asserts that,

> The dawn was coming up like thunder
> . . . Bagpipes and kettledrums
>
> were the only thing missing . . . (256)

The Major is angry enough at the averted collision, but his primary complaint addresses the driver's expletive.

> . . . I am not a honky.
> A donkey perhaps, a jackass, but I haven't spent
>
> damned near twenty years on this godforsaken rock
> to be cursed like a tourist. Do you understand? (256)

As soon as Hector realizes that it is the Major he has offended, he apologizes, and the two are soon reconciled. It is at this point that Dennis cautions Hector about his recklessness and his responsibilities as a prospective father, the encounter previously foreshadowed at the instant of Hector's fatal crash (225).

After dropping Maud off at the Roman Catholic cathedral on the east side of Columbus Square, Dennis parks the Rover in front of the library and strolls a few blocks down Bridge Street to while away the time at the

docks.[7] He recalls having witnessed a sunrise in Lisbon years ago as he
wondered where he and his new bride would eventually settle. It occurs
to him that his pace repeats the tread of Midshipman Plunkett, an earlier
century in a Dutch harbor. After all his dreams of world travel, he is now as
permanently moored in this island as the old freighter he sees rusted to its
wharf. Stopping off to purchase freshly baked loaves before picking up his
wife at the cathedral, he muses that she has become his "Bread of Heaven"
(259). Unfortunately, Plunkett's comfortable reverie cannot last. Shortly
thereafter, Maud smells mortality among her beloved oleanders and takes
to her bed.

On the morning of Maud's death from cancer, Major Plunkett surveys
the imagery preserved in his accumulated love letters. As he stretches out
beside her, he notices volumes of Macaulay and Gibbon, "an empire's
bookends" (260). In having the Major register these particular historians,
Walcott succinctly juxtaposes two empires: Edward Gibbon (1737–1794)
compiled the five-volume *Decline and Fall of the Roman Empire* (1776–
1788); Thomas Babington Macaulay (1800–1859) wrote the five-volume
History of England (1849–1861). Plunkett's mind drifts back over the names
and places that delineate his heritage of imperial service. There are all the
potentates, viceroys, commissioners, Dragoons, extravagantly uniformed
native armies, exotic music, Maud's collection of *Airs from Erin;* famous
military campaigns from the relief of Mafeking to Gordon in Khartoum
and Clive in India.[8] An integral portion of his commemorative review also
turns on mundane images: colonial power has declined as the sunflower
follows the setting sun in obscure provinces

> where a pig totters across a village midden
> over the sunset's shambles, Rangoon to Malta,
> the regimental button of the evening star. (263)

In the act of accepting God's will, Dennis finds that all the associations of
his life are now consummated in Maud.

---

7. Columbus Square (since 1893)—with its Memorial, fountain, benches, and
sidewalks as Walcott describes them—was officially renamed Derek Walcott Square
in 1993.

8. Mafeking, a town in South Africa that was relieved from a Boer siege lasting 217
days between 1899–1900. Charles George "Chinese" Gordon (1833–1885), a British
general and governor of Egypt and Sudan who, after a brilliant career as a soldier and
diplomat, died at the siege of Khartoum. Robert Clive (1725–1774), a British officer
and twice governor of Bengal in India.

By way of cementing the integral connection between autobiography and fiction in his self-reflexive epic, at this point, Walcott personally intrudes into the narrative of Maud's funeral to assert that the Plunketts are derived from his own mother and father. In addition to imaginative parallels, he notes that the morning-glories and bougainvilleas growing before the Plunketts' house replicate flowers attached to his own childhood home. Not surprisingly, floral imagery is prominent in the description of his mother's house in *Another Life*.[9] As the intimate confession progresses, he alludes once again to *The World's Great Classics* belonging to his father's barber (205). By this point, the collage of personal experience and classical knowledge that shapes *Omeros* can hold little surprise. Walcott's purpose for this particular editorial interruption seems to be motivated, however, by his growing desire to underscore the primacy of real life over literary invention. This is what prompts him to state explicitly that more than the incidental parallels—"Plunkett in my father" (Warwick's untimely death making Walcott a lonely Telemachus), his "mother in Maud," his Helen of the West Indies rather than Troy, his Seven-Seas version of a "khaki Ulysses," and "an empire's guilt / stitched in the one pattern of Maud's fabulous quilt" (263)—he knew individual people before he saw fictional designs into which they might fit.

In this sixth book, Walcott has already begun to distance himself from the wrong kind of aesthetic love, the artificial perspective that distances subject matter (249). By this gesture, we are invited to observe the process by which he transforms *Omeros*. If the poem seems to begin as a demonstration that dispossessed West Indians are worthy of epic treatment, in the propagandistic tradition of Virgil's *Aeneid*, then its intertextual self-interrogation takes precedence in the latter stages. Walcott's questioning of the quality of his own love for St. Lucia is but the first in a series of crucial reversals. As heralds of Western culture, both he and Major Plunkett have taken it upon themselves to immortalize Helen as a literary icon. In raising the issue of his artistic distance from the people about whom he wishes to write, Walcott ultimately redefines the purpose of *Omeros*, and he does so explicitly.

Stepping forth candidly and explaining his own change of heart contributes to the immediacy of Walcott's authorial presence. His narrative

9. In the second chapter of *Another Life*, Walcott celebrates the bougainvillea and allamanda, rather than morning glories, growing around his mother's home at 17 Chaussee Road. See discussion of the imagery in Edward Baugh's *Derek Walcott: Memory as Vision: Another Life*, 26.

stance, at least, projects an air of ready accessibility. When he returns
to the story, as one of the mourners at Maud Plunkett's funeral, his new
emphasis is on the human bond among his various characters and especially
the Major's deepening humility. In his guise as narrator, Walcott registers
amazement, not that Helen, Achille, and Philoctete attend the ceremony,
but that Achille, who shoveled pigpens for the Major, should be moved to
tears. He wonders,

> . . . Where was it from,
> this charity of soul, more piercing than Helen's
>
> beauty? runnelling his face like the road to the farm?
> We sang behind Plunkett, and I saw Achille perspire
> over the words, his lips following after the sound. (265)

In the solemnity of the occasion, the poet reaches for words as expressive
as Japanese calligraphy or impressionist brush strokes such as those in *Les
Nympheas.*[10] Mentioning his need to write out his feelings, he capitalizes
on the irony of being a participant in his own creation:

> I was both there and not there. I was attending
> the funeral of a character I'd created;
> the fiction of her life needed a good ending.
>
> as much as mine. (266)

Insisting once again on the interchangeability of characters, he admits
that in earlier lamp-lit scenes (65, 89) it was he who had gazed upon
Maud through the Major's eyes and seen the image of his own mother. He
scratches out his impressions now, with an instrument sharp as Maud's
sewing needle or as the swift's beak embroidered into her quilt.

One crucial advantage to this variegated depiction of the solemn cer-
emony is that it allows Walcott to range freely among several strands of
plot. As the funeral temporarily closes off one story line, he nonchalantly
rekindles the temporarily suspended relationship between Achille and

---

10. Claude Monet's painting of water lilies (1918–25) uses impressionistic technique
to shatter the chromatic spectrum into fragments of color in a flat plane wherein objects
and surrounding atmosphere coalesce into patterns within the observer's eye.

Helen. Outside the church, she lifts her veil to inform Achille that she is coming home (267). Yet, significant as this momentous reconciliation may be, Walcott reserves its consummation for the final chapter of book six. For the moment, he is more interested in further exploitation of his self-reflexive persona. On the day following Maud's funeral, Walcott becomes involved in a conversation with the Major at the local bank. Plunkett's voice has not changed since he used to drill the college's young Cadet Force queued up for inspection. Inadvertently, the Major slips into British affectation when he asks, "Been travellin' a bit, what?" It is not so much the word as the tonal register, but he is betrayed by the kind of idiomatic tic he and Maud abhorred from phony expatriates in the staid, old Victoria Club (25). Unable to retract the utterance, he is forced to move along, volunteering the conciliatory observation that he too has "Been doin' a spot of writing meself" (269). Walcott recoils from the class-conscious turn of phrase, but the incident prompts a lengthy examination of the cultural barriers inherent in colonial domination.

His point of departure entails nothing less than a reexamination of the very foundation of *Omeros* itself. Reminding the reader of that eventful day early in the epic when he and Major Plunkett had been moved to account for Helen's diffident arrogance (23, 30), he now concludes that they had both undertaken their ambitious projects with invalid premises. In his own way, each had presumed to honor Helen according to a preconceived frame of reference. Walcott prefers to think that his approach was more intuitive, basically literary—Olympian machinery cast in native dialect. The Major's ploy, on the other hand, "tried to change History to a metaphor" by making Helen the object of the Battle of the Saints, her yellow dress the standard of Rodney's flagship. If Dennis Plunkett had attempted to elevate a remarkable housemaid through association with Aegean legends, Walcott with equal hubris had been inspired by a Greek girl to cast the same housemaid in a Homeric mold. Both are guilty of "forced coincidence," since the cannonballs left in St. Lucia have nothing to do with Olympic games and the pyrite-encrusted bottle displayed in the local museum did not spill from De Grasse's *Ville de Paris* (270–71).

Having condemned the very literary and "Historical" (capitalized) traditions that have sustained *Omeros* up to this point, Walcott now draws attention to the natural subject matter that remains: Helen, the woman, and the text itself.

> . . . There, in her head of ebony,
> there was no real need for the historian's
> remorse, nor for literature's. Why not see Helen
>
> as the sun saw her, with no Homeric shadow,
> swinging her plastic sandals on that beach alone,
> as fresh as the sea-wind? Why make the smoke a door? (271)

As he purges himself of "[a]ll that Greek manure" (271), he contemplates with fresh enthusiasm the story that remains to be committed to paper.

> But it was mine to make what I wanted of it, or
> what I thought was wanted. A cool wood off the road,
> a hut closed like a wound, and the sound of a river. (272)

The St. Lucian flavor of his renewed impetus manifests itself immediately in the island rituals celebrated in the final chapter of book six. Two holidays are juxtaposed in such a way that the characters are shown participating in ceremonies with markedly divergent roots.

Chapter fifty-five opens with Philoctete and blind old St. Omere enjoying Ma Kilman's sumptuous Christmas feast. Although origins of this Judeo-Christian observance in the West Indies are inextricable from the tragedy of slavery and colonial servitude, the simple message of faith and salvation still carries deep conviction among the people. In addition, Boxing Day, the day after Christmas, draws upon a totally different tradition. Taking up African masks, costumes, and musical instruments, celebrants pour into the streets to reclaim lost centuries of their racial identities. The origin of this festival, known as Jonkonnu or Junkanoo, is obscure. Its name may derive from the French *gens inconnus,* meaning masked or unknown people, or from the tenacious West African chieftain Jananin Canno, who managed to revive this tribal custom among his fellow slaves in the New World in the 1500s or 1600s. To start this special day, Achille lathers up in his primitive shower and vigorously scrubs his body down to that same heel he once caught in a thorn-vine in his African dream.[11] Then the muscular fisherman

---

11. This episode occurs at the end of the twenty-eighth chapter: "vine looped his tendon, encircling the heel / with its own piercing chain" (148). The chain metaphor confirms yet another of the various racial wounds in *Omeros;* additionally, involvement of the tendon and heel evokes the mortal flaw in Homer's Achilles.

Achille as Winner of the Games. Watercolor by Derek Walcott (Larry Fink, photo).

struggles into Helen's yellow dress. He and Philoctete transform themselves with women's clothing, wigs, and discarded banana refuse into fantastic "androgynous / warriors" (276). When Helen finds the whole impression to be humorous, it affords Achille an opportunity to explain the significance of his disguise. The explanation draws upon his sun-induced dream of ancestral Africa (133–56) with all its overtones of racial memory.

> At first she had laughed, but then, with firm tenderness,
> Achille explained that he and Philo had done this
> every Boxing Day, and not because of Christmas,

but for something older; something that he had seen
in Africa, when his name had followed a swift,
where he had been his own father and his own son. (275)

When he and Philoctete join the masquerading stilt-walkers and athletic dancers in the infectious rhythms of fife, chac-chac, and drum, they are reenacting the scene Achille had witnessed in his tribal dream (143).

Whatever the ancient ritual had meant to their ancestors, in Achille's and Philoctete's contemporary performance, Walcott emphasizes its cathartic powers. As they whirl, dip, and strenuously high-step down the street, they exorcise the degradation of the Middle Passage. The spectacular exhibition draws tears of joy from Philoctete; for Walcott points out that even though they have outgrown their pain, they have not forgotten the past. Thus their communal dance becomes Walcott's third consecutive depiction of ablution in this sixth book. Philoctete's racial wound has been cleansed in baptism, Walcott's narrator has begun to expurgate some of his textual adulterations, and in his proud dance, Achille dramatically revives the warrior that has lain dormant in his veins. Taken together, these symbolic acts confirm the pervasive homecoming motive of books six and seven. As the ghost of Warwick had foretold in chapter thirty-six (188), the journey of the swift is following its circular pattern.

8 Home from the Sea

 As book seven opens, Walcott depicts himself back again in January, the dual-visioned month of his birth, gazing seaward from his hotel balcony in St. Lucia. His eye is caught this time by an object floating on the tide. In the unreliable light of dawn, he is struck by the visual transformations that seem to take place with the imagery playing through his mind. What appears to be a coconut husk one moment looks more like a drifting log at next glance and then reminds him of a plaster head in the foam. The passing fancy picks up impetus as the thought of sculpture reminds him of a woman's vaselike throat. Upon hearing someone blow a conch shell in the village, he catches himself enunciating "Omeros," the way he had once been instructed by a Greek girl.

Stream-of-consciousness thought carries him along, turning the driftwood into the form of old Seven Seas, beckoning him to follow. Shades of Proteus fill the scene as the metamorphosis proceeds from log to blind seaman to Homeric bust. Entering the dream, Walcott himself becomes insubstantial, realizing that he casts no shadow. He interprets his own transparency to signify the inner vision associated with St. Lucia's blind patron saint. With her eyes, he sees through the phantom of himself. On the heels of the statue, he ascends Philoctete's pathway past "every wound," reaches the spot where Ma Kilman discovered the healing plant, and stops to address the issue of his foreign travels (282). Two itinerant drifters have found themselves on the same shore.

It is easy to initiate a conversation with the statue, because both of them have seen much of the world and they share a common interest in the craft of writing. Walcott mentions seeing Seven Seas in London, clutching the worn manuscript of his odyssey on the steps of St. Martin-in-the-Fields.

His Homeric guide responds that the curate who chased him away did not care for him because he was a heathen. Condescending to word play, "The Aegean's chimera / is a camera, you get my drift, a drifter / is the hero of my book," he forces from Walcott the admission that he has never actually read his mentor's work, "Not all the way through." Omeros registers momentary injury, but admitting that the gods and demigods are negligible, he insists the rest of the book should still be read. In an apology closely echoing Dante's homage to Virgil in the first canto of the *Inferno*,[1] Walcott admits his poetic indebtedness:

> . . . "I have always heard
> your voice in that sea, master, it was the same song
> of the desert shaman, and when I was a boy
>
> your name was as wide as a bay, as I walked along
> the curled brow of the surf; the word 'Homer' meant joy,
> joy in battle, in work, in death, then the numbered peace
>
> of the surf's benedictions, it rose in the cedars,
> in the *laurier-cannelles,* pages of rustling trees.
> Master, I was the freshest of all your readers." (283)

The freshness of which the pupil speaks in the closing line reflects both the exigencies of common humanity and the nascent West Indian culture Walcott wishes to reify in his poetic line.

Walcott obviously projects his own appreciation of earthy reality into the persona of his animated statue when they discuss the girl who first taught him the appropriate Greek pronunciation of Omeros. After insisting that "A girl smells better than a book," recalling Helen's smell and casually dismissing the Trojan war as nothing more than "an epic's excuse," the statue abruptly asks, "Did you, you know, do it often?" Feeling his virility challenged, Walcott lies in the affirmative. As though touched with nostalgia for a lost love, Omeros then asks whether men still fight wars. With regret, Walcott responds, "Not over beauty, . . . Or a girl's love." By way of compensation, Omeros suggests a theme closer to Walcott's heart,

1. Dante Alighieri, *Dante Alighieri: Inferno,* 1.79–87.

"Love is good, but the love of your own people is

greater."
    "Yes," I said. "That's why I walk behind you.
Your name in her throat's white vase sent me to find you."
    "Good. A girl smells better than the world's libraries." (284)

In this exchange, Walcott's Homeric guide validates his epic impulse. Although they both inscribe their reactions in written form, each has been inspired not by historical or literary scholarship but by the physical experience of an actual woman, by the rhythm of the sea, by birth in a specific place. Thus, Walcott "walks behind" the image of Homer metaphysically: following his example as a man, if not his style as a heroic poet.

Having qualified his indebtedness to Homeric example in this manner, Walcott asserts the authenticity of his own vision while he continues to exploit Western literary convention. Beginning with the fifty-seventh chapter, when he initiates the obligatory journey into the underworld, he reflects his affinity with traditional classical authors who have manipulated epic forms according to their own designs. Despite specific local place-names, unmistakable Dantean influences mark Walcott's inferno. His West Indian Hades appears to be the darker side of a surreal St. Lucia rather than a subterranean netherworld. In place of Dante's Sibyl, he has the marble statue of Seven Seas guide him to a black canoe standing just offshore. The ocean along the coast of the island is his Acheron, and the "grizzled oarsman" (285) who ferries them to the sulfur pits of Soufrière is a black, Charon. Walcott's grinning, dialect-speaking boatman is a locally familiar, invincible domino player with grave-digger's breath.

Their ethereal canoe slides effortlessly among and through bathers, who can sense only the chilly wake of their invisible passage. As they glide past Castries and the same wharf where he had once conversed with his father's ghost, the narrator joins the statue in singing praises of the island. Their calypso takes in the Genoese sailor (Columbus) who named it for a blind saint, describes the natural beauty that elicits associations with an unfaithful wife (Helen of Troy), includes African fishermen who harvest its wooded mountains for their canoes (depicted in the opening chapter of *Omeros*), and the healing properties of its sulfuric volcano (confirmed in Ma Kilman's restorative "seawater and sulphur" baptism of Philoctete, 247). Their southerly progress along St. Lucia's coastline eventually brings them to land in Marigot Bay. There, Seven Seas conjures parallels with a ghostly British fleet lying in wait for the opposed French: he contends,

> " . . . This is like Troy
> all over. This forest gathering for a face!
> Only the years have changed since the weed-bearded kings.
>
> Beyond these stone almonds I can see Compte de Grasse
> pacing like horned Menelaus while his wife swings
> her sandals by one hand, strutting a parapet,
>
> knowing that her beauty is what no man can claim
> any more than this bay. Her beauty stands apart
> in a golden dress, its beaches wreathed with her name." (288)

Although Walcott established early on the historical significance of the Battle of the Saints, he has taken considerable geographical liberty here by alluding to Britain's spectral fleet while entering Marigot Bay. Since Walcott mentions the Comte de Grasse in this scene, he may be mistaken about an actual battle maneuver or he may be superimposing two different campaigns. If Rodney did not shelter in Marigot Bay prior to the Battle of the Saints, British Admiral Samuel Barrington deceived French commander d'Estaing by anchoring his fleet there in 1778. Barrington's ploy of disguising masts as trees may have been in Walcott's mind when he has Seven Seas describe the ships as "This *forest* gathering for a face" (288, italics added), or he may simply be using a natural metaphor for this grove of wooden masts.[2] Just prior to the Battle of the Saints (April 1782), Rodney's fleet actually lay at anchor off Gros Îlet (now Rodney Bay) north of Castries. Marigot, on the other hand, is situated approximately halfway between Achille's Gros Îlet village and his nightmare's destination at Sufrière, further south on the Caribbean side of the island. Perhaps he telescopes the locations of the real landscape in order to condense his Dantean vision of "hell in paradise" (289).

---

2. According to Harriet Durham, "Barrington eluded the enemy—we dare not suggest he was hiding—by taking his fleet into Marigot and disguising his ships as trees by lashing palm fronds to the masts," Durham and Lewisohn, *St. Lucia Tours and Tales,* 13.

Time and space at any rate are manipulated so that when they beach their canoe, Walcott and his marble guide are able to tour the forbidding environs of Soufrière where Bennett & Ward once pursued their futile enterprise. Within the volcanic inferno lie the Malebolge of damned souls who are punished for their various sins. First, in the Pool of Speculation are assorted traitors, "who had sold out their race," suffering at the hands of Hephaestus or Ogun, the Greek and African gods of the forge (289). These include elected officials who sold land to developers to create menial jobs for the poor while advancing their own sons professionally; businessmen who granted coastal trawlers the right to dredge the life from the sea; casino owners and gamblers contemptuous of "black people's laziness" (290). Because (drawing from the chimera/camera pun, 282–83), these traitors snap up the "postcard archipelago" of the superficial photographer rather than the magical imagery of the chimera, they have lost their souls to tourism.

In order to increase the narrator's understanding of his function as a man and a writer at this juncture, Seven Seas repeats the didactic role of all previous epic guides. He begins by explaining why Walcott has learned nothing of great significance from all his world travels. In a metaphor reminiscent of Penelope's tapestry, he notes that the flight of the swift ravels and unravels its own web. Similarly, Walcott has one beach, one island, one oar—the pen—with which he has plied one speech, one truth since childhood. Peeling back layers of self-reflection, he points out that the boy who first contemplated the rolling surf has always remained on his native shore, sending abroad only the phantom of himself.

> Mark you *he* does not go; he sends his narrator;
> he plays tricks with time because there are two journeys
> in every odyssey, one on worried water,
>
> the other crouched and motionless, without noise.
> for both, the "I" is a mast; a desk is a raft
> for one, foaming with paper, and dipping the beak
>
> of a pen in its foam, while an actual craft
> carries the other to cities where people speak
> a different language, or look at him differently,
>
> while the sun rises from the other direction
> with its unsettling shadows, but the right journey
> is motionless; as the sea moves round an island

that appears to be moving, love moves round the heart—
with encircling salt, and the slowly travelling hand
knows it returns to the port from which it must start.

Therefore, this is what this island has meant to you,
why my bust spoke, why the sea-swift was sent to you:
to circle yourself and your island with this art. (291)

Blood circulates through the heart; the reciprocal motion of the waves
encompass an island just as the poet encloses his subject. This, Seven Seas'
longest speech, delineates Walcott's mission in undertaking *Omeros,* just as
Anchises reinforces Aeneas and the shade of Virgil encourages his wayward
pilgrim to complete their respective journeys.

Following the example of other epic protagonists who encounter shades
of deceased companions in the underworld—Odysseus, his Elpenor; Ae-
neas, his Palinurus and Dido; Dante, a number of friends and foes—
Walcott singles out his fictive countryman Hector for particular attention.
He elaborates on Hector's punishment not only because of its appropri-
ateness but also because it affirms Hector's belief in an afterlife. Since
this road warrior abandoned the sea to drive a taxi, he essentially con-
demned himself to stand, shouldering an oar, beneath the geyser of a
comet. As is the case with Dante's sinners, he pays now for having made
the wrong choice. Walcott insists, "for me not to have seen him there
would question / a doctrine with more conviction than my own dream"
(292). He also seizes the opportunity to distinguish Hector's Catholic
purgatory (a transitory state) from the eternity of Christian hell. Since
Christ's net gathers all confirmed believers, "his spectre's punishment was
/ a halt in its passage towards a smokeless place" (292). The only other
individuals named in Walcott's inferno are the two colonial opportunists
Bennett & Ward, who are forced to excrete an ampersand-shaped ther-
mometer.

As the shade of Omeros has anticipated, progress grows increasingly
difficult due to the blinding sulfur fumes and because of his burdensome
self-doubt. Just as the Major and Philoctete suffer from their injuries,
Walcott's spiritual wound now makes him falter. In spite of his insistence
on Hector's eventual salvation, the next bolgia forces him to confess, "I
had lost faith both in religion and in myth." What he finds distressing

are the superficial, self-aggrandizing poets who plunder life in the name
of art.

> And that was where I had come from. Pride in my craft.
> Elevating myself. I slid, and kept falling
>
> towards the shit they stewed in; all the poets laughed,
> jeering with dripping fingers; then Omeros gripped
> my hand in enclosing marble . . . (293)

Fortunately his guide assists him to higher ground, but his proximity to
the envious, backbiting crew of poets compels him to search his own soul,
begging for a second chance. Omeros cautions,

> "You tried to render
> their lives as you could, but that is never enough;
> now in the sulphur's stench ask yourself this question,
>
> whether a love of poverty helped you
> to use other eyes, like those of that sightless stone?" (294)

The interrogation weighs all the more heavily because it is left suspended.
We do know that Walcott has previously repudiated the hypocritical ro-
manticization of poverty as a nostalgic luxury (227–28). The ambiguous
question leaves the possibility, however, that consideration of the poor has
broadened his perspective; or his fascination with the natural beauty of
simple peasants may have predisposed him to emulation of Homer in the
first place.

The result of this internal debate is that it terminates his nightmare.
Having had his soul exorcised, he finds himself still on the divided crest
of January as he had been at the opening of book seven. He has been
rejuvenated, savoring anew the Edenic world he shares with Achille.

> . . . The sea was my privilege.
> And a fresh people. The roar of famous cities
> entered the sea-almond's branches and then tightened
>
> into silence, and my crab's hand came out to write—
> and down the January beach as it brightened

> came bent sibyls sweeping the sand, then a hermit . . .
> . . . .
> Philoctete made with his ablutions, and that "Ah!"
> for the New Year's benediction. Then Philoctete
>
> waved "Morning" to me from far, and I waved back. (295)

Walcott feels closer than ever to Philoctete in that their common wound
has responded to the same cure. The image of his hand as a crab echoes the
metaphor from *Another Life,* where he disparages the "sidewise crawling"
linear motion of writing across a page.[3] Nevertheless, elated with this
January morning's freshness, he responds to the "thunderous myths" of
the ocean (295). He exults that the ocean retains no memory of *Gilgamesh*
or of the *Iliad,* because it erases and creates every line of its epic tale with
each rolling wave, from Africa to the New World: "Our last resort as much
as yours, Omeros" (296).

In its power to erase and generate life, the ocean provides Walcott's
paradigm. To his rhetorical question, then, "Why waste lines on Achille, a
shade on the sea-floor?" he immediately cites the example of self-sustaining
coral. Organic architecture beneath the sea offers him a parody of man's
practice of building atop old ruins. Thus, Achille furnishes the skeletal
framework for Walcott's dispossessed protagonist.

> From that coral and crystalline origin, a simply decent
> race broke from its various pasts, from howling sand
> to a track in a forest, torn from the farthest places
> . . . .
>   . . . History has simplified
>
> him. Its elegies had blinded me with the temporal
> lament for a smoky Troy, but where coral died
> it feeds on its death, the bones branch into more coral (297)

Even if "History" makes no pilgrimages to his coral pantheons, Achille
embodies the struggle of a remarkable people. Grateful for the inspiration
necessary to execute this worthy story, Walcott then produces the requisite
apostrophe to his epic muse.

3. Walcott, *Another Life,* 59.

> O Sun, the one eye of heaven, O Force, O Light,
> my heart kneels to you, my shadow has never changed
> since the salt-fresh mornings of encircling delight
>
> across whose cities the wings of the frigate ranged
> freer than any republic, gliding with ancient
> ease! I praise you not for my eyes. That other sight. (298)

The closing qualification not only emphasizes the primacy of spiritual insight or imagination but also gains further poignancy because of its oblique tribute to the blindness of the patron saint of St. Lucia.

Never content to sustain a mood indefinitely, Walcott descends from heavenly evocation rather abruptly to describe his protagonist's angry response to an intrusive tourist. Achille is incensed when a photographer shows unwarranted interest in the misspelling of *In God We Troust*. He, Philoctete, and their fellow fishermen work hard enough against the relentless forces of nature without having to suffer curious idlers seeking local color. Achille not only refuses to pose for snapshots but also creates a minor scene by hurling insults and imaginary weapons at his antagonists.

> It was the scream of a warrior losing his only soul
> to the click of a Cyclops, the eye of its globing lens,
> till they scuttered from his anger as a khaki mongrel
>
> does from a kick. It was the last form of self-defense. (299)

Walcott's major point is neither the reference to a naive fear of photography nor his parody of Odysseus' insult to Polyphemus; rather, he is more concerned with the laughter of servile waiters who begin mocking Achille's futile display. The derision of these liveried menials betrays their simplistic frame of reference: "They laughed at simplicities, the laugh of a wounded race" (299). Walcott reminds us that they are like "Lawrence of St. Lucia," the waiter who once served the Plunketts at the beach hotel (23). Not only do Achille's exhausted fishermen suffer obstreperous tourists, descending like scavenging gulls around their beached canoes; they are afflicted with the condescending scorn of their own countrymen.

Achille's anger, following as it does Walcott's nightmare visit to Soufrière's inferno, provides the motive for his abbreviated quest in chapter sixty for a new home. Human deprivations combined with unaccustomed vagaries of recent weather patterns causes Seven Seas to prophesy coming disasters. He reads omens suggesting that people may be the next endangered species; then the earth itself might be doomed. It is all the more disconcerting for Achille to realize that, while he might sustain his own integrity, his finite strength could not extend to others. In frustration, Achille and Philoctete launch their canoe in quest of some haven beyond the incursions of rapacious entrepreneurs. They pass trawlers dredging the wealth of the sea as miners once stripped the land of its minerals. Insatiable seines depopulate the ocean of its lobsters, albacore, dolphins, and shrimp as Aruac and Carib peoples were eradicated from their habitat. Wondering if he is the last of a vanishing breed of fishermen who love the source of their livelihood, he resolves to sail southward, leaving behind the hotels, marinas, and sunbathing tourists,

> . . . and find someplace,
> some cove he could settle like another Aeneas,
> founding not Rome but home, to survive in peace (301)

From Gros Îlet, he and Philoctete sail the same coastal voyage on which Omeros had led him—past cliffs, beaches, inlets, villages such as Anse La Raye and Canaries—until they land to spend the night among the fishermen of Soufrière. By firelight, Achille reflects on these hoary remnants of a heroic calling who bear the scars of "loving the sea over their own country" (302).

Having failed to locate a satisfactory homestead on the first day, Achille and Philoctete determine to extend their search farther southward toward the Grenadines. However, while they are still miles short of this group of islands, they are struck by a sight that drastically alters their objectives. Without warning, they chance upon gleaming dark shoals where there should be open sea. As suddenly as they realize that the reefs are actually moving through the water faster than their canoe, it becomes evident that they are surrounded by a pod of whales. In the moment it takes to recognize their awesome peril, one monster breaches, then sounds so near *In God We Trust* that they are almost swamped in the cresting swell. Their fragile canoe rights itself, and they are able to bail out the excess water, but they read this near-death experience as a sign. Observing the indifferent wave surge northward toward St. Lucia, Achille reexamines his impetuous decision to escape:

> . . . He has seen the shut face of thunder,
> he has known the frightening trough dividing the soul
>
> from this life and the other, he has seen the pod
> burst into spray. The bilge was bailed out, the sail
> turned home, their wet, salted faces shining with God. (303)

Offensive as the alien influences may be in his beloved island, it is his home and the source of all that is meaningful to him.

As we leave Achille to retrace his ill-conceived voyage, the narrative turns for the last time to the grieving Dennis Plunkett. Memories of his late wife are all associated with nineteenth-century Ireland. The accumulated detritus of their colonial sojourn strikes him as so *fin de siecle* that he wonders if "he'd fought the wrong war in / the wrong century" (304). By candlelight, his daguerreotype of Maud resembles a Victorian cameo, and there is the image of Helen in the shadows—large eyes, head in madras tie. His mood translates itself into one of the sentimental period studies by William Etty or Laurence Alma-Tadema.[4] As he calmly strokes his purring tomcat, reverie carries the Major back to the time he and Maud lay on a grassy hillside overlooking the camouflaged troop-ships that were to transport his regiment to North Africa. The occasion is memorable because Maud first offers herself to him and, although he is tempted, he gallantly refuses to engage in premarital sex. Offering the quaint notion that he needs something to believe in while he is away and wishing to avoid the fate of soldiers who knocked up cheap women, Dennis resists Maud's urging. Supposing that he must think she wishes to trap him into marriage, since she has boldly guided his hand between her legs, Maud is embarrassed to the point of anger. To reassure her injured pride, Dennis promises they will have a son at the proper time and after the war they will retire to an exotic island.

Plunkett's daydream merges seamlessly with the present as we find him engaged in a private séance in the back of Ma Kilman's rum shop. The ancient sibyl's paraphernalia offends the Major at first, and he expects to witness some facile chicanery. When she mentions a vision of Maud dressed in white walking beside a vast, still lake, he assumes that anyone

4. William Etty (1787–1849), English painter of mythological subjects in a style resembling Delacroix. Sir Laurence Alma-Tadema (1836–1912), Dutch-born, naturalized English painter of meticulously exact, often anecdotal historical scenes.

could extrapolate such a picture from any calendar's reproduction of Glenda-Lough. From the moment of Maud's death, he has conceived of her soul whirring away, across the sea to the ruined castles of Ireland. Without even realizing he has verbalized the question, he finds himself asking, "Heaven?" Ma Kilman's response, "Yes, if heaven is a green place," wins his heart utterly. As Walcott phrases it, "That moment bound him for good to another race" (307). Rather than serve as medium to deliver his message, Ma Kilman assures him that he can speak for himself and Maud will hear his words. Nevertheless, he asks her to convey his apologies for any pain he may have caused his wife and leaves twenty dollars in payment for Ma Kilman's services.

Smiling at his own foolishness for having indulged in this séance, Dennis is caught by surprise when he recognizes the image of Maud holding aside the beaded door-curtain for his exit. His head wound freezes as all the birds copied from Maud's guidebook are released from her silken quilt to metamorphose into the clouds overhead. In the next moment, he and Maud are seated together in the Land Rover and he relives simultaneously their trip to the bakery (259) and their encounter on the mountain road with the old woodsman with his bag of snakes' heads (61). Over the following days, the Major's wound slowly heals. He experiences the peace of Maud's faith and speaks with her as though she were present. His obsessive interest in history, which "had cost him a son and a wife," dwindles from memory, and he learns to talk among his workmen no longer as

> . . . boys who worked with him, till every name
>
> somehow sounded different; when he thought of Helen
> she was not a cause or a cloud, only a name
> for a local wonder. . . . (309)

The unspectacular disclosure of this epiphany is in sharp contrast with the ambitious fanfare with which he set out to commemorate Helen by writing her own story; he has now learned to appreciate her intrinsically, without the trappings of the past.

With the Major's revised plans, it begins to become evident that Walcott is gradually altering the epic trajectory of each of his remaining protagonists. We have already seen Walcott's narrator awaken to a renewed love of St. Lucia after touring his own nightmarish inferno. Although Achille is so alienated by obtrusive tourists and corrupted islanders that he undertakes a quest for a new homeland, his encounter with brute nature convinces him that home, with its imperfections, is superior to exile. Each of these characters, in turn, has sought a sense of belonging that is similar to that described in Robert Frost's "The Gift Outright":

> The land was ours before we were the land's.
> . . . .
> But we were England's, still colonials,
> Possessing what we still were unpossessed by,
> . . . .
> Until we found out that it was ourselves
> We were withholding from our land of living.

Walcott's homing instinct departs in one crucial respect from Frost's. In a 1995 review of a collection of Frost's poems, "The Road Taken," he observes that when New England's colonial settlers took possession of the land, they conveniently overlooked the existence of the indigenous natives who had to be dispossessed. As early as *Dream on Monkey Mountain,* Walcott imagines a less monopolistic quality of "ownership" for Makak. Elaborating on Makak's revelation, he explains to J. P. White that despite Makak's poverty, he learns to celebrate his belonging to a place. "I'm not talking about poverty, I'm talking about the sense of ownership that allows him to feel that when he walks on that road, it belongs to him. That is the condition of the West Indian. That sense of finally putting your foot down on a piece of earth that is yours."[5] Now in *Omeros,* despite the impossibility of escaping the depredations of "progress," Achille makes his way back home. Canceling his well-meaning desire to impose historical designs on Helen and her island, the Major learns to embrace the unfolding experience of being part of the island itself. As with Frost's Americans, they have had to relinquish their efforts to possess Helen before they may be possessed by her.

By accretion, Walcott lays the groundwork for general reconciliation in the closing chapters of *Omeros.* After Achille and the Major have effected their respective accommodations, chapter sixty-two broadens the

---

5. Robert Frost, *Complete Poems of Robert Frost,* 467; Derek Walcott, "The Road Taken," 29; White, "An Interview with Derek Walcott," 29.

application. Seven Seas may be physically blind, but he uses his ears and his mind's eye to furnish a panoramic inventory of his island. At the pulpit-helm of his stone ship the black priest makes the sign of the swift over his congregation while the village is besieged by yachts in the marina. The landscape has been transformed by the camera lens into an elegiac booklet of postcards. One captures Seven Seas and his dog in the shade; some depict the humorous misspellings on pirogues—*In God We Troust, Blue Genes, Artlantic City;* one captures Philoctete as he is first seen in *Omeros,* revealing his scarred shin, refusing to explain its cure; and another preserves Hector's grave, marked with shells and a single oar. Curiosity seekers may take in Ma Kilman's No Pain Cafe, the museum (with its pyrite-encrusted bottle, engravings of the Battle of the Saints, and logbook where the Major discovered his namesake), and the abandoned cannons gaping seaward from the redoubt.

In keeping with the fluid perspective throughout *Omeros,* Seven Seas' account grows increasingly poetic and soon yields to Walcott's philosophical musings. Whereas in the past he has called the fire-belching cannon an "iron lizard" (83), and St. Lucia was once named Iounalao "where the iguana is found" (4), Walcott now has a lizard question whether this New World island could have been the object of imperial contention. He wonders if a black Helen carrying cheap, plastic sandals could have been the instigation of armed conflict.

> . . . Were both hemispheres the split breadfruit of
> her African ass? . . .
> . . . .
> Who gives her the palm? Did sulking Achille grapple
> with Hector to repeat themselves? Exchange a spear
>
> for a cutlass; and when Paris tosses the apple
> from his palm to Venus, make it a *pomme-Cythère,*
> make all those parallels pointless. Names are not oars
>
> that have to be laid side by side, nor are legends. (312–13)

Much as he and Major Plunkett have made of traditional parallels, Walcott obviously reaches the conclusion that past and present run separate courses. Contemplating the two Helens—one of ancient marble, hewn in classic features; the other in ebony, wearing a yellow cotton dress—he prefers the living one, sleeping on a straw mattress in a beach shack, who has never seen fabled Troy.

To verify his assertion that stories do not have to be laid side by side, once again he catalogs Maud Plunkett's island-bred birds and cites the succession of imperial fleets occupying her coves.

> . . . Now there were hundreds of Frenchmen
>
>> and British listening in their separate cemeteries,
>> who died for a lizard, for red leaves to belong
>> to their ranks, for that green flash that was History's.
>> (314–15)

While these heroic dead have left their languages, their grave markers, their deeds and portraits in official texts, the names of workers who actually constructed society on the island go unrecorded. Achille, Hector, and Philoctete's ancestors are remembered only in the names of their progeny, in the children who burst enthusiastically out of classrooms each day, filling the streets with their voices.

A domestic scene in Ma Kilman's cafe illustrates their simple continuity. As Seven Seas basks in the warm sunlight, he enjoys the presence of Christine, a new young Helen. The daily pace has slowed so that they savor the most mundane details. Christine is a promising country maiden, seeking domestic employment. Ma Kilman mentions that she has recently heard from the girl's uncle Maljo, the failed political candidate known as "Statics," who now gathers citrus in Florida. The appearance of Helen herself in the shop prompts the old gardeuse to mention that Achille wants to give Hector's expected child an African name. In response to Helen's resistance to the idea, Ma Kilman remarks that she must still learn to accept her origins. When mention is made of Philoctete's standing as the baby's godfather, Seven Seas builds to what may be seen as a communal benediction: Philoctete has been cured, Major Plunkett is recovering, and he anticipates eventual healing for them all.

> He hummed in the silence. The song of the chanterelle,
> the river griot, the Sioux Shaman. Asphalt
> rippled its wires, like a harp. The street was still. (318)

We leave Seven Seas reposing at the window, quiet as a marble bust, listening to the rhythm of the sea and the creaking hinge of a passing swift.

Mundane as this domestic catalog may appear to be in comparison with its background of imperial battles, slavery, genocide, international travel, and classical allusions, it is at the heart of Walcott's epic material. The essence of his protagonists' heroism is not in the worldly renown of glorious deeds, but rather in the beauty of their simple humanity. If their exploits are not spectacular or superhuman, they are nonetheless remarkable examples of the resilience of the human spirit. Not content with merely recording the testimony of their lives, however, Walcott goes the extra step of delving into his own recording process. The argument can be made that Walcott's classical paraphernalia ultimately subverts his tribute to West Indian culture, rendering him vulnerable to the charge that he has succumbed to Western hegemony. A corollary to this line of reasoning is that he strikes the posture of self-examination in order to disarm postcolonial critics who would otherwise condemn his imitation of influential masters.

The problem with this interpretation is that it is too facile. Walcott could have avoided imitation altogether; instead, he offers a more sophisticated version of the artifice first exhibited in his autobiographical *Another Life*. In a 1975 interview, he describes this earlier poem as the "biography of an 'intelligence,' a West Indian intelligence."[6] As is to be expected, the naive narrator in *Another Life* matures as he learns from experience. In keeping with conventional bildungsroman practice, we observe the youngster in the process of acquiring knowledge and wisdom. Walcott takes the greater risk in *Omeros* of tendering multiple protagonists who, with the best of intentions, undertake enterprises that prove to be ill-conceived. Initially, the unwitting reader who is in the habit of accepting the authority of the text sympathizes when the Walcott narrator and Major Plunkett both seize upon the idea that Helen deserves to be legitimized within formal historical and literary traditions. As a consequence of this erroneous complicity with the narrative perspective, the reader becomes disabused at the same time the protagonists recognize their injustice to Helen. A poet wishing to project the image of authorial omniscience could have avoided this necessary corrective

6. Hamner, "Conversation with Derek Walcott," 411.

insight just as easily as potentially equivocal classical parallels could have
been avoided. Walcott rejects these options in order to explore the process
of self-discovery.

Although Walcott's exploitation of epic comparisons permeates *Omeros*
from the beginning, his scattered disclaimers are not entirely ingenuous.
On various occasions and through more than one persona, he has extended
and then withdrawn the conventional structure underlying his multilevel
narrative. It is as though he imitates predecessors for the express purpose of
emphasizing his deviation from the established pattern. Familiar tracings
register with the reader only to be isolated for contrast within the textual
fabric. Given the number of times he disrupts the literary context for
self-examination, his own authorial interpretations and motives open
themselves to question. When he explains himself, as he does once again
in the closing pages, he compensates for initial flaws that have plagued his
primary narrators from the beginning. Both he and Major Plunkett have
attempted to impose alien dimensions on Helen and their island. Upon
discovering their common error, Walcott ultimately repudiates classical
aspirations for his black heroine, and Dennis Plunkett learns humbly to
accept St. Lucia's Helen for the remarkable woman she is without reference
to external models.

As a result, readers must contend with the ambiguity of shifting perspec-
tives, fluidity of intermingled narrative lines, and the self-reflexive nature
of the text itself. Significantly, the culminating gesture by which Walcott
achieves epic closure is an effortless transition from physical description to
open introspection. The squeaking hinge of the swift that Seven Seas hears
as he reposes at Ma Kilman's window (319) is simultaneously a familiar
motif and a metaphorical link between a thought and its graphic expression
on the page. Walcott is explicit about the connection:

> I followed a sea-swift to both sides of this text;
> her hyphen stitched its seam, like the interlocking
> basins of a globe in which one half fits the next. (319)

The meridian of her flight links Old and New Worlds, Africa and
Caribbean islands, the complementary poles of his expansive world. Having
drawn attention to the act of writing one last time in this manner, he briefly
catalogs virtues of his epic tale. Achille, his hardy, barefoot protagonist,

never owned a passport or rode an elevator, was never subservient to
anyone, will never read his own story; and as a warrior, he engaged in the
slaughter of fish only to survive.

Nearing the end of his voyage, the poet himself claims that he can
imagine no greater tribute than to have Achille act as his pallbearer. His
casket-pirogue could settle beside those of Hector and Maud, lulled with the
rhythm of Caribbean waves (321). Helen is last seen moving among diners
at the Halcyon Hotel, which should be recognized as the hotel Walcott
visits in "The Light of the World."[7] Men admire and women study her
feline grace, "a fine local woman" who might well inspire a famous battle
or the name of an island (322). The poet asserts that for three years this
woman's name has kept his pen wandering across the page. In the recording
of her fable, he has searched out his own inheritance.

> Like Philoctete's wound, this language carries its cure,
> its radiant affliction; reluctantly now,
> like Achille's, my craft slips the chain of its anchor,
> . . . .
> And Achille himself had been one of those children
> whose voices are surf under a galvanized roof;
> sheep bleating in the schoolyard; a Caribbean
>
> whose woolly crests were the backs of the Cyclops's flock,
> with the smart man under one's belly. Blue stories
> we recited as children lifted with the rock
>
> of Polyphemus. From a plaster Omeros
> the smoke and the scarves of mare's tails, continually
> chalked associate phantoms across our own sky. (323)

When he reiterates these rich allusions here, once again, the association
is not only with the literary figures of Odysseus and Polyphemus but also
with the expansive land, sea, and sky under which myths arise. All the
ingredients that inspired Homer are equally available in Walcott's vital
Caribbean. In reaching the conclusion of *Omeros,* however, he sheds the
last vestiges of ancient correspondences in order to root Achille firmly in
his native landscape. After a grueling day at sea, he scales and guts his cargo

7. Walcott, *The Arkansas Testament,* 51. The Sandals Halcyon Hotel is located on
Choc Beach, St. Lucia.

of fish. Making sure that *In God We Troust* is beached and secured for the
night, he sloughs off the dried scales and rinses himself under the depot
standpipe before walking homeward to Helen. Even in closing, however,
Walcott preserves the continuity of Achille's story; his final line assures us
that "When he left the beach the sea was still going on" (325).

Given the intertextuality of *Omeros,* this open image is certainly appro-
priate. With the exception of Hector, who lived to regret abandoning the
sea, each of the main characters of Walcott's epic of the dispossessed has
worked his or her way through adversity to reconciliation. By definition, this
word implies resignation to undesirable conditions, but it also suggests the
reestablishment of peace, equilibrium, the achievement of new harmony.
For that which is lost, there is compensation. Just as his Greek namesake
had his injury healed and was reintegrated into his community, St. Lucia's
Philoctete is cured of his physical and racial wound. Ma Kilman, the
gardeuse who suffers the burden of all her people, recalls the African herbal
remedy that alleviates Philoctete's degradation. Although Achille suffers the
loss of his friend and nemesis Hector, he recovers his African name and
welcomes the prospect of living peacefully with Helen, who is carrying
Hector's unborn child. Helen has been unfaithful and she waits tables at
the Halcyon Hotel, yet her beauty and pride are undiminished as she basks
in Achille's unselfish love. Major Plunkett loses his identity as a colonist, his
treasured Maud dies, and he abandons his plans to commemorate Helen;
nevertheless, his old wound also heals and he gains both a surrogate son
and a sense of belonging to his adopted island. Seven Seas/Omeros, as blind
as the patron saint of his island and his Homeric counterpart, enjoys the
inner vision of the prophetic seer.

In the persona of the author himself, the intertextuality also exhibits
vestiges of continuity and reconciliation. Walcott has had to accommodate
both the classical and indigenous aspects of his dual heritage. Borrowing
or adapting sources confirms his attachment to established tradition. At
the same time, however, the liberties he takes with convention serve to
reconstitute a genre that might otherwise have grown moribund. When
William Shakespeare plagiarizes from extant works, he breathes life into
skeletons, invents flesh, enhances language, and "gives to aery nothing /
a local habitation and a name."[8] As a West Indian equally versed in the

8. William Shakespeare, *A Midsummer Night's Dream,* 5.1.16–17.

Western canon and calypsonian tradition, Walcott, too, exploits, parodies, complements, transforms, and occasionally transcends his original sources. The intertextuality of his self-reflexive epic includes the recycling of conventional influences and the intermeshing of real life with literary tropes on the written page. In spite of Walcott's disclaimers, *Omeros* is not only a credible extension of the world's store of epics, it also enriches that venerable genre and exposes unexpected, rarely used resources. *Omeros,* the West Indian epic, deserves to be compared with its predecessors—the *Iliad,* the *Odyssey,* the *Aeneid,* the *Divine Comedy, Paradise Lost, Leaves of Grass,* the *Cantos,* the *Bridge,* and others—because it represents the postcolonial world as these masterpieces address their respective ages.

Bibliography

Adcock, Craig E. *Marcel Duchamp's Notes from the Large Glass: An N-Dimensional Analysis.* Ann Arbor: UMI Research Press, 1983.

Aeschylus. *The Agamemnon.* In *The Orestes Plays of Aeschylus,* translated by Paul Roche, 27–99. New York: New American Library, 1962.

Anderson, William Scovil. *The Art of the Aeneid.* Englewood Cliffs: Prentice-Hall, 1969.

Babuts, Nicolae. "Text: Origins and Reference." *PMLA* 107, no. 1 (January 1992): 65–77.

Bachelard, Gaston. *The Poetics of Space.* Translated by Maria Jolas. New York: Orion Press, 1964.

Barthes, Roland. *Criticism and Truth.* Edited and translated by Katherine Pilcher Keuneman. Minneapolis: University of Minnesota Press, 1987.

Baugh, Edward. *Derek Walcott: Memory as Vision: Another Life.* London: Longman, 1978.

Benfey, Christopher. "Coming Home." Review of *Omeros,* by Derek Walcott. *New Republic* 203 (October 23, 1990): 36–39.

Bensen, Robert. "Catherine Weldon in *Omeros* and 'The Ghost Dance': Notes on Derek Walcott's Poetry and Drama." *Verse* 11, no. 2 (summer 1994): 119–25.

Blackmur, R. P. "New Thresholds, New Anatomies." In his *Form and Value in Modern Poetry,* 269–85. Garden City, N.Y.: Doubleday, 1957.

Bloom, Harold. *The Anxiety of Influence: A Theory of Poetry.* New York: Oxford University Press, 1973.

Brown, Robert, and Cheryl Johnson. "An Interview with Derek Walcott." *Cream City Review* 14, no. 2 (winter 1990): 209–23.

Bruckner, D. J. R. "A Poem in Homage to an Unwanted Man." Review of *Omeros,* by Derek Walcott. *New York Times,* October 9, 1990.

Burris, Sidney. "An Empire of Poetry." *Southern Review* 27, no. 3 (summer 1991): 558–66.

Chandler, David, ed. *Dictionary of Battles: The World's Key Battles from 405 B.C. to Today.* New York: Henry Holt, 1987.

Conrad, Joseph. *Heart of Darkness.* Edited by Robert Kimbrough. New York: Norton, 1963.

Crane, Hart. *The Complete Poems and Selected Letters and Prose of Hart Crane.* Edited by Brom Weber. New York: Liveright, 1966.

———. *The Letters of Hart Crane, 1916–1932.* Edited by Brom Weber. New York: Hermitage House, 1952.

Culler, Jonathan. *Structuralist Poetics: Structuralism, Linguistics and the Study of Literature.* Ithaca: Cornell University Press, 1975.

Dante Alighieri. *Dante Alighieri: Inferno.* Translated by Allan Gilbert. Durham: Duke University Press, 1969.

De Vries, Jan. *Heroic Song and Heroic Legend.* Translated by B. J. Timmer. London: Oxford University Press, 1963.

Durham, Harriet F., and Florence Lewisohn. *St. Lucia Tours and Tales.* New York: Robertson Printing, 1971.

Eakin, Paul John. *Fictions in Autobiography: Studies in the Art of Self-Invention.* Princeton: Princeton University Press, 1985.

Ferry, Anne Davidson. *Milton's Epic Voice.* Cambridge: Harvard University Press, 1963.

Frost, Robert. *Complete Poems of Robert Frost.* New York: Holt, Rinehart and Winston, 1967.

Froude, James Anthony. *The English in the West Indies: or the Bow of Ulysses.* London: Longmans, 1888.

Gordon, John. *Finnegans Wake: A Plot Summary.* Syracuse: Syracuse University Press, 1986.

Graves, Robert. *The Crowning Privilege: Collected Essays and Poetry.* Freeport, N.Y.: Books for Libraries, 1970.

Hamilton, Richard. "The Large Glass." In *Marcel Duchamp,* edited by Anne D'Harnoncourt and Kynaston McShine, 57–67. New York: Museum of Modern Art, 1989.

Hamner, Robert D. "Conversation with Derek Walcott." *World Literature Written in English* 16, no. 2 (November 1977): 409–20.

———. *Derek Walcott, Updated Edition.* New York: Twayne, 1993.

Hargreaves, Reginald. *The Bloodybacks: The British Serviceman in North America and the Caribbean 1655–1783.* New York: Walker, 1968.

Hutcheon, Linda. *Narcissistic Narrative: The Metafictional Paradox.* New York: Methuen, 1984.

Ingalls, Jeremy. *The Epic Tradition and Related Essays.* Tucson: Capstone Editions, 1989.

Ismond, Patricia. "Walcott's *Omeros*—a Complex, Ambitious Work." *Caribbean Contact* 18, no. 5 (March–April 1991): 10–11.

James, C. L. R. *The Black Jacobins: Toussaint L'Ouverture and the San Domingo Revolution.* 2d ed. New York: Vintage, 1963.

Johnson, Dorothy. *Some Went West.* New York: Dodd, Mead, 1965.

Joyce, James. *Finnegans Wake.* New York: Viking Press, 1955.

King, Bruce. *Derek Walcott and West Indian Drama.* Oxford: Clarendon Press, 1995.

Kroeber, Karl. *Romantic Narrative Art.* Madison: University of Wisconsin Press, 1966.

Leithauser, Brad. "Ancestral Rhyme." Review of *Omeros,* by Derek Walcott. *New Yorker,* February 11, 1991, 91–95.

Lord, Albert B. *The Singer of Tales.* Cambridge: Harvard University Press, 1960.

Marcus, G. J. *Heart of Oak: A Survey of British Sea Power in the Georgian Era.* London: Oxford University Press, 1975.

Mason, David. Review of *Omeros,* by Derek Walcott. *Hudson Review* 44, no. 3 (autumn 1991): 513–15.

Merchant, Paul. *The Epic.* London: Methuen, 1971.

Miller, James E., Jr. "She's Here, Install'd Amid the Kitchen Ware: Walt Whitman's Epic Creation." In his *The American Quest for a Supreme Fiction,* 31–49, 336–37. Chicago: University of Chicago Press, 1979.

———. "Whitman's 'Leaves of Grass' and the American Lyric Epic." In *Poems in Their Place: The Intertextuality and Order of Poetic Collections,* edited by Neill Fraistat, 287–307. Chapel Hill: University of North Carolina Press, 1987.

Milton, John. *Complete Poems and Major Prose.* Edited by Merritt Y. Hughes. New York: Odyssey Press, 1957.

Moore, Thomas. *Airs of Old Erin.* New York: Edward B. Marks Music Corp., 1936.

———. "Bendemeer's Stream." In *Folk Songs of Many Peoples,* vol. 2, edited by Florence Hudson, 112–13. Botsford, New York: Women's Press, 1922.

Mukherjee, Arun. *Towards an Aesthetic of Opposition: Essays on Literature, Criticism and Cultural Imperialism.* Ontario: Williams-Wallace, 1988.

Natkiel, Richard, and Anthony Preston. *Atlas of Maritime History.* Greenwich, Conn.: Bison Books, 1986.

O'Brien, Sean. "In Terms of the Ocean." Review of *Omeros,* by Derek Walcott. *Times Literary Supplement* 4563 (September 14–22, 1990): 977–78.

Okpewho, Isidore. *The Epic of Africa: Toward a Poetics of the Oral Performance.* New York: Columbia University Press, 1979.

Pantin, Raoul. "Any Revolution Based on Race Is Suicidal." *Caribbean Contact* 1, no. 8 (August 1973): 14, 16.

Parry, Milman. *The Making of Homer's Verse: The Collected Papers of Milman Parry.* Edited by Adam Parry. New York: Oxford University Press, 1987.

Pearce, Roy Harvey. *The Continuity of American Poetry.* Princeton: Princeton University Press, 1961.

Poe, Edgar Allan. "The Poetic Principle." In *The Complete Works of Edgar Allan Poe,* vol. 14, edited by James A. Harrison, 266–92. New York: AMS Press, 1965.

Presson, Rebekah. Interview with Derek Walcott. "Derek Walcott" (with Reading from *Omeros*). *New Letters on the Air: Contemporary Writers on Radio.* Audiotape, 29 minutes. University of Missouri–Kansas City, 1991.

———. "The Man Who Keeps the English Language Alive: An Interview with Derek Walcott." *New Letters* 59, no. 1 (1992): 8–15.

Quinn, Vincent. *Hart Crane.* New Haven: Twayne, 1963.

Said, Edward. *Culture and Imperialism.* New York: Alfred A. Knopf, 1993.

Schellenberger, J. "More Early Nineteenth-Century Epics." *Notes and Queries* 30, no. 3 (June 1983): 213–14.

Sen, Nabaneeta Dev. "Thematic Structure of Epic Poems in the East and West: A Comparative Study." In *Proceedings of the International Comparative Literature Association, II: Comparative Literature Today: Theory and Practice,* edited by Eva Kuschner and Roman Struc, 607–12. Stuttgart: Bieber, 1979.

Shakespeare, William. *A Midsummer Night's Dream.* In *The Riverside Shakespeare,* edited by G. Blakemore Evans, 222–46. Boston: Houghton Mifflin, 1974.

———. *The Tragedy of King Lear.* In *The Riverside Shakespeare,* edited by G. Blakemore Evans, 1255–95. Boston: Houghton Mifflin, 1974.

Smith, Rex Allen. *Moon of Popping Trees*. Lincoln: University of Nebraska Press, 1981.

Stanford, W. B. *The Ulysses Theme: A Study in the Adaptability of a Traditional Hero*. 2d ed. Oxford: Basil Blackwell and Mott, 1963.

Stevens, William Oliver, and Allan Westcott. *A History of Sea Power*. Garden City, N.Y.: Doubleday, 1942.

Suzuki, Mihoko. *Metamorphoses of Helen: Authority, Difference, and the Epic*. Ithaca: Cornell University Press, 1989.

Taylor, Patrick. *The Narrative of Liberation: Perspectives on Afro-Caribbean Literature, Popular Culture, and Politics*. Ithaca: Cornell University Press, 1989.

Terada, Rei. *Derek Walcott's Poetry: American Mimicry*. Boston: Northeastern University Press, 1992.

Vestal, Stanley. *New Sources of Indian History 1850–1891*. Norman: University of Oklahoma Press, 1934.

Virgil. *The Aeneid of Virgil*. Translated by C. Day Lewis. New York: Oxford University Press, 1952.

Vogler, Thomas A. *Preludes to Vision: The Epic Venture in Blake, Wordsworth, Keats, and Hart Crane*. Berkeley: University of California Press, 1971.

Walcott, Derek. *Another Life*. New York: Farrar, Straus and Giroux, 1973.

———. "The Antilles: Fragments of Epic Memory." *New Republic* 207 (December 28, 1992): 26, 28–32.

———. *The Arkansas Testament*. New York: Farrar, Straus and Giroux, 1987.

———. "Caligula's Horse." *Kunapipi* 11, no. 1 (1989): 138–42.

———. "The Caribbean: Culture or Mimicry?" *Journal of Interamerican Studies and World Affairs* 16, no. 1 (February 1974): 3–13.

———. *The Castaway*. London: Jonathan Cape, 1965.

———. "A Dilemma Faces W. I. Artists." *Sunday Guardian* (Trinidad), January 12, 1964.

———. *Dream on Monkey Mountain and Other Plays*. New York: Farrar, Straus and Giroux, 1970.

———. *Drums and Colours: An Epic Drama*. Commissioned for the opening of the First Federal Parliament of the West Indies, April 23, 1958. *Caribbean Quarterly*, Special issue, 7, no. 1–2 (March–June 1961): 1–104.

――――. "Epitaph for the Young: A Poem in XII Cantos." Bridgetown, Barbados: Advocate Co., 1949.

――――. *The Fortunate Traveler.* New York: Farrar, Straus and Giroux, 1981.

――――. "The Ghost Dance." Unpublished typescript. [Performed Hartwick College, Oneonta, N.Y., 1989].

――――. *The Gulf.* New York: Farrar, Straus and Giroux, 1970.

――――. *Hart Crane. Voices and Visions Series.* Directed by Laurence Pitkethley. Videocassette, 57 minutes. New York: New York Center for Visual History, 1988.

――――. *Henri Christophe: A Chronicle in Seven Scenes.* Bridgetown, Barbados: Advocate Co., 1950.

――――. *In a Green Night: Poems 1948–60.* London: Jonathan Cape, 1962.

――――. *The Joker of Seville.* In his *The Joker of Seville and O Babylon!* 3–151. New York: Farrar, Straus and Giroux, 1978.

――――. *The Last Carnival.* In his *Three Plays,* 3–101. New York: Farrar, Straus and Giroux, 1986.

――――. "Leaving School." *London Magazine* 5, no. 6 (1965): 4–14.

――――. "Meanings." *Savacou* 2 (1970): 45–51.

――――. *Midsummer.* New York: Farrar, Straus and Giroux, 1984.

――――. "The Muse of History: An Essay." In *Is Massa Day Dead?* edited by Orde Coombs, 1–28. Garden City, N.Y.: Doubleday, 1974.

――――. "A Note on Production." In his *Dream on Monkey Mountain and Other Plays,* 208. New York: Farrar, Straus and Giroux, 1970.

――――. *The Odyssey.* New York: Farrar, Straus and Giroux, 1993.

――――. *Omeros.* New York: Farrar, Straus and Giroux, 1990.

――――. *Pantomime.* In his *Remembrance and Pantomime,* 89–170. New York: Farrar, Straus and Giroux, 1980.

――――. "Poetry—Enormously Complicated Art." *Trinidad Guardian,* June 18, 1962.

――――. "The Road Taken." *New Republic,* November 27, 1995, 29–34, 36.

――――. *The Sea at Dauphin.* In his *Dream on Monkey Mountain and Other Plays,* 43–80. New York: Farrar, Straus and Giroux, 1970.

――――. *Sea Grapes.* London: Jonathan Cape, 1976.

――――. *Selected Poems.* New York: Farrar, Straus and Company, 1962.

――――. *The Star-Apple Kingdom.* New York: Farrar, Straus and Giroux, 1979.

――――. *25 Poems.* Bridgetown, Barbados: Advocate Co., 1949; 1st ed., Port-of-Spain, privately printed, 1948.

————. "What the Twilight Says: An Overture." In his *Dream on Monkey Mountain and Other Plays*, 1–40. New York: Farrar, Straus and Giroux, 1970.

————. "Young Trinidad Poets." *Sunday Guardian*, June 19, 1966.

Weber, Brom. *Hart Crane*. New York: Bodley Press, 1948.

White, J. P. "An Interview with Derek Walcott." *Green Mountain Review* ns., 4, no. 1 (spring–summer 1990): 14–37.

Winters, Yvor. "The Significance of *The Bridge*, by Hart Crane." In his *On Modern Poets*. New York: Meridian Books, 1959.

Works Consulted

Adams, Percy G. "The Epic Tradition and the Novel." *Southern Review* 9, no. 1 (January 1973): 300–310.

Arlett, R. M. "The Dialectical Epic: Brecht and Lessing." *Twentieth Century Literature* 33, no. 1 (spring 1987): 67–79.

Beebe, Maurice. "Ulysses and the Age of Modernism." In *Ulysses: Fifty Years*, edited by Thomas F. Staley, 172–88. Bloomington: Indiana University Press, 1974.

Benstock, Bernard. *James Joyce*. New York: Frederick Ungar, 1985.

Bernstein, Michael Andre. *The Tale of the Tribe: Ezra Pound and the Modern Verse Epic*. Princeton: Princeton University Press, 1980.

Beye, Charles R. *"The Iliad," "The Odyssey" and the Epic Tradition*. Garden City, N.Y.: Doubleday, 1966.

Bhabha, Homi K. "DissemiNation: Time, Narrative, and the Margins of the Modern Nation." In his *Nation and Narration*, 291–322. London: Routledge, 1990.

Bien, Peter. "The Demoticism of Kazantzakis." In *Modern Greek Writers*, edited by Edmund Keely and Peter Bien, 145–69. Princeton: Princeton University Press, 1972.

Bolt, Sidney. *A Preface to James Joyce*. New York: Longman, 1981.

Bowra, C[ecil] M. *Homer*. London: Duckworth, 1972.

Brecht, Bertolt, ed. *Brecht on Theatre*. Translated by John Willett. New York: Hill and Wang, 1966.

Breen, Henry H. *St. Lucia: Historical, Statistical and Descriptive*. London: Longman, 1844. London: Frank Cass, 1970.

Breiner, Laurence A. "Lyric and Autobiography in West Indian Literature." *Journal of West Indian Literature* 3, no. 1 (January 1989): 3–15.

Brewster, Anne. *Towards a Semiotic of Post-Colonial Discourse: University Writing in Singapore and Malaysia 1949–1965*. Center for Advanced Studies, Occasional Paper, National University of Singapore: Heinemann, 1989.

Brooks, Peter. "The Idea of a Psychoanalytic Literary Criticism." *Critical Inquiry* 13 (winter 1987): 334–48.

―――. *Reading for the Plot*. New York: Knopf, 1984.

Brydon, Diana. "The Myths that Write Us: Decolonising the Mind." *Commonwealth: Essays and Studies* 10, no. 1 (1987): 1–14.

Burden, Dennis H. *The Logical Epic: A Study of the Argument of Paradise Lost*. Cambridge: Harvard University Press, 1967.

Césaire, Aimé. *Cahier d'un retour au pays natal*. Introduction by Andre Breton. Paris: Présence Africaine, 1971.

―――. *Discourse on Colonialism*. Translated by Joan Pinkham. New York: Monthly Review Press, 1972.

Cikovsky, Nicolai, Jr. *Winslow Homer*. New York: Abrams, 1990.

Clinton, DeWitt. "A Guide to Historical/Epic Poems Published in English, 1980–1985." *Salthouse* 14–17 (1986): 1–27.

Corliss, Richard. "Club Adriatic." Review of *The Odyssey*, by Derek Walcott. *Time* 144, no. 18 (October 31, 1994): 78.

Cornevin, Robert. "African Epic Poems and the Living Epic." *Présence Africaine* 60 (1966): 134–39.

Cowles, Frank Hewitt. "The Epic Question in Vergil." *Classical Journal* 36, no. 3 (December 1940): 133–42.

Cox, James M. "Autobiography and America." In *Aspects of Narrative: Selected Papers from the English Institute*, edited by J. Hillis Miller, 143–72. New York: Columbia University Press, 1971.

Crane, Hart. *The Bridge*. New York: Liveright, 1970.

Crawford, Robert. "Homing." Review of *Omeros*, by Derek Walcott. *Poetry Review* 80, no. 4 (winter 1990–1991): 8–10.

Culler, Jonathan. *On Deconstruction: Theory and Criticism after Structuralism*. Ithaca: Cornell University Press, 1982.

Cumming, Mark. "Carlyle, Whitman, and the Disimprisonment of Epic." *Victorian Studies* 29, no. 2 (winter 1986): 207–26.

Davidson, Basil, et al. *A History of West Africa to the Nineteenth Century*. Garden City, N.Y.: Anchor Books, 1966.

Delaney, Frank. *James Joyce's Odyssey: A Guide to the Dublin of Ulysses*. New York: Holt, Rinehart and Winston, 1981.

Delasanta, Rodney. "The Classical Exemplum." In his *The Epic Voice*, 37–56. Hague: Mouton, 1967.

de Man, Paul. "Autobiography as De-facement." *Modern Language Notes* 94, no. 5 (1979): 919–30.

Demaray, John G. *The Invention of Dante's Comedy*. New Haven: Yale University Press, 1974.

D'Harnoncourt, Anne, and Kynaston McShine, eds. *Marcel Duchamp*. New York: Museum of Modern Art, 1989.

Dunn, N. E. "The Common Man's *Iliad*." *Comparative Literature Studies* 21, no. 3 (fall 1984): 270–81.

Eble, Kenneth. *Ezra Pound*. Boston: Twayne, 1979.

Eliot, T. S. "Ulysses, Order, and Myth." In *James Joyce: Two Decades of Criticism*, edited by Seon Givens, 198–202. New York: Vanguard Press, 1939.

Ellmann, Richard. *Ulysses on the Liffey*. Oxford: Oxford University Press, 1972.

Fagles, Robert. "Epilogue: Homer and the Writers." In *Homer: A Collection of Critical Essays*, edited by George Steiner, 160–71. Englewood Cliffs, N.J.: Prentice-Hall, 1962.

Falconio, Donald. "Critics of Kazantzakis: Selected Checklist of Writings in English." *Journal of Modern Literature* 2 (1972): 314–26.

Flanagan, Brenda. "An Interview with Derek Walcott." *Voices of the African Diaspora: CAAS Research Review* 7 (1991): 17.

Foerster, Donald M. *The Fortunes of Epic Poetry*. Washington: Catholic University of America Press, 1962.

Forsyth, Neil. "Homer in Milton: The Attendance Motif and the Graces." *Comparative Literature* 33, no. 2 (spring 1981): 137–55.

Friedman, Norman. "Point of View in Fiction." *PMLA* 70, no. 5 (December 1955): 1160–84.

Fussell, Edwin. "Dante and Pound's *Cantos*." *Journal of Modern Literature* 1, no. 1 (1970): 75–87.

Gasché, Rodolphe. Foreword. "Autobiography and the Problem of the Subject." *Modern Language Notes* 93, no. 4 (May 1978): 573–74.

Gates, Henry Louis, Jr. "Authority, (White) Power, and the (Black) Critic; It's All Greek to Me." In *The Nature and Context of Minority Discourse*, edited by Abdul R. JanMohamed and David Lloyd, 72–101. New York: Oxford University Press, 1990.

Genette, Gérard. *Narrative Discourse*. Translated by Jane E. Lewin. Ithaca: Cornell University Press, 1980.

Genovese, Eugene. *Roll Jordan Roll: The World the Slaves Made*. New York: Pantheon, 1974.

Gilman, Richard. *The Confusion of Realms*. London: Weidenfeld and Nicolson, 1970.

Goldberg, S. L. "Homer and the Nightmare of History." In his *The Classical Temper: A Study of James Joyce's Ulysses*, 145–210. New York: Barnes and Noble, 1963.

Greenblatt, Stephen, ed. *The Power of Forms in the English Renaissance*. Norman: University of Oklahoma Press, 1982.

Griffiths, Gareth. "Imitation, Abrogation and Appropriation: The Production of the Post-colonial Text." *Kunapipi* 9, no. 1 (1987): 13–20.

Hadas, Moses. "Aeneas and the Tradition of the National Hero." *American Journal of Philology* 69 (1948): 408–14.

Hamner, Robert D. *Critical Perspectives on Derek Walcott*. Washington: Three Continents Press, 1993.

Harbsmeir, Michael. "Early Travels to Europe: Some Remarks on the Magic of Writing." In *Europe and Its Others*, vol. 1, edited by Francis Baker et al., 73–88. Colchester: University of Essex, 1985.

Harvey, A. D. "The English Epic in the Romantic Period." *Philological Quarterly* 55, no. 2 (spring 1976): 241–59.

Hornbeck, John F. "St. Lucia." In *Islands of the Commonwealth Caribbean: A Regional Study*, edited by Sandra W. Meditz and Dennis M. Hanratty. Area Handbook Series. Washington, D.C.: Library of Congress, 1989.

Hudgins, Andrew. "*Leaves of Grass* from the Perspective of Modern Epic Practice." *Midwest Quarterly* 23, no. 4 (summer 1982): 380–90.

Huggan, Graham. "Blue Myth Brooding in Orchid: A Third-World Reappraisal of Island Poetics." *Journal of West Indian Literature* 1, no. 2 (June 1987): 20–28.

Jameson, Fredric. "Metacommentary." *PMLA* 86, no. 1 (January 1971): 9–18.

Jay, Paul C. "Being in the Text: Autobiography and the Problem of the Subject." *Modern Language Notes* 97 (1982): 1045–63.

Kain, Richard M. "Years Dreams Return: The Epic Structure." In his *Fabulous Voyager: James Joyce's Ulysses*, 35–47. Chicago: University of Chicago Press, 1947.

Kenner, Hugh. "Pound and Homer." In *Ezra Pound among the Poets,* edited by George Bornstein, 1–12. Chicago: University of Chicago Press, 1985.

Kroeber, Karl. "American Ethnopoetics: A New Critical Dimension." *Arizona Quarterly* 45, no. 2 (summer 1989): 1–13.

Kuberski, Philip. "Ego, Scriptor: Pound's Odyssean Writing." *Paideuma* 14, no. 1 (spring 1985): 31–51.

Lacan, Jacques. *Speech and Language in Psychoanalysis.* Edited by Anthony Wilden. Baltimore: Johns Hopkins University Press, 1968.

Lejeune, Philippe. "Autobiography in the Third Person." Translated by Annette and Edward Tomarken. *New Literary History* 9, no. 1 (autumn 1977): 27–49.

Litz, A. Walton. *The Art of James Joyce.* London: Oxford University Press, 1961.

Mandel, Oscar. *Philoctētēs and the Fall of Troy.* Lincoln: University of Nebraska Press, 1981.

Maresca, Thomas E. *Epic to Novel.* Columbus: Ohio State University Press, 1974.

McClatchy, J. D. "Robert Lowell: History and Epic." *Southwest Review* 72, no. 2 (spring 1987): 238–45.

Merchant, Paul. "Children of Homer: The Epic Strain in Modern Greek Literature." In *Aspects of the Epic,* edited by Tom Winnifrith, Penelope Murray, and K. W. Gransden, 92–108. London: Macmillan, 1983.

Michalopoulos, Andre. *Homer.* Boston: Twayne, 1966.

Miller, J. Hillis. *Aspects of Narrative: Selected Papers from the English Institute.* New York: Columbia University Press, 1971.

Miller, James E., Jr. *A Critical Guide to "Leaves of Grass."* Chicago: University of Chicago Press, 1957.

———. "An Epic of the Modern Consciousness: Hart Crane's *Bridge.*" In his *The American Quest for a Supreme Fiction,* 163–99. Chicago: University of Chicago Press, 1979.

Murray, Penelope. "Homer and the Bard." In *Aspects of the Epic,* edited by Tom Winnifrith, Penelope Murray, and K. W. Gransden, 1–15. London: Macmillan, 1983.

Nelson, Emmanuel S. "Black American and the Anglophone Afro-Caribbean Literary Consciousness." *Journal of American Culture* 12, no. 4 (winter 1989): 53–58.

Newman, Robert D. *Transgressions of Reading: Narrative Engagement as Exile and Return.* Durham: Duke University Press, 1993.

Newton, Rick M. "Homer and the Death of Kazantzakis' Odysseus." *Classical and Modern Literature: A Quarterly* 9, no. 4 (1989): 327–38.

Nimis, Stephen A. *Narrative Semiotics in the Epic Tradition: The Simile.* Bloomington: Indiana University Press, 1987.

Nwonga, D[onatus] Ibe. "The Limitations of Universal Critical Criteria." In *Exile and Tradition: Studies in African Literature,* edited by Rowland Smith, 8–30. New York: African Publishing, Dalhousie University Press, 1976.

Owens, Craig. "The Discourse of Others: Feminists and Postmodernism." In *The Anti-Aesthetic: Essays in Postmodern Culture,* edited by Hal Foster, 57–81. Port Towsend, Wash.: Bay Press, 1983.

Parrinder, Geoffrey. *African Mythology.* New York: Peter Bedrick Books, 1982.

Parry, Benita. "Problems in Current Theories of Colonial Discourse." *Oxford Literary Review* 9, no. 1–2 (1988): 27–58.

Pearce, Roy Harvey. "Pound, Whitman, and the American Epic." In *Ezra Pound: A Collection of Critical Essays,* edited by Walter Sutton, 163–77. Englewood Cliffs, N.J.: Prentice-Hall, 1963.

Prescott, Joseph. "Homer's *Odyssey* and Joyce's *Ulysses.*" In his *Exploring James Joyce,* 29–50. Carbondale: Southern Illinois University Press, 1964.

Questel, Victor D. "The Fate of Writing." *Caribbean Quarterly* 28, no. 1–2 (March 1982): 76–84.

Raleigh, John Henry. "Bloom as a Modern Epic Hero." *Critical Inquiry* 3, no. 3 (spring 1977): 583–98.

Read, Forrest. "Pound, Joyce, and Flaubert: The Odysseans." In *New Approaches to Ezra Pound: A Co-ordinated Investigation of Pound's Poetry and Ideas,* edited by Eva Hesse, 125–44. Berkeley: University of California Press, 1969.

Richards, I. A. *Principles of Literary Criticism.* New York: Harcourt, Brace, 1948.

Ritoók, Zs. "The Views of Early Greek Epic on Poetry and Art." *Mnemosyne* 42 (1989): 331–48.

Robbins, Bruce. "Death and Vocation." *PMLA* 107, no. 1 (January 1992): 38–50.

Said, Edward W. "Molestation and Authority in Narrative Fiction." In

Aspects of Narrative: Selected Papers from the English Institute, edited by J. Hillis Miller, 47–68. New York: Columbia University Press, 1971.

———. *Orientalism.* London: Routledge and Kegan Paul, 1978.

———. *The World, the Text and the Critic.* Cambridge: Harvard University Press, 1983.

Scipper, Mineke. "Eurocentrism and Criticism: Reflections on the Study of Literature in the Past and Present." *World Literature Written in English* 24, no. 1 (summer 1984): 16–26.

Seidel, Michael. *Epic Geography: James Joyce's Ulysses.* Princeton: Princeton University Press, 1976.

Seidel, Michael, and Edward Mendelson. *Homer to Brecht: The European Epic and Dramatic Traditions.* New Haven: Yale University Press, 1977.

Sicari, Stephen. "The Secret of Eleusis or How Pound Grounds His 'Epic of Judgment.'" *Paideuma* 14 (fall–winter 1985): 303–21.

Simpson, George E. *Religious Cults of the Caribbean: Trinidad, Jamaica, and Haiti.* Puerto Rico: Institute of Caribbean Studies, University of Puerto Rico, 1980.

Simpson, Roger. "Epics in the Romantic Period." *Notes and Queries* 33, no. 2 (June 1986): 160–61.

Slemon, Stephen. "Post-colonial Allegory and the Transformation of History." *Journal of Commonwealth Literature* 23, no. 1 (1988): 157–68.

Slemon, Stephen, and Helen Tiffin, eds. *After Europe: Critical Theory and Post-Colonial Writing.* Sydney: Dangroo Press, 1989.

Smith, Stan. "Neither Calliope Nor Apollo: Pound's Propertius and the Refusal of Epic." *English* 34 (autumn 1985): 212–31.

Soyinka, Wole. *Myth, Literature and the African World.* London: Cambridge University Press, 1976.

Steadman, John M. *Milton's Epic Characters: Image and Idol.* Chapel Hill: University of North Carolina Press, 1968.

Stuart, Gilbert. *James Joyce's Ulysses: A Study.* New York: Alfred A. Knopf, 1952.

Tagopoulos, Constance V. "Joyce and Homer: Return, Disguise, and Recognition in 'Ithaca.'" In *Joyce in Context,* edited by Vincent J. Cheng and Timothy Martin, 184–200. Cambridge: Cambridge University Press, 1992.

Thiong'o, Ngugi wa. *Decolonizing the Mind: The Politics of Languages in African Literature.* London: James Currey, 1986.

Tiffin, Helen. "Commonwealth Literature: Comparison and Judgement." In *History and Historiography of Commonwealth Literature,* edited by Dieter Riemenschneider, 19–35. Tübingen: Gunther Narr Verlag, 1983.

————. "Post-Colonialism, Post-Modernism and the Rehabilitation of Post-Colonial History." *Journal of Commonwealth Literature* 23, no. 1 (1988): 169–81.

Treves, Sir Frederick. *The Cradle of the Deep: An Account of a Voyage to the West Indies.* New York: E. P. Dutton and Co., 1928.

Wade-Gery, H. T. *The Poet of the Iliad.* Cambridge: Cambridge University Press, 1952.

Walcott, Derek. "Berlin: The A. B. C. of Negritude." *Sunday Guardian* (Trinidad), October 8, 1964.

————. *A Branch of the Blue Nile.* In his *Three Plays: The Last Carnival, Beef, No Chicken, A Branch of the Blue Nile,* 211–312. New York: Farrar, Straus and Giroux, 1986.

————. "Carnival: The Theatre of the Streets." *Sunday Guardian* (Trinidad), February 9, 1964.

————. "A Colonial's Eye View of the Empire." *Triquarterly* 65 (winter 1986): 73–84.

————. "The Great Irony." *Sunday Guardian* (Trinidad), September 25, 1966.

————. "Magnificence and Art in the Carnival Spectacle." *Trinidad Guardian,* March 5, 1962.

————. "Native Women under Sea-Almond Trees: Musings on Art, Life and the Island of St. Lucia." *House and Garden* 156, no. 8 (August 1984): 114–15, 161–63.

————. "Necessity of Negritude." *Trinidad Guardian,* September 28, 1964.

————. "On Robert Lowell." *New York Review of Books* 31 (March 1, 1984): 25, 28–31.

————. "A Self-Interview Raises Questions of Identity." *Sunday Guardian* (Trinidad), October 16, 1966.

————. "Spiritual Purpose Lacking." *Sunday Guardian* (Trinidad), January 5, 1964.

[————]. "West Indian Writers." *Times Literary Supplement,* May 23, 1952.

————. "W. I. Writers Must Risk Talent." *Trinidad Guardian,* June 6, 1963.

West, Cornel. "Minority Discourse and the Pitfalls of Canon Formation." *Yale Journal of Criticism* 1, no. 1 (fall 1987): 193–201.

White, Hayden. *The Content of Form: Narrative Discourse and Historical Representation.* Baltimore: Johns Hopkins University Press, 1987.

———. *Metahistory: The Historical Imagination in Nineteenth-Century Europe.* Baltimore: Johns Hopkins University Press, 1973.

White, J. P. "Derek Walcott: The Spirit of a Post-Elizabethan Globalist." *Green Mountain Review* ns., 4, no. 1 (spring–summer 1990): 11–13.

Whitman, Cedric H. *Homer and the Heroic Tradition.* Cambridge: Harvard University Press, 1958.

Wilkinson, Nick. "A Methodology for the Comparative Study of Commonwealth Literature." *Journal of Commonwealth Literature* 13, no. 3 (April 1979): 33–42.

Wolf, Eric R. *Europe and the People without History.* Berkeley: University of California Press, 1982.

The World's Great Classics. 50 vols. New York: Colonial Press, 1899–1901. Reprint, New York: Grolier, 1969.

Young, Robert. "Post-structuralism: An Introduction." In his *Untying the Text: A Post-structuralist Reader,* 1–28. Boston: Kegan Paul, 1981.

Yu, Anthony C. "Homer and the Scholars Once More." In his *Parnassus Revisited: Modern Critical Essays on the Epic Tradition,* 3–25. Chicago: American Library Association, 1973.

Index

Achille: Greek parallels, 4, 59, 67, 79, 81, 84, 117; African heritage, 6, 51, 52, 59, 70, 71, 72, 73, 76–77, 78, 79–80, 84, 108, 121, 123, 132, 145, 146, 150, 161, 165; Antillean roots, 7, 29, 37, 38, 39, 53, 54, 58, 62, 66, 70, 72, 77–78, 79–80, 84, 85, 87, 123, 134, 142, 145, 146, 153, 154, 155, 161, 163, 164, 165; contest for Helen, 27, 40, 42, 44, 45, 46, 47, 51, 66, 67, 68, 69, 70, 71, 73, 81, 90, 91, 95, 129, 130, 132, 135, 142–43, 159, 160, 161, 165; authorial mask, 48, 50, 75, 81, 126, 127; predecessors in earlier works, 48; reclaiming name, 59, 72, 76, 81, 83, 91; African odyssey, 75–83, 86, 91, 101, 107–8, 124–25, 144, 146; as buffalo soldier, 84, 91; American counterpart, 96, 100, 101; seeks new home, 155–59
Achilles: allusion, 23, 30, 40, 67, 132, 132n4, 144n10; in naming of Achille, 59
Aeneas, 3, 4, 23, 47, 55, 76, 136, 152, 156
Aeneid: traditional form, 8, 9, 13, 33, 76, 141, 166; influence on *Omeros*, 29
Afolabe: Achille's ancestor, 4, 59, 75–76, 83, 108, 121; American counterpart, 96, 146
Africa: diaspora, 3, 34, 42, 56, 74, 80, 82, 84, 94, 97, 106, 121, 122, 127, 128, 133, 136, 137, 144, 161; influence, 4, 6, 11, 16, 37, 43, 51, 56, 69, 73, 77, 101, 106, 107, 117, 121, 122, 127, 130, 134, 144, 149, 151, 154, 161, 163, 165; return to, 6, 36, 56, 70, 72, 98, 126; epic potential, 9, 10, 31, 74, 84, 101, 160; Makak's heritage, 21, 75, 78, 98; Shabine's dream, 25; Plunkett's military service, 66, 121, 157; Achille's return, 70, 75–83, 86, 91, 94, 101, 107, 108, 121, 126, 144, 145–46, 165
Agamemnon, 81
Alma-Tadema, Laurence, 157
Anchises, 4, 55, 56, 152

Antigone (Greek sculptress), 42, 42n6, 132, 147, 148
Arawak (Aruac), 28, 37, 62, 80, 85, 95, 156
Autobiography: in literature, 6, 11; in *Another Life*, 17, 21, 162; in *Omeros*, 45, 48, 54–55, 69, 72, 73, 83, 85, 88, 91, 95, 104, 106, 125, 135, 141; in James Joyce, 114

Battle of the Saints, 4, 59–60, 59n1, 61, 63, 65, 82, 98, 109, 111, 143, 150, 160, 164
Bloom, Leopold, 11–12, 115, 116
Boston, 85, 88, 89, 91, 95, 99, 100, 101, 106, 122, 123, 125

Carib, 28, 37, 85, 95, 156
Césaire, Aimé, 19, 128
Charon, 4, 149
Circe, 47, 81–82, 138
Classical: influences, 1, 3, 7, 20, 33, 47, 59, 66, 102, 118, 165; epic formula, 11, 22, 92, 94, 149, 162; tragic formula, 19; parallel, 36, 40, 46, 49, 63, 66, 69, 81, 119, 141, 160–61, 162, 163
Clive, Robert, 140
Cody, William "Wild Bill," 96
Colonial: effects of colonialism, 4, 21, 22, 24, 25, 96, 104, 105, 106, 108, 110, 112, 115, 122, 131, 140, 143, 144, 152, 157, 159; educational system, 11, 66, 112; artistic contributions, 16, 18, 105, 115, 131; identity, 48, 91, 115, 165; independence, 54, 159
Columbus, Christopher, 13, 14, 20, 23, 108, 139, 149
Comet: precursor in earlier work, 26; Hector's van, 66, 67, 68, 130, 139; as symbol, 69, 131–32, 152
Conrad, Joseph, 5, 35, 110, 128
Crane, Hart, 10, 11, 12–15

148, 149, 150, 151, 154, 155, 160, 163, 164; contribution to epic tradition, 2, 3, 4, 6–7, 9, 11, 13, 29, 31, 32, 33–36, 40, 43, 59, 60, 64, 67, 70, 75, 76, 78, 83–84, 93, 94, 95, 98, 103, 104, 118–19, 120, 127, 137, 138, 141, 148, 149, 162, 163, 165–66; encounters father, 4, 54–58, 75, 102–103, 104, 146, 162; persona in *Omeros*, 4, 6, 7, 25, 41–42, 48, 54–56, 62, 65, 69, 72, 73–74, 75, 80, 81, 83, 85, 86, 88, 90, 92, 95–96, 97, 99–100, 101, 105, 106, 108, 109, 115, 119, 120, 121, 122, 123, 125, 126, 129, 130, 135, 138, 141, 143, 146, 147, 151, 153, 154, 162, 164, 165; writes epic for Caribbean Helen, 4, 7, 15, 16, 18, 21, 26, 45, 48, 49, 51, 84, 112, 143, 146, 149, 152, 158, 162, 163; structure of *Omeros*, 4–6, 12, 35, 36, 41–42, 44, 45, 46, 51, 54, 58, 60, 62, 65, 66, 67, 70, 71, 72, 73, 74, 75, 78, 79, 80, 81, 82, 83, 85, 86, 90, 91, 96, 97, 98, 101, 102, 103, 106, 107, 109, 110, 111, 112–13, 114, 115, 116, 117, 118, 119–20, 122, 124, 129, 131–32, 133, 138, 139, 140, 141, 142, 143, 146, 151, 154, 158, 159, 162, 163, 165–66; presence in *Omeros*, 4, 54–57, 58, 66, 85, 102–103, 104, 126, 141, 148; on imitation, 11–13, 18, 88, 93, 95, 106–7, 121, 162; on value of accident, 37–39, 120; age reversal, 62, 102; American identity, 88–89, 92, 93, 94, 106, 107; colonial schizophrenia, 105, 121, 122, 134; tours inferno, 149–52, 155, 158

—Works: *Another Life*, 17, 21–22, 48, 54, 76, 99, 141, 154, 162; *The Arkansas Testament*, 23*n22*, 24, 26–27, 49, 50; *The Castaway*, 93–94; *Dream on Monkey Mountain*, 20, 21, 75, 78, 98, 159; *Dream on Monkey Mountain and Other Plays*, 18, 19, 33, 48, 74, 82; *Drums and Colours*, 20, 21, 32, 82; "Epitaph for the Young": predecessor to *Another Life*, 17, 18, 21–22, 32; "The Ghost Dance," 24, 27, 29, 98–99; *The Gulf*, 91; *Henri Christophe*, 18–20, 21, 32, 82; *In a Green Night*, 15, 18, 107; *Midsummer*, 107, 112; *The Odyssey*, 18, 29–31; *The Sea at Dauphin*, 18, 48, 113; *Sea Grapes*, 76, 91, 107

Warrior: latent, 20–21, 131, 132, 137, 145, 146, 152, 155, 164; of epic tradition, 33, 40, 65; African, 78, 79; native American, 124, 125

Weldon, Catherine, 6, 27–29, 94, 95–96, 97–99, 122–23, 124, 125, 126, 127, 132

Whitman, Walt, 10, 12, 13, 14, 15

Wound: Philoctete's, 4, 36, 39, 42, 43, 66, 69, 81, 91, 133, 136, 137, 164; symbolic dimensions, 42, 71, 91, 146, 147, 155, 165; search for cure, 43, 154, 164; Plunkett's, 44, 45, 53, 158, 165; Achille's, 47, 48, 69; Malebolge at Soufrière, 52; Walcott's, 57, 89, 136, 144, 152; Hector's, 133; compared with Philoctētēs' injury, 137

Zagajewski, Adam, 123, 123*n12*

Zeus, 52

About the Author

Robert D. Hamner is Senior Professor of English and Humanities at Hardin-Simmons University in Abilene, Texas. He is the author or editor of six books, including *Derek Walcott*.